A Unique Time of God

A Unique Time of God

Karl Barth's WWI Sermons

Karl Barth

Translated and Edited by William Klempa

© 2016 William Klempa

First edition
Published by Westminster John Knox Press
Louisville, Kentucky

17 18 19 20 21 22 23 24 25—10 9 8 7 6 5 4 3 2

Translated by William Klempa from the German *Predigten 1914* (Karl Barth, *Gesamtausgabe*, vol. 1), published by Theologischer Verlag Zürich, Zurich 1999.

All rights reserved. No part of this book may be reproduced or transmitted in any form or by any means, electronic or mechanical, including photocopying, recording, or by any information storage or retrieval system, without permission in writing from the publisher. For information, address Westminster John Knox Press, 100 Witherspoon Street, Louisville, Kentucky 40202-1396. Or contact us online at www.wjkbooks.com.

Unless otherwise indicated, Scripture quotations are from the Revised Standard Version of the Bible, copyright © 1946, 1952, 1971, and 1973 by the Division of Christian Education of the National Council of the Churches of Christ in the U.S.A., and used by permission. Scripture quotations marked NRSV are from the New Revised Standard Version of the Bible, copyright © 1989 by the Division of Christian Education of the National Council of the Churches of Christ in the U.S.A., and used by permission.

Book design by Sharon Adams
Cover design by Marc Whitaker / MTWdesign.net
Cover photo: © Imperial War Museums (Q 5100)

Library of Congress Cataloging-in-Publication Data

Names: Barth, Karl, 1886–1968, author. | Klempa, William, editor.
Title: A unique time of God : Karl Barth's WWI sermons / Karl Barth ; translated and edited by William Klempa.
Description: First edition. | Louisville, KY : Westminster John Knox Press, 2017. | Includes bibliographical references and index.
Identifiers: LCCN 2016032994 (print) | LCCN 2016047885 (ebook) | ISBN 9780664262662 (pbk. : alk. paper) | ISBN 9781611647952 (ebook)
Subjects: LCSH: World War, 1914-1918—Sermons. | Sermons, German—Translations into English. | Bible—Sermons.
Classification: LCC BX4827.B3 A5 2017 (print) | LCC BX4827.B3 (ebook) | DDC 252/.042—dc23
LC record available at https://lccn.loc.gov/2016032994

♾ The paper used in this publication meets the minimum requirements of the American National Standard for Information Sciences—Permanence of Paper for Printed Library Materials, ANSI Z39.48-1992.

Most Westminster John Knox Press books are available at special quantity discounts when purchased in bulk by corporations, organizations, and special-interest groups. For more information, please e-mail SpecialSales@wjkbooks.com.

*To the memory of my father, Miko, who fled Europe
and in particular Austrian-Hungarian conscription before the war, and
to my mother, Mary, who fled Europe shortly after the Great War*

*And also to my father-in-law, Major James Stewart,
who went with the Canadian forces to the Great War in Europe,
and to my mother-in-law, Margaret Findley, Scottish war bride,
who came to Canada with her husband to lead a new life*

With honor, gratitude, and affection

Contents

Preface		ix
Acknowledgments		xv
Time Line		xvii
Introduction		1
Sermons		47
July 26, 1914	Ephesians 2:4–7	49
August 2, 1914	Mark 13:7	59
August 9, 1914	Philippians 4:6	69
August 16, 1914	John 15:14–15	77
August 23, 1914	Revelation 6:4 and Matthew 10:28	85
August 30, 1914	Isaiah 30:15	95
September 6, 1914	Psalm 102:26–28	105
September 13, 1914	Matthew 8:23–26	115
September 20, 1914	Jeremiah 22:29	125
October 11, 1914	Mark 10:17–23	135
October 18, 1914	Romans 8:38–39	145
October 25, 1914	Psalm 119:142	155
November 1, 1914	John 17:20–21	165
Notes		173
Select Bibliography		185
Index of Persons		191
Index of Places		194
Index of Subjects		197

Preface

The Great War of 1914–1918 was the most horrendous, catastrophic, and unprecedented happening in all of history. As a unique clash of men and armaments, it defined the twentieth century. The war's consequences were immense, and in our day we still experience its dreadful effects.

World War I, as it was later called, in its vast literature of some 25,000 books and articles—and counting—has received numerous striking appellations and descriptions. It has been called "Armageddon,"[1] "the Great Cataclysm,"[2] and "Europe's Last Summer."[3] It has been described as the "seminal catastrophe"[4] and the defining event of the century. The most striking and perhaps the most perplexing designation given to it was by a young Swiss pastor who was to become the century's leading Protestant theologian, Karl Barth. He gave the war a strikingly positive interpretation by calling it a *Gotteszeit*, "a time of God,"[5] not only a time of God, but *eine Gotteszeit, wie nur je eine*, "a unique time of God." He knew the war's wickedness and destructiveness, but he held out hope for redemption and restoration. As we might expect, Barth's take on the war was profoundly moral and religious. Barth saw the war through eyes of faith, focused on the one sovereign God who holds the "whole world in his hands." Not all readers will agree with his views, but his contribution cannot be readily dismissed. Barth's status as the century's preeminent Protestant theologian and major political thinker, plus the strong persuasiveness of his moral analysis and religious interpretation, ought to merit him our attention.

It was Barth's conviction that, in this unique time of God, God had drawn nearer to humanity. Barth does not state explicitly how and why God's mysterious presence was evident. Hints, however, are given. The "how" is indicated by the religious phenomena that were associated with the outbreak of the Great War in Germany and in Russia. Barth mentions that something comparable to a new Pentecost had occurred. He is clearer about the "why": God has come nearer than ever in recent memory to address Europe in judgment and in mercy. If there is one theme pounding through the thirteen sermons like the relentless beating of a drum, it is the gospel ethic: "God is not mocked, for you reap whatever you sow" (Gal. 6:7 NRSV). Europe had heard this warning many times but had not heeded it. In consequence, it would have to face the full force of its failure and negligence in massive slaughter, destruction, and misery. It was Barth's conviction that we live in a moral universe upheld by God's righteousness and justice, and to displease God by departing from God's ways is, as it was for Israel of old, to incur judgment. With Barth, however, judgment is never the ultimate, but only the penultimate, word. God's grace always abounds over God's judgment. Though God's word is a judging one, it is even more a saving one.

In sermons preached beginning July 26, 1914—the date of Austria-Hungary's forty-eight-hour ultimatum to Serbia—and continuing to the first Sunday of Advent, he took a dialectical approach to the war, contrasting its force of judgment with its expression of God's grace. As Barth said, "God will not soon come so near to us again as he does now with this generous call to mend our ways and to change our minds."[6] Moreover, Barth said that God had spoken to Europe so clearly in the first two months of the war that it would be difficult not to understand this message.[7]

Barth's theology has received the appellation "crisis theology" because of his frequent use of this term in his *Römerbrief* commentary. This term described an aspect of Barth's theology but is not as comprehensive as the term "dialectical theology." Bruce McCormack has used the designation "realistic dialectic theology." However, Barth's theology was not realistic from the outset but became so only later. The frequently used term "neo-orthodoxy" is the least accurate and most unsatisfactory one of the three.

"The past is never dead. It's not even past,"[8] as the American novelist William Faulkner rightly said; and these sermons from the past still make for compelling reading today. They are not at all like the mental impressions typically evoked by the word "sermon." They are vital, brilliant, and gripping analyses of the causes and events of the First World War and a running commentary on its conduct and events.

Years later, Barth criticized his war sermons as an excessive and needless pursuit of relevance. His desire for relevance was not without cause; presumably, he wanted to interest and appeal to the wartime newcomers to his church services, though his sermons eventually prompted the rebuke, "The preacher needs to get back to the Bible."[9] Perhaps at the time, and certainly in retrospect, Barth was conscious that he had departed from the high road he had first chosen to follow. As he wrote later in his *Homiletics*, relevance should not be a preacher's primary aim, and his warning that the preacher must "aim [higher] than relevance" was made partly in reference to these early sermons,[10] though the contemporary reader can be grateful that he saw so clearly the importance of the Great War and that he preached on it so passionately, so lengthily, and so ably.

Not everyone in his congregation was so grateful. He received another rebuke at the beginning of Advent, when a parishioner told Barth that she was tired of hearing about the war. He stopped, as it were, in his wartime tracks. The war continued to rage on, but no longer in his sermons. Barth's preaching took its own course; the war and his preaching converged again from time to time, but never with the same intensity as in its first four months. When closure came to the war on November 11, 1918, Barth breathed a sigh of relief and wrote, "Now has the devil evidently departed."[11] Perhaps, but if so, not for long. Was Barth underestimating the strength and tenacity of evil? In fact, the devil and his minions continued their awful work during the years of the Weimar Republic. A firm foothold was gained by these forces of evil during the Third Reich, and nights of terror, bloodbaths, exterminations of the weak and infirm, and "final solutions" perpetrated their horrors in ways difficult to imagine at the time. There is no equal in world history to what Hannah Arendt termed "the banality of evil" in the twentieth century.[12]

Barth, the cheerful theologian, however, did not despair. He trusted in the triumph of God's purposes and was convinced that God's kingdom would be established. Throughout his World War I sermons, as well as his later works, he never lost sight of the fact that the true and ultimate relevance is to be found in exposing the life and conduct of individuals and nations to God's light, which is revealed in Jesus Christ, who is the "Light of life."

Barth's war sermons have a threefold significance. First, they establish Barth as a significant critic of World War I. He joins the distinguished company of its major critics, such as Romain Rolland,[13] the French Nobel laureate in literature who became a pacifist, was forced to flee France, and went to work for the Red Cross in Geneva during the war; Stefan Zweig,[14] the Austrian literary figure who joined the army as a young man but later became a pacifist and wrote a pacifist drama entitled *Jeremiah* that played in Zurich; Leonard Ragaz, the Swiss pastor and religious socialist, editor of the journal *Neue Wege* (New Way), who in his preaching and literary work strongly opposed the war; Bertrand Russell,[15] the brilliant Cambridge philosopher, who was imprisoned for six months by the British government for his strong pacifist views; Keir Hardie, a founder of Scotland's Labour Party, who protested the war alongside the suffragettes; and the French socialist Jean Jaurès, who was assassinated near the war's beginning.

Second, the sermons reveal Barth's mature historical understanding and his keen political acumen. Early in August, he saw the significance and worldwide dimensions of the Great War and spoke of it as one of the most monumental events since the beginning of humankind. He believed it would be not a short but a long war, that millions of soldiers would be slaughtered, that the destruction and devastation would be horrific, and that Europe would lose its central place in the world, giving way to the emergence of the United States as the great world power.

While he employed the categories of justice and injustice to understand the war, he was not content with this sanitized view of it but interpreted it as a European power struggle, the result of narrow nationalism, racial pride, and a false Christian religiosity that identified God with the ancient pagan god Wotan. Barth lamented that the war had occurred between supposedly Christian nations ruled by Christian monarchs. To him, it represented the failure of the European churches and of socialism to prevent it. He predicted that historians would continue to argue about the origins and causes of the war for years to come; indeed, a century later this debate continues.

Third, the sermons are thoroughly theological in character and are indispensable for an understanding of the beginnings and development of Barth's dialectical theology. The beginnings are usually identified with his essays published in *The Word of God and the Word of Man* (1928). Yet it is clear that in Barth's early preaching, and in these war sermons in particular, are the true beginnings of Barth's later theology. The doctrines that are discussed more fully in the *Church Dogmatics*—God, Jesus Christ, the Holy Spirit, creation, providence, sin, judgment, the supremacy of God's grace over sin, the "new world of the Bible," and eschatology—are to be found *in nuce* in these war sermons. Although they remain under the influence and are couched in the terms of liberal theology, it is also discernible that Barth was gradually departing from his liberal roots.

Near the end of his life, Barth pinpointed his break with liberal theology as the moment when he saw to his horror the names of his two revered teachers, Adolf von Harnack and Wilhelm Herrmann, in the appeal of the ninety-three German intellectuals (published in October 1914) in support of Kaiser Wilhelm II's war policies. Undoubtedly, the shaking of the foundations of the house of liberal theology, in which Barth lived as a student and as a young pastor, took place at that time; but its eventual collapse probably did not occur until the spring of 1915, when he had important meetings and conversations with Friedrich Naumann and Christoph Blumhardt. These talks prompted him to turn his back on the former and to follow the teaching of the latter.

Friedrich-Wilhelm Marquardt, the late professor of systematic theology at the Free University of Berlin, has stated that the 1974 publication of the 1914

Sermons (*Predigten 1914*) was the most important posthumous Barth publication.[16] The importance of these sermons, and particularly the war sermons, cannot be overstated. Through these addresses, a revolutionary theology was born out of the necessity and struggle of proclaiming the Christian message during the first few months of the Great War. In them the war is given a moral and religious interpretation, an element often missing in other historical studies. These interpretations must be taken into account as we remember and reflect upon this armageddon, this apocalyptic event of a century ago. It is a matter of gratitude that these sermons, unlike so many, were preserved and later published. It is also a matter of pride that thirteen of these sermons are translated and published here in English for the first time.

Acknowledgments

I am grateful for my dear late wife Lois Stewart's encouragement and support of this project. She followed its progress with great interest and read and commented on a number of the translated sermons. When she was afflicted with cancer in 2011, I postponed the project, originally intended to be completed by the autumn of 2013. Shortly before she died in May 2013, she urged me to resume my work on it. I did so at first with a measure of reluctance, but I continued out of the conviction that these sermons should be made available to English readers.

I am grateful to Ms. Anneka Voeltz and Mr. Henry Unruh for their initial help in translating some of the sermons. Above all, I am grateful to Professor Iain Nicol, a noted translator, for his assistance with the translation of some of these sermons. He has corrected and tidied up my translated prose to make it publicly presentable. Any errors or infelicities of language that still remain are my own doing.

I want to thank Dr. Hans-Anton Drewes, the Karl Barth archivist in Basel, for his hospitality and help. I had an enjoyable week of research work in the Barth archives. At the same time, I want to thank the two pastors of the Safenwil congregation for showing me the church and the parsonage where Karl Barth and his family lived. This visit to Safenwil gave the place "a local habitation and a name." I also want to thank Dr. Clifford Anderson, now of Vanderbilt, who managed the Barth Collection while at Princeton Seminary, for his valuable help. Librarians have also been exceedingly helpful; I am grateful to the librarians of Princeton Theological Seminary, Harvard Divinity School, and McGill University for their help. In particular, I want to thank Dr. Daniel Shute, librarian at the Presbyterian College in Montreal, for his help and assistance. I am also grateful to my daughter, Catherine Klempa, and my son, Michael, for their help with the manuscript, and to Ms. Kirsten Shute for her assistance.

Finally, I can appreciate the feeling of satisfaction Barth felt after his father permitted him to study in Marburg under Wilhelm Herrmann in 1908, since I myself had the fine opportunity to study under Karl Barth in Basel during the short summer semester of 1960. I am grateful to my *Doktorvater* Thomas F. Torrance for arranging a grant from the University of Edinburgh to make this study possible. Barth's lectures on the doctrine of baptism, his seminar on the first eight chapters of Calvin's *Institutes*, and his English seminar are still vivid in my mind some fifty years later. I am appreciative to the German government for providing a *Deutscher Akademischer Austauschdienst Stipendium* that enabled me to study at the University of Göttingen and to acquire a facility in the German language, for which I shall always be grateful.

I want to express my gratitude to three people who read this manuscript and made suggestions for changes: Professor David Demson of Wycliffe College, Toronto; Mary-Margaret Klempa at Cornell University; and Professor John Vissers of Knox College, Toronto. I owe a great debt of gratitude to Professors George Hunsinger and Bruce McCormack of Princeton Seminary, David Demson once again, and other members of the North American Barth Society for all that I have learned from them. *Danke sehr.*

Finally, I want to express my gratitude to Dr. Robert Ratcliff and Westminster John Knox Press for accepting my book for publication and especially to Dr. Ratcliff for his extra efforts to ensure its publication in 2016.

Time Line

Week and Event	Sermon Text and Theme	Barth's Literary Activity
July 26–August 1 July 28—Austria-Hungary declares war; Russia mobilizes on Austrian and German borders July 31—Germany warns Russia to stop mobilization August 1—Germany declares war on Russia and asks France to stay neutral	Ephesians 2:4–6 God's people are set in the heavenly realm.	Barth writes a review of the 1913 issues of *Die Hilfe* (*The Help*, ed. Friedrich Naumann)
August 2–8 August 2—Germany invades Luxembourg; Kaiser Wilhelm's speech to the soldiers: "I no longer know parties, only Germans." August 3—Germany declares war on France; Belgium refuses entry; Chancellor Bethmann-Hollweg defends German violation of Belgian neutrality	Mark 13:7 When you hear of war and rumors of war, do not be alarmed.	

Week and Event	Sermon Text and Theme	Barth's Literary Activity
August 2–8 (*continued*) August 4—Germany invades Belgium; Great Britain warns Germany concerning Belgium, then declares war August 5—Germany begins assault on Liège, starting the Battle of the Frontiers; Austria-Hungary declares war on Russia; Serbia declares war on Germany August 7—The British Expeditionary Force arrives in France	Mark 13:7 (*continued*) When you hear of war and rumors of war, do not be alarmed.	
August 9–15 August 11—France declares war on Austria-Hungary August 12—UK declares war on Austria-Hungary	Philippians 4:6 Do not worry about anything; faith in God should overcome human anxieties.	August 13—Karl Barth writes to Martin Rade, noting that Germany's operation in Belgium caused tension between the two men. He writes that the August 2–8 issue of *Die Christliche Welt* (*The Christian World*) must have been lost or delayed in the tumult of war. August 15—Barth's review of *Die Hilfe* is published in *CW*.
August 16–22 August 16–19—Battle of Cer—Serbs defeat Austro-Hungarians August 17—Russia enters East Prussia August 20—Germany unsuccessfully attacks Russians in East Prussia	John 15:14–15 Friends or servants of Jesus?	

Week and Event	Sermon Text and Theme	Barth's Literary Activity
August 23–29 August 23—Japan declares war on Germany; Germany enters France August 23–30—Russian army badly defeated by Germans in Tannenberg August 25—German army raids Louvain in Belgium, executing civilians as suspected snipers and burning its historic library	Revelation 6:4 and Matthew 10:28 The war is God's judgment, represented by Revelation's rider on the red horse who takes peace from the earth.	August 26—Eduard Thurneysen writes to Barth, commending his June 7 sermon published in *Neue Wege* and his comments on Friedrich Naumann in *Christliche Welt*, noting that this second magazine at least "inwardly" supports the war. August 29—Barth replies, expressing his regret for lives wasted in the war and his distress at the attitudes expressed in *CW*, especially Martin Rade's apparent endorsement of the war. Rade had reprinted Luther's essay on soldiers and salvation.
August 30–September 5 August 29–30—Allied retreat at Battle of St. Quentin September 2–11—Austro-Hungarian defeat at Battle of Rava Russka September 5—Beginning of Battle of the Marne, in which France finally resists German forces, upsetting the Schlieffen Plan	Isaiah 30:15 Quietness and neutrality in the face of war	August 31—Barth expresses his disappointment to Rade about the last three issues of *CW* and asked why Rade had changed his attitude towards the war. He argues that *CW*, instead of speaking from a standpoint of faith, is blindly following the rest of Germany which mixes patriotism, love of war, and the Christian faith in a hopeless mess. September 4—Barth writes in a letter to Thurneysen: "The unconditional truths of the gospel are simply suspended for the time being, and in the meantime a German war theology is put to work, its Christian trimming consisting of a lot of talk about sacrifice and the like."* In his letter he included two of his recent sermons, calling them experiments rather than finished products.

*Karl Barth, Sept. 4, 1914, letter, in *Revolutionary Theology in the Making*, ed. and trans. James D. Smart (Richmond, VA: John Knox Press, 1964), 26.

Week and Event	**Sermon Text and Theme**	**Barth's Literary Activity**
September 6–12 September 9—German Chancellor Betthman-Hollweg describes Germany's war aims September 12—Battle of the Marne concludes with French forces halting Germany's advance, preventing the takeover of Paris, but with severe casualties on both sides.	Psalm 102:26–28 Trust in God rather than in victories and defeats; God is eternal and transcends national rivalries	
September 13–19 September 13–15—In France, the First Battle of the Aisne ends in a draw; the system of trench warfare used there will continue for most of the war September 14—Erich von Falkenhayn succeeds Helmuth von Moltke the Younger as Germany's Chief of Staff September 19—Start of Battle of Flirey in France	Matthew 8:23–26 Jesus' power to still the storm of war; the need for repentance	
September 20–26 "Race to the City" continues from the First Battle of the Aisne—German and French troops try to outflank each other Trench warfare is largely at a stalemate September 24—Siege of Przemyśl, the longest siege in WW1 (133 days), begins	Jeremiah 22:29 O land, hear the word of the Lord!	September 25—Barth writes to Thurneysen that Rade is surprised and upset by Barth's (and his brother Peter's) criticism of *CW*, more so than Barth had expected. September 25—Rade writes back to Barth, suggesting that Barth's previous letter and his counterargument be printed in *Neue Wege* if Leonard Ragaz agrees. His letter is brief but friendly.

Time Line

Week and Event	Sermon Text and Theme	Barth's Literary Activity
September 27–October 10 September 22–29—Battles continue along the western front as part of the so-called "Race to the Sea" September 28–October 10—Germany attacks and captures Antwerp, Belgium October 4—Manifesto of the 93 Intellectuals is published, in which German intellectuals defend their nation's invasion of Belgium	(Barth on study leave for two weeks)	October 1—Barth replies to Rade that he would prefer to have their debate published in a more widely read German paper (rather than the Swiss *NW*) such as *CW* or the *Zeitschrift für Theologie und Kirche*, but allowed for *NW* as an alternative. October 5—Rade answers that the year's volumes of the *ZThK* are already planned. He will send Barth's letter to Ragaz (editor of *NW*) the next day at the latest, along with his reply, asking Barth to arrange for publication. Rade writes that they can also continue the dispute in the 1915 *ZThK*, since he thinks Barth does not understand the German national spirit.
October 11–17 October 11—Battle of Flirey ends in German victory, blocking many French roadways to Verdun October 16—Battle of the Yser in Belgium begins	Mark 10:17–23 The rich young ruler and the question of eternal life	
October 18–24 October 19—"Race to the Sea" ends at Belgian coastline of North Sea; First Battle of Ypres begins	Romans 8:38–39 War reveals good character but is also caused by human failure; God rules above all	
October 25–31 October 29—Turkey begins hostilities against Russia	Psalm 119:142 The formula "Necessity knows no law" leads to injustice, as opposed to God's righteousness	October 27—Thurneysen writes to Barth, saying that church historian Paul Wernle criticized socialist pastors sharply by saying they only parrot others' sayings.

Week and Event	Sermon Text and Theme	Barth's Literary Activity
November 1–7 November 2—Russia declares war on Turkey November 2—British navy begins the naval blockade of Germany November 3—First German naval attack on British coast November 5—Great Britain and France declare war on Turkey	John 17:20–21 Reformation Sunday and importance of Christian unity	November 4—Barth writes to Wilhelm Hermann, asking if he has read the latest issue of *NW* and hoping for some understanding despite disagreements. He asks three things: how to maintain belief in German scholarly objectivity in face of the pro-war attitude in academia; if "experience" is a constitutive part of the Christian faith, how to justify the fact that Germans experience their war as a holy war; and how Germans can remain in Christian communion with neutral and enemy peoples if they keep insisting on their military rightness. He ends by expressing his respect for the German character but disagreeing with German propaganda, preferring the writings of French pacifist Romain Rolland.

Introduction

THE GREAT WAR AND ITS CONSEQUENCES

It is said with some justification that the twentieth century began not according to the calendar in 1900, celebrated by the six-month-long Paris Exposition that attracted fifty million visitors,[1] but in August 1914, marked by the Great War. This disastrous European war quickly escalated and engulfed most of the world, inaugurating a century of calamities. It so convulsed the great European empires of Russia, Germany, and Austria-Hungary that the scepters fell from the hands of Nicholas II, Kaiser Wilhelm II, and Emperor Franz Joseph, bringing to an end these ancient European monarchies.

Another empire, the Ottoman, which became the fateful ally of Germany, fell when the latter fell, and great was its fall, leaving only the Turkish region of its empire intact. Kaiser Wilhelm II had cleverly courted the Ottomans. He made a visit to the Middle East as early as 1892 and pledged his undying friendship to the Ottomans. He knew that if a war occurred, it would be a two-front one that involved Russia and France, since they were members of the Entente powers along with the United Kingdom. It was therefore crucial that the Bosporus and the Dardanelles be kept in Ottoman hands and Russian ships be prevented from sailing between the Black Sea and the Mediterranean.

The Great War created the conditions that produced the totalitarian movements of both the right and the left, leading to the Second World War and the Holocaust, a host of smaller wars, including the Korean War, and the wars within Israel, and that culminated in the cold war that continued nearly to the end of the century. The first two decades of the twenty-first century witnessed a resurgent radical Islamic movement, in the fourfold form of the Taliban, Al-Qaeda, ISIS, and Boko Haram, that declared jihad against Western democracies and in particular what it called its Christian crusaders. This clash of religious civilizations is likely to continue for at least another decade.

The Great War brought sweeping social, economic, political, and religious changes whose effects we continue to experience daily. The First World War was a catastrophic event, and we continue to live with its consequences.

IMPACT ON STATESMEN AND SOLDIERS

A British historian active in the antinuclear movement of the 1960s, A. J. P. Taylor, has commented in the preface to his book on the First World War that the (then called) Great War "cut deeply into the modern consciousness."[2] This was true of those who were both directly and indirectly involved with the war.

It includes European leaders and diplomats who scrambled and largely stumbled to prevent the war, such as British foreign secretary Sir Edward Grey, who shortly before Britain's entry into the war said, "The lamps are going out all over Europe, we shall not see them lit again in our lifetime." This was obviously an exaggeration, but it testifies to the horror of the war that Grey feared. It includes Chancellor Bethmann-Hollweg, who had the unenviable task of defending Germany's violation of Belgian neutrality and did so under great personal stress, especially since his wife had died earlier in 1914. It includes Helmuth von Moltke the Younger, who botched the Schlieffen Plan and bore the responsibility for its failure, being sacked by the German military staff in October 1914. It includes General John French, head of the British Expeditionary Force, who was fired by Lord Kitchener and replaced by General Douglas Haig. It includes the officers and soldiers who manned the trenches on both sides; nine million were killed, twenty million were wounded, and another twenty million returned home bearing the trauma of the war. It includes the war's critics: Keir Hardie, Bertrand Russell, the British suffragettes, the French Nobel laureate Romain Rolland, the French socialist Jean Jaurès who was assassinated on the eve of the First World War, Stefan Zweig in Austria, Leonard Ragaz in Switzerland, and Albert Einstein in Germany. It includes the leaders of the churches, who for the most part defended their countries' policies, and, especially, it includes the theologians. I will single out three theologians who were deeply affected by the outbreak and course of the Great War—Adolf von Harnack, Paul Tillich, and Karl Barth—before discussing Barth and his war sermons in particular.

IMPACT ON HARNACK, TILLICH, AND BARTH

The Great War cut deeply into the consciousness of these three theologians. They were all sons of pastors, and each achieved the achievements of his father. However, they also differed in many other respects: the first two were German Lutherans and the third a Swiss German Reformed pastor. Adolf von Harnack (1851–1930) was a dominant voice in German liberal theology. He was born in Estonia and educated at the universities of Tartu in Estonia and Leipzig in Germany. His father opposed his becoming a Lutheran minister, because he had ceased to believe in the resurrection of Jesus; so instead he taught at the universities of Giessen and Marburg before taking up his position at the University of Berlin. Shortly after his arrival in Berlin, he created a controversy over the Apostles' Creed, which he claimed said both too little and too much. Rejecting its authority, he favored a shorter statement of faith.

Harnack's great achievement was his seven-volume history of dogma, *Dogmen Geschichte*, which was characterized by its view that the simple gospel of Jesus had been overlaid with the concepts of Greek philosophy in a process that he called the hellenization of Christianity. In his view, Protestantism was a protest against this approach to dogma, as it insisted on the simple gospel of Jesus. It was this theme that Harnack set forth in a series of lectures to students of all faculties at the University of Berlin, which was later published as *Das Wesen des Christentums* (*What Is Christianity?*). In this series of lectures, he summed up Jesus' simple gospel in three statements: the fatherhood of God and the coming of the kingdom, the brotherhood (and sisterhood) of humankind, and the infinite value of the human soul. This became the manifesto of the social gospel movement that dominated the first two decades of the twentieth century. Paul Tillich, who had moved to Berlin in 1900 when he was only fourteen years old, once remarked in his lectures at Harvard University that he witnessed boxcars loaded with Harnack's *Das Wesen des Christentums* being transported to all parts of Europe.

While in Berlin, Harnack wrote a history of the Prussian Academy and later became general director of the German National Library. He was a fervent German nationalist and a confidante of Kaiser Wilhelm II; in his political philosophy, he used social Darwinism to justify the expansion of the German state. On August 2, 1914, the day after Germany declared war on Russia and the day before it declared war on France, the kaiser spoke to the troops departing from Berlin to Belgium. He called upon Harnack to write his speech, and Harnack made use of Frederick the Great's appeal to the German military. Harnack had the kaiser say, "I no longer know parties. I know only Germans."[3] Apparently Russia and France's threatened aggression had united all Germans in a common cause.

Harnack was greatly vexed with Chancellor Bethmann-Hollweg for stating that though the violation of Belgian neutrality was a necessity (*Not kennt kein Gebot!*), Germany would make restitution after the conclusion of the war. Harnack also saw this action of invading Belgium as a necessity—he quoted the German proverb "necessity cuts iron"—yet he saw no need for restitution. He justified Germany's action by comparing it to the Old Testament account of David and his companions eating the shewbread when they were famished.[4]

In his October 25 sermon, Karl Barth praised Chancellor Bethmann-Hollweg for being an honorable man for his frank admission about Belgium and implied that Harnack was less so; though Barth never mentioned Harnack's name, he referred to his defense of Germany's military action. It was out of the conviction that Germany was defending itself and that its actions in Belgium were simply a response to Belgian provocation that Harnack became a signatory to the Appeal and Manifesto of the ninety-three German intellectuals. Harnack continued to believe that Russia was responsible for the war, and to the very end of his life he insisted that Germany had only fought a defensive war.

Paul Tillich (1886–1965) was born in a village in Brandenburg, studied at the University of Berlin, and took his doctorate at the University of Breslau, with the view of assuming an academic career. He married Margarethe Wever in late September 1914 and enlisted in October 1914 as a chaplain in the German military, probably believing the propaganda that the war would be over before Christmas. This was not to be so. The Great War proved to be a horrific experience for the young Tillich. He was sent to the Western front, where he preached to the German troops, conducted funerals for the soldiers who had been killed, and in many cases had to dig the graves and cover the bodies. As a chaplain, he was awarded the Iron Cross, but he suffered two nervous breakdowns during the war and was given sick leave and psychiatric therapy.

Philip Jenkins, in his book *The Great and Holy War*, writes that Tillich's experiences, particularly of "the horrors of Verdun," gave him this "life-changing epiphany": "The World War in my own experience was the catastrophe of idealistic thinking in general. . . . If a reunion of theology and philosophy should again become possible, it could be achieved only in such a way as would do justice to this experience of the abyss of our existence."[5] It is impossible to understand Tillich's theology without taking into account the impact of the First World War. Besides his personal troubles at this time—his first marriage ended in divorce in 1919—the war prompted him to switch from an orthodox to a psychological-philosophical approach to theology, as he sought to understand human weakness in terms of alienation rather than sin.

Karl Barth (1886–1968), unlike Tillich, did not see the war's combat firsthand but was still deeply affected by the outbreak and events of the Great

War. As is evident from his writings, it preoccupied his thoughts, pervaded his lectures, peppered his letters to his friend Eduard Thurneysen, and finally propelled him to produce his theological bombshell, the *Commentary on Romans* (Oxford University Press), which, as Karl Adam aptly said, "exploded on the playground of the theologians."[6] To situate Barth politically and theologically and to understand the sermons he preached at the outbreak of the war, it may be helpful to give an overview of his early life and years as a pastor.

KARL BARTH EARLY LIFE

Education

Barth's roots were in Basel, and he always felt he belonged to this Swiss city, even though he lived less than half of his life in it. He was born in Basel on May 10, 1886, but his family moved to Bern three years later, and he did not return until 1935, when he came to teach at the university, retiring in 1962. He died there on December 10, 1968.

It almost seems as if he were destined to become a Reformed pastor and theologian. His grandfathers on both his father's and mother's sides were Reformed pastors, as was his father, Fritz Barth. Through his mother, Anna Sartorius, he was distantly related to Jacob Burckhardt, the Swiss historian, and Heinrich Bullinger, the Zurich reformer. He was brought up in a religiously conservative and pious home in which concern for the poor was stressed. The young Karl loved the out-of-doors and had a fondness for such rough sports as boxing and wrestling. Though he was a voracious reader, he found school burdensome. He had an appreciation for music and recalled later the first time he heard bars from Mozart's *The Magic Flute* and how they went through him and into him.

At the age of sixteen, on the eve of his confirmation, Barth decided to become a theologian. A major influence in this decision was a Bernese pastor, Robert Aeschbacher, who in his confirmation classes had excited the young Barth about the content of the Christian faith. Barth wanted to penetrate into its theological basis and to understand it thoroughly from within. But an even stronger influence than Aeschbacher was his own father, Fritz Barth, who taught early Christianity and church history in Bern's theological faculty.

Karl Barth began his theological studies at the University of Bern in 1904. The beginning of the twentieth century marked the high tide of German liberal theology. The German liberal school, which stemmed from Friedrich Schleiermacher and Albrecht Ritschl, was like a giant octopus that held most German theological faculties in its power and even extended its tentacles into Switzerland. Barth began, as he said later, to take liberal theology "in bucketsful,"[7] first at Bern and then later at Berlin and Marburg. In these strongholds of liberal theology, "old orthodoxy" was always castigated, the historical-critical method was extolled, and the scientific (*wissenschaftlich*) character of theology was claimed and praised. Barth and his fellow students were taught "that all God's ways begin with Kant, and if possible, must also end there."[8]

After four semesters in Bern, Barth was ready for study abroad. Abroad, of course, meant Germany, the fountainhead of modern theology, and not England or France. He wanted to go to Marburg, the leading liberal school, but his father preferred that he should go to Halle, where positive theology was taught. A compromise was reached: Berlin, which was seen as neutral. During the 1906–7 winter semester Barth studied intensively in Berlin under Hermann Gunkel and Franz Kaftan but avoided Reinhold Seeberg and Karl Holl. His major study was, however, the history of dogma under the leading liberal theologian of the time, Adolf von Harnack. Barth was the youngest member of his seminar on the Acts of the Apostles. He gave up the sightseeing and cultural activities typically enjoyed by visitors to Berlin in order to devote himself fully to his studies. He produced a 158-page essay on Acts.[9] From Berlin he wanted to go to Marburg to study under Wilhelm Herrmann, whose book on *Ethics* he had read with enthusiasm.

When the young Barth returned to Bern, his father was alarmed by his son's devotion to liberal theology. Therefore, he sent him off to Tübingen in October 1907 to study some positive theology under Adolf Schlatter. But this exercise did not have its desired effect, since Barth was already pointed in the liberal direction. He disliked Schlatter and even called the Tübingen theological faculty "a low dive."[10] A redeeming feature of his unhappy semester in Tübingen was that he met Christoph Blumhardt for the first time. It was Blumhardt who would eventually prove to be helpful in rescuing Barth from what he called "the swamp" of liberal theology.

After this purgatorial time in Tübingen, Barth's father finally relented and allowed him to go to Marburg, his "Zion." The three semesters Barth spent in Marburg from April 1908 to August 1909 were his "happiest student memory."[11] While in Marburg, he studied under Wilhelm Herrmann, Horst Stephan, the Schleiermacher scholar Martin Rade, and the neo-Kantian philosophers Herrmann Cohen and Paul Natorp. In autumn 1908 he took up the post of editorial assistant to Martin Rade, editor of *Christliche Welt*, the leading journal of liberal theology.

On November 4, 1908, Barth was ordained in the Bern Cathedral, with his father preaching the ordination sermon. He returned to attend lectures and seminars in Marburg and to work closely with Martin Rade, with whom he established a close friendship. During his time there he became friendly with Rudolf Bultmann, a doctoral student, and Eduard Thurneysen, a Swiss student whose father was a Reformed pastor and a friend of Barth's father.

Assistant Pastor in Geneva

For the next two years, beginning in September 1909, Barth served the German-speaking congregation in Geneva. As a "Herrmannian of a higher order," to use Hendrikus Berkhof's description,[12] and with what Barth called his "satchel" of modern liberal theology, he assumed the duties of the pastoral ministry. He was not unaware of the difficulties that this posed for him as a pastor. An issue facing established churches at that time was the paucity of applicants from modern theological faculties for the work of foreign missions. Barth contributed to this discussion with a 1909 essay entitled "Modern Theology and Work for the Kingdom of God."[13] He admitted that it was incomparably more difficult for someone like himself who had studied at Berlin and Marburg to make the transition to the parish ministry than for a graduate of a more positive or conservative theological school like Halle or Greifswald. While graduates of the latter institutions were able to affirm the contents of the creed with good conscience, it was not such a simple matter for the graduates of Marburg and Heidelberg. They had imbibed the worldview of religious individualism and had accepted the relativizing implications of historical criticism. They knew that the New Testament must be investigated like any literature of a world religion, such as Zoroastrianism. They were also aware that there is no privileged religious doctrine that is immune from this analysis and criticism. Yet this did not produce a feeling of inferiority on Barth's part but rather a sense of superiority and a certitude in the rightness of modern theology. Barth counseled that the graduates of liberal schools should not jettison their theology to conform to the expectations of parishioners but instead must press forward with integrity to instruct them in it. This provocative essay elicited two responses by professors of practical theology, Ernst Christian Achelis of Marburg and Paul Drews of Halle. They misunderstood Barth and sought to defend Ritschlian theology from what they thought was Barth's attack.

While in Geneva, Barth made two acquaintances that were significant to him for the remainder of his life. The first was his acquaintance with Nelly Hoffmann, who was a member of his confirmation class. She was the youngest of five sisters who had come from Zurich to Geneva in 1905. She was only seventeen when she became engaged to Karl Barth in May of 1911.

The second acquaintance was with the theology of John Calvin. While in Geneva during the four-hundredth anniversary of Calvin's birth, Barth began working through his *Institutes* along with his reading of Schleiermacher's sermons and letters. As Barth confessed later, he read his work with the "peculiar glasses of [his] student years." In fact, he admitted that "Calvin would hardly have been very pleased at the sermons which I preached in his pulpit then." He even toyed with the idea of combining idealist theology with Reformation theology but later abandoned the project as unfeasible.[14] In any event, Barth's engagement with Calvin's theology was not a later development but began with his vicarship in Geneva. It deepened during his Safenwil pastorate, through his use of Calvin's commentaries in the preparation of his sermons and lectures and through his close friendship with Eduard Thurneysen, who shared his interest in the Reformed leader.

Douglas John Hall, my highly esteemed colleague at McGill, has spoken rather negatively of a Calvinizing/Presbyterianizing of Barth's later theology. The old dictum is that theology was born in Germany, corrected in Scotland, and corrupted in the States. Professor Hall's version is that Barth's theology was born in Germany, corrected by Reinhold Niebuhr and Paul Tillich at Union Seminary in New York, and corrupted by Calvinism. This, however, misrepresents Barth by implying that he departed from his roots. In fact, Barth began as a Calvinist under the tutelage of his father, Fritz, and continued to immerse himself in Calvin throughout his long career. Though often critical of Calvin, Barth was convinced that, next to the apostles, he was the best teacher available.

The Safenwil Pastorate

Barth was called to the agricultural and industrial village of Safenwil in the canton of Aargau in July 1911. It was a village of fewer than two thousand residents of whom over 90 percent were Protestants, mainly of the Reformed faith. His installation as pastor took place on July 9, his father preaching the induction sermon. In his own inaugural sermon, Karl Barth laid down what he intended to make the hallmark of his ministry in Safenwil: he would not speak of God only because he was a pastor; rather, he was a pastor because he *must* speak of God.[15] For the newly inducted minister, that meant making the preaching office central. Yet, as he discovered, this was not as simple as it seemed. In a 1922 essay in which he reflected on his Safenwil pastorate, he summarized the pastor's dilemma in three short sentences typical of his dialectical approach: "*As ministers we ought to speak of God. We are human, however, and cannot speak of God. We ought therefore to recognize both our obligation and our inability and by that very recognition give God the glory*" (italics in original for emphasis).[16] For Barth, this dilemma, which every preacher faces, can be overcome as the minister proclaims that "*God* becomes *man*" and states this as

God's Word, as God himself speaks it.[17] The Word of God is the necessary yet impossible task of the minister.

Eduard Thurneysen testified that Karl Barth took the preaching office with the utmost seriousness. "In preparation for this work," Thurneysen wrote, "he sat down before the Bible each day of the week and in his own new way ploughed it like a farmer who goes out into his fields in the early morning and makes furrow after furrow."[18] His sermons were lengthy and intellectually demanding.[19] Attendance at worship services was poor except on special occasions and during the first few Sundays of the First World War, when church attendance surged. Barth, nevertheless, persistently carried out this important work. It was precisely this struggle with the task of speaking of God that changed the direction of twentieth-century Protestant theology.

The "Red" Parson: Barth and Socialism

Barth came up against the social question in a new and stark way when he became the pastor of a working-class village congregation. In an autobiographical piece written in 1927, Barth recalled, "In the class conflict which I saw concretely before me in my congregation, I was touched for the first time by the real problems of real life. The result was that for some time . . . my only theological work consisted of the careful preparation of sermons and classes. What I studied were factory acts, safety and trade unionism."[20]

Gary Dorrien's statement that Barth's theological transformation began with his conversion to Religious Socialism in Safenwil is misleading.[21] It is more accurate to speak of the young pastor deepening his social concern and putting theory into practice. There are many indications that Barth was already a socialist. He was brought up in a home where concern for the destitute was stressed. His father, Fritz, was apparently influenced by the Christian socialism of Friedrich Naumann and subscribed to his journal *Die Hilfe* ("Help for God, help for one's brother and sister, help for the state, help for oneself").[22] In a collection of essays published in 1894, Fritz Barth wrote of the "great and severe" social "emergency" and issued a challenge to "change what has to be changed."[23] Like his father, Karl Barth joined the student association Zofingia. Imbued with a similar social concern, Karl Barth gave a lecture in January 1906 in Bern on "Zofingia and the Social Question" that provoked considerable debate.

The lecture took as its point of departure the high fees Zofingia exacted, in effect excluding poorer students from membership. He referred to Leonhard Ragaz (1868–1945), then the pastor of the Basel Münster church and a Swiss Religious Socialist leader who had drawn attention in one of his sermons to the class struggle. "We have to agree," Barth said, "the gulf between capital and labor . . . in short, between rich and poor . . . is growing continually larger."[24] The social question was part of the human problem that Jesus addressed and that found its religious solution in the Reformation and its political outcome in the French Revolution. While neither of these two historical events brought in the kingdom of God, they were its "necessary premises."[25] Barth called on his fellow students to gain a better understanding of the class struggle and to be filled with the spirit of social responsibility to the lower strata of society.[26]

The Zofingia lecture was long on social responsibility but short on socialist theory. This deficiency would be remedied later after Barth had carefully read Werner Sombart and Heinrich Herkner at the beginning of his Safenwil ministry. Still, there is this perceptive bit of social analysis: "Social activity with the secondary purpose of preserving 'throne and altar' is and remains an absurdity. It is, in effect, 'putting a new piece of cloth on an old garment' or 'pouring new wine in old wineskins.'"[27] The term "prophetic socialism" best describes Barth's position at this stage of his development.[28]

Before beginning his studies at Marburg in 1908, Barth had attended a student conference at Aargau where he heard a stirring address by Ragaz, who contended that God was meeting humanity today through socialism. Socialism and its offshoot Christian socialism had gained ground in Germany in the latter half of the nineteenth century. It was promoted at first by Friedrich Naumann's journal *Die Hilfe* and Adolf Stöcker's Evangelical Social Congress, of which Adolf von Harnack was president from 1902 to 1912. Nevertheless, it did not have the support of many Lutheran pastors, because, among other reasons, they perceived it as hostile to religion. The reverse was true in Switzerland. As Barth recalled in 1950: "Every Swiss pastor who was not asleep or living somehow behind the moon or for whatever reason errant, was at that time in the narrower or wider sense a 'Religious Socialist.'"[29]

The Religious Socialist movement in Switzerland largely owed its impetus to two Swiss Reformed pastors, Hermann Kutter (1863–1931) and the aforementioned Leonhard Ragaz. In 1903, Kutter, pastor of Neumünster church in Zurich where Zwingli had ministered, wrote a short, stirring prophetic book, *They Must: An Open Word to Christian Society*.[30] Kutter had obtained his doctorate in Bern and during his studies had close contact with Fritz Barth. Although Karl Barth would later become dissatisfied with Kutter, who supported Kaiser Wilhelm and Germany in the war, he gratefully learned from him to think of socialism as a parable of the kingdom of God.

Barth was also greatly indebted to Ragaz. In 1906, the year of Barth's Zofingia address, Ragaz had delivered a lecture at a pastor's conference in Basel on "The Gospel and the Current Social Struggle," in which he had analyzed the social struggle and issued a challenge to Christians to become involved in it.³¹ Shortly afterwards, Ragaz, Kutter, and Hans Bader, another Reformed pastor, had organized the Swiss Religious Socialists and planned annual conferences. Ragaz founded a journal, *Neue Wege*, to which Barth later contributed articles. The Swiss Religious Socialists took a stand against both "positive" conservative theology and theological liberalism. Undoubtedly, this created tensions for Barth as he became more passionately involved in the social struggle during his first few years in Safenwil.

An important influence on Swiss Religious Socialism was Christoph Blumhardt (1842–1919). Barth had met him when he studied in Tübingen in 1907, but Blumhardt's crucial impact on Barth's theology of the kingdom of God would not occur until his Safenwil pastorate. Yet Blumhardt's influence was already being powerfully felt in Swiss Religious Socialism. In 1909, Ragaz had his first direct contact with him. Blumhardt's great emphasis was on "waiting" for the kingdom of God, though by "waiting" he did not mean with folded hands but by "action in waiting"—to employ a title of Barth's later essay on him.³² From 1900 to 1906, he served as a Social Democratic Party member of the Württemberg regional parliament. He and his father, Johann Christoph Blumhardt, made a deep impact on Swiss Religious Socialism. They gave it an ability to speak of God as the living God, they contributed an eschatological understanding of the kingdom of God, and they deepened its Christology. Accordingly, Barth's theology came to be shaped in these three ways.

Not only did Barth study leftist sociology and align himself with the working-class members of the village; he also subscribed to trade-union newspapers and journals. Barth began giving lectures to the worker's association, beginning in October. On December 17, 1911, he gave a lecture on "Jesus Christ and the Movement for Social Justice."³³ In it he stated his conviction that socialism was not only the "most urgent word of God to the present" but also a "direct continuation of the spiritual power which . . . entered into history and life with Jesus."³⁴ He was concerned about establishing the inherent connection between Jesus and socialism. Both are movements "from below to above." Both are characterized by solidarity with the poor. There are not two worlds, one spiritual and the other material, "but the one reality of the Kingdom of God." Barth was careful not to make Jesus into a Social Democrat or to defend all socialist behavior but only to argue that the goals of socialists matched those of Jesus. Jesus, Barth went on to explain, wanted four things: "to help those who are least, . . . to establish the Kingdom of God upon this earth, . . . to abolish self-seeking property [ownership]," and to "make persons into comrades."³⁵

In his *Final Testimonies*, Barth recollected: "I was never a doctrinaire socialist. What interested me about socialism in Safenwil was especially the union movement."³⁶ Certainly Barth's approach to socialism was motivated by the need to help his parishioners, and it would become more nuanced after its betrayal by the German Social Democrats, who voted for war credits (like war bonds, these were used to finance military operations) along with the other political parties. Yet one would not go amiss in interpreting Barth's claim in his lecture that capitalism stands in the way of the coming of God's kingdom, and that the goal to eliminate private property as a means of production is radically socialistic in nature. Although he did not join the Social Democratic Party until 1915, he allied himself with its cause much earlier. He idolized the German socialist leader August Bebel, who followed an orthodox Marxist philosophy. Bebel was imprisoned for almost three years for treason against the German state. He exerted a considerable influence on Karl Barth. Vladimir Lenin, who later led the revolution in Russia and who at that time resided in Zurich, greatly admired Bebel as well.

As early as 1911, Bebel was convinced that Germany was heading toward a catastrophic war that would cause "mass bankruptcy, mass misery, mass unemployment and great famine."[37] This probably influenced Barth's early view of the war. A year before it, when Bebel died in August 13, 1913, of a heart attack, Barth devoted part of an August sermon, and a September sermon two weeks later, to his legacy. He placed Bebel alongside Luther and Calvin as a spiritual leader, arguing that although all three had flaws of character and philosophy, God had spoken through each one. The Swiss Germans of the Safenwil congregation were inclined to regard Bebel as a renegade and were displeased with Barth's glowing eulogy. Barth remarked in the September sermon that he had received complaints concerning the August one but would go ahead despite their protests. All this indicates that during his Safenwil pastorate he was a hardline socialist, though he may have become more moderate later. At the same time Barth never committed himself to a Marxist standpoint that prescribed the use of revolutionary methods to achieve socialist goals.

Unsurprisingly, Walter Hüssy, a manufacturer, who owned factories in Safenwil, interpreted Barth's lecture as radical socialism verging on communism. His family had been the major contributors to the building of the Safenwil church some forty years earlier. After reading Barth's lecture in the socialist daily, the *Free Aargau*, he wrote an open letter to the Zofingen daily newspaper ridiculing Barth as an ill-informed, wide-eyed idealist and attacked his lecture "as a long rabble-rousing speech, garnished with an incredible number of religious quotations,"[38] which in fact were biblical passages drawn mainly from Jesus' teaching. There is, he said, a difference between theory and praxis that "even the most ancient, and hence today no longer pertinent, Bible sayings do not help to remove."[39]

Barth was, of course, not one to step away from a fight and in his open response letter entered the fray, as he said, "in my shirt sleeves rather than my frock coat."⁴⁰ After stating that Mr. Hüssy had not understood anything at all in his lecture, Barth affirmed his faith in "progress," but progress away "from economic egoism toward an economic sense of community."⁴¹ Barth concluded that the issue was between Mr. Hüssy's shrewdness, which separated theory from praxis, as well as socialism from the Bible, in which justice replaces private profit.⁴²

It was a sharp, in fact, harsh, reply. The upshot was that Mr. Hüssy's cousin, who was president of the Safenwil church officers, resigned in protest. A couple of years later, all of the six church officers resigned in protest, perhaps spurred by Barth's sermons on Bebel or other socialist themes. Unusually, they were replaced by people who were more favorable to the "red" pastor.

During his ten years in Safenwil, Karl Barth helped organize three unions where none had existed previously. A concrete example may help to gain a better understanding of Barth's efforts on behalf of his working-class parishioners, which he viewed as integral to his pastoral task. In September 1917, fifty-five women employees in the Safenwil knitting mill organized themselves into a union. They were then threatened with a general notice of dismissal. Barth went to the manufacturer's villa to talk with him—as he said, "like Moses with Pharaoh"—to plead their cause. The outcome was a flat rejection, a declaration of war, and Barth being told that he was the "worst enemy" that the manufacturer (presumably Walter Hüssy) had had in his whole life.⁴³ (Barth had been interested in Bebel's work *Women under Socialism*.)

Later Barth reported to his good friend Eduard Thurneysen that the general notice of dismissal had been replaced by individual notices, but surprisingly wages had been increased. Afterwards a union was organized. Barth shared this news with Thurneysen, since he also was a Religious Socialist and a friend of Hermann Kutter. The latter visited often with both of them in their parishes. Along with a common, consuming interest and involvement in the movement for social justice, the two young pastors worked in close association on biblical exposition, sermon preparation, and theological and philosophical studies. They came to share a common theological "vision" that led to their launching of a new theological movement.⁴⁴ We now turn to consider this unique theological relationship.

Barth and Eduard Thurneysen

"No theologian is an island, entire of itself; every theologian is a piece of the continent, a part of the main," to adapt John Donne's memorable words.⁴⁵ The theological task is primarily communal rather than individual, performed in dialogue and close collaboration with other theologians. It is carried out for the edification and upbuilding of the church and not for self-aggrandizement. This close cooperation with others characterized Barth's theological work from the outset: first with Eduard Thurneysen, and then after 1925 with Charlotte von Kirschbaum. In the former case the collaboration was so close that in the two volumes of sermons they published jointly as *Seek God and You Shall Live* (1917) and *Come, Holy Spirit* (1925) it is difficult to distinguish which are Barth's and which are Thurneysen's.

These two young Reformed pastors became neighbors when Thurneysen was called to the Leutwil village church in 1913. They had met as students in Marburg. Eduard Thurneysen's father, also a Reformed pastor, was best man at Karl Barth's parents' wedding. A two-and-a-half-hour walk along valleys and high ridges separated the villages of Leutwil and Safenwil. When Thurneysen was first installed, Barth walked to Leutwil for the service of installation. This walking back and forth became a frequent occurrence. When the two pastors were unable to visit each other they exchanged letters and postcards. These letters have been published and some have been translated into English under the evocative title *Revolutionary Theology in the Making*.[46] They show the remarkable theological and personal oneness between the two. "We had the imperative need," Thurneysen wrote later, "to discuss with each other in real brotherhood everything that was happening in Church, world, and Kingdom of God."[47] They came to share a common perspective, namely, the conviction that God's revelation is found in Holy Scriptures. This led both of them to wrestle with Scripture with a new earnestness, working through not only historical-critical commentaries but also earlier ones, particularly those of the Reformers. Karl Barth later paid this high tribute to his friend: "Eduard Thurneysen was perhaps the very first of all to recognize the necessity for a Church-theology. . . . I myself must confess that I received from him the stimulus to work in this direction."[48] What the two did was try to learn their theological ABCs all over again, beginning by reading and interpreting the writings of the Old and New Testaments more thoroughly than before. "And behold," Barth remembered many years later, "they began to speak to us."[49]

Barth's Break with Liberal Theology

Barth's breakaway from liberal theology involved a move away from the social, political, and religious views of Friedrich Naumann toward those of Christoph Blumhardt. His years in the pastorate, first in Geneva and then in Safenwil preceding the outbreak of the war, were a time of searching, disquiet, and even theological turmoil for Barth, as he struggled with the question of how theology is related to praxis, an issue that was uppermost in his mind as he was on the eve of making his transition from the theological classroom to "work for the Kingdom of God."[50] Barth had become involved in the workers' struggle, which meant a turn to the more practical. Pressure had been building up for a breakaway from liberal theology, and the sources of pressure were at least threefold: first, Barth's growing dissatisfaction with liberal theology's proclivity to preach love without judgment; second, Barth's recently discovered "new world in the Bible" and his view that the Bible is the Word of God and not simply testimonies of religious experience; and third, Barth's shock and dismay over his liberal teachers Harnack, Herrmann, and Rade supporting Kaiser Wilhelm's *Weltpolitik* and war policies.

To be sure, positive theologians such as Reinhold Seeberg of Berlin and Adolf Schlatter of Tübingen also supported Kaiser Wilhelm, but in any case Barth did not regard positive theology as a real alternative. It seems that there were very few peace-loving theologians and clergy in Germany. Statistics show that out of a population of some 65 million, only 10,000 or so belonged to peace societies, whereas in France, with a population of 38 million, there were about 300,000 connected with peace organizations before 1914.[51]

Barth was looking for a totally new direction, which he later found in what Bruce McCormack has called, in the title of his book, Barth's "critically realistic dialectical theology." Strains and tensions began to develop in his thinking. The religious individualism of modern theology collided with the communalism of his pastoral and socialist praxis; the relativizing nature of the historical-critical approach to the Bible collided with the revelation of the sovereign God in Scripture; and the reliance on religious experience collided with his new understanding that theology ought to proceed from God to humanity rather than from humanity to God. As Barth said later in a lecture, "One can *not* [sic] speak of God simply by speaking of man in a loud voice."[52]

There was also an inner contradiction in his Marburg-acquired theology that was now exposed. Colin Gunton has pointed out that Barth had learned from both Harnack and Herrmann the importance of the centrality of Christ. Yet they held, as Barth did also, to Schleiermacher's notion that God is immediately known through religious experience. This position, however, was inherently unstable. If God is immediately perceivable by all people of all religions, then one does not need Christ. Christ becomes superfluous. Communion with God does not need a mediator or require revelation and redemption through Jesus Christ. Barth came to realize that you cannot consistently hold onto both the immediacy and centrality of religious experience and the centrality of Christ.[53]

"Things fall apart, the center cannot hold": this line from William Butler Yeats's poem "The Second Coming" offers a clue to what was happening to Barth's theological position. The happy balance between God and the world that had been integral to Barth's theological outlook learned at Marburg began to fly apart. Barth came to see that pastoral and socialist praxis demanded a radically different foundation than modern liberal theology. The occasions for the breakaway were Barth's 1915 meetings with Friedrich Naumann and Christoph Blumhardt. These meetings made clear to Barth that he had come to a fork in the road and had to make a choice between continuing on the road marked "Naumann" or turning at the road marked "Blumhardt." Unquestionably, Barth was aware at the time of the significance of this twofold meeting, but he did not give literary expression to it until 1919 in his obituary for the two men, who had died in the same year.[54]

Naumann, a Lutheran pastor, became sympathetic with the plight of industrial workers during his time as an industrial chaplain in Frankfurt am Main. In the 1890s he founded the newspaper *Die Hilfe*, which was at first a forum for Christian Socialism. However, as a theological liberal he began to adopt the liberal politics of his day, supporting nationalism and militarism. Barth noted that Naumann had become more pragmatic and less Christian in his political accommodation to the world. The German sociologist Max Weber criticized the Christian element in Naumann's socialism, and Naumann was strongly influenced by Weber's economic theories. Social Democracy, on the other hand—as Barth argued—takes the absoluteness of God with political seriousness.[55] Moreover, Christian hope makes Christians aliens in a sinful world and induces a spirit of longing for something better.

During the early summer of 1914, Barth busied himself with a review of the 1913 issues of *Die Hilfe*[56] for *Die Christliche Welt*—edited by Martin Rade (the journal's name translates as *The Christian World*). Barth had a great deal of respect for the paper, ever since as a schoolboy he had seen it on his father's desk.[57] At the outset of his lengthy article reviewing these issues of *Die Hilfe*, Barth gave an appreciative account of Naumann's progressivism and his advocacy for unemployment insurance, unions, and property reforms, but he noted that Naumann had become pragmatic in his concessions to mainstream politics and that he no longer saw the importance of Christianity for political action. Barth conceded that politics involved compromise but that Christians should not be satisfied with these compromises, since they hoped in something greater.

As Bruce McCormack writes, "For Barth, it was impossible that a Christian should ever think of making a final peace with the world as it is."[58] Barth held that the true Christian is an alien in this world and, at the same time, an advocate for its betterment. To refuse to adjust silently to current conditions, to preserve a "revolutionary unrest,"[59] was the religious drive in socialism that Barth advocated and that Naumann had regrettably abandoned. On the whole, the review criticized *Die Hilfe's* lack of this "revolutionary unrest." Barth's review showed, as George Hunsinger has written, that "[b]y the eve of the First World War, the fault lines of Barth's break with liberalism had become manifest."[60]

The clearest evidence of Barth's break from liberal theology occurred in April 1915, on the occasion of Barth's and Eduard Thurneysen's visit to Marburg to attend the wedding service of Barth's brother Peter to Martin Rade's daughter Helene. This was the occasion during which Barth met Rade's brother-in-law Friedrich Naumann and a lively discussion ensued. It is not known what subjects were discussed, but we can infer from Barth's later writings that it concerned Germany's war aims. In 1915 Naumann had published a book called *Mitteleuropa*, in which he envisioned an industrialized Germany controlling central Europe, including the neutral countries of Belgium, the Netherlands, and Switzerland as well as Turkey, in a postal and free-trade union.[61] Barth disagreed vehemently with this vision, which may have been a factor in their argument. An August 24, 1916, article in the *New York Times* reports Friedrich Naumann's argument in the latest edition of *Die Hilfe* that Germans no longer knew what they were fighting for in the war; that ordinary citizens, suffering unexpected privations, distrusted the government's war aims. In contrast to the view of these "small" people, Naumann was convinced that Germany had to continue the war, hold on to the occupied territories it possessed, and persevere in the struggle against the enemy that was determined to crush Germany.[62]

As for Barth's visit in April 1915, shortly after the wedding he and Thurneysen traveled to Bad Boll in Württemberg to visit Christoph Blumhardt and spend five days at his retreat center. While at Bad Boll, Barth heard a meditation by Blumhardt on Jesus' words "Peace be with you" and talked with him at length. From these talks, Barth saw the significant connection between knowing God and hoping in the future of God's kingdom through belief in God as the renewer of the world. In September 1916, Barth wrote an essay on Blumhardt, entitled "Action in Waiting for the Kingdom of God," in which he pointed out that Blumhardt always began with God, rather than climbing up to God by means of deliberations; since God is the beginning and end, we can wait for him confidently, even though we can see only the beginning.[63]

In Barth's obituary for Naumann and Christoph Blumhardt, who both died in 1919, he pronounced a "No" to Naumann's theology and praxis and a "Yes" to Blumhardt's; for Barth, Naumann now represented the past and Blumhardt the future. Their paths, he wrote, had run parallel for some time and then had diverged greatly. Barth details Naumann's descent from his early revolutionary Christianity into a nationalist socialism. Naumann gradually turned from his earlier understanding of God to "veneration of nature and of culture," including the worship of steel and concrete.[64] His conclusion from his visit to Palestine that Jesus was not a social reformer, his departure from socialism to embrace liberalism, and his adoption of Kaiser Wilhelm's *Weltpolitik* all led to an overriding belief in nationalism and German expansionism. The New Testament, which at one time had opened his eyes to social realities, had become a "closed book" to him.

Naumann achieved such a high reputation that he was being considered for the new presidency of the Weimar Republic, but he died unexpectedly in 1919 while on a Baltic holiday. (General Paul von Hindenburg was elected president in 1925 and in 1933 called on Adolf Hitler, leader of the largest elected party, to become the chancellor of the Weimar Republic.) As a whole, Barth considered that Naumann had "lost that fundamental insight to which he had once come so near,"[65] that of the transformational power of God, and had replaced it with a hope in the time-bound world of nations and politics. As a result, he could represent only the past and not the future.

In contrast, Christoph Blumhardt represented a more vital Christianity than Naumann, and it was he who exerted a positive influence on Barth's new theological direction. In speaking of Blumhardt, Barth first mentions his father, Johann Christoph. From him, Barth learned the important biblical truth that "Jesus is victor." On December 28, 1843, the elder Blumhardt had healed a young woman named Gottliebin Dittus by exorcising demonic spirits that had tormented her for two years. Johann Blumhardt recorded hearing the words "Jesus is victor" from Gottlieben's sister; these words he considered a "cry of despair" from the defeated "angel of Satan," which convinced him that the victory of Jesus is sure in the present as well as the future.[66] Likewise, his son Christoph discerned in all of creation a longing for redemption, and was convinced that, because God reigns, humanity must "awake" from its show of honor, piety, and superficial relationships in order to let the meaning of God's Word permeate all of life.[67]

Like Naumann, Blumhardt was aware of the nature and limitations of humanity, but unlike him, he believed that people could and would necessarily be transformed by the Holy Spirit:

> Because [Blumhardt] believed in God, he also believed in man [*sic*], and because he believed in man, he also believed in the renewal of the world. If the gift "from above" were to be understood again and find a ready soil, all things would be possible. In the meantime, however, he affirmed joyfully and hopefully, as signs and harbingers of the coming victory of Jesus Christ, everything that seemed to him to point toward the renewal of the world which was in preparation.[68]

Christoph represented Württemberg as a Social Democrat in the provincial legislature, but, as Barth said, this was more an act of confession than of politics.[69] This risky step combined action and waiting—two of the qualities Barth emphasized in Blumhardt—in the hope of God's kingdom. To Barth, this was the way the future church must think and act.

THE UNEASY PEACE BEFORE THE GREAT WAR

Karl Barth was aware of Europe's inner turmoil preceding the First World War, unlike his contemporary, the distinguished writer Stefan Zweig. In his August 23 sermon, Barth spoke of the hidden war that had been going on in the European continent, marked by militarism and the arms race, mutual suspicion and hatred, and selfish economic competition.[70] By contrast, in his 1942 autobiography, Zweig had spoken of the years before the war as the golden age of security.[71] It was indeed an age of security for Zweig as a young man, who was born into a wealthy Jewish family, enjoyed the cultural opportunities of one of Europe's major cities, and was privileged to pursue doctoral studies at the University of Vienna to become Europe's most famous and translated writer in the 1920s and 1930s. He would never again experience such a peaceful existence. The First World War brought untold turmoil to Zweig's life. Caught up in war enthusiasm, he joined the Austrian army, only to leave it a year later and, under the influence of his friend Romain Rolland, to become a pacifist. He wrote a pacifist play entitled *Jeremiah*, which, with the help of the Swiss Religious Socialist Leonhard Ragaz, he staged in Zurich in 1917.

The Second World War and Hitler's persecution of the Jews brought even more turmoil, and Zweig despaired of life. Faced with the prospect of a post–World War II world, he and his young wife, the daughter of a rabbi, sadly took their lives in a suicide pact in Brazil in 1942. His autobiography *The World of Yesterday* was published after his death (for Zweig, it was always a world of yesterday and only rarely a world of today and tomorrow). Zweig had also written a book on John Calvin called *The Right to Heresy*, in which he praised Calvin's Basel critic Castellio and castigated Calvin's role in the execution of the heretic Servetus. In his view, Calvin's Geneva was a totalitarian state comparable to Hitler's Germany.

As we will see later, Barth was familiar with the work of Romain Rolland; though he does not refer to him here, his view of what was occurring in Europe was similar. For more than a decade, the prospect of war had hung like the sword of Damocles over Europe, with many nations and alliances struggling for the mastery of the continent. In 1912, in his serial novel *Jean-Christophe*, Rolland foresaw a European war:

> The fire smouldering in the forest of Europe was beginning to burst into flames. In vain did they try to put it out in one place; it only broke out in another. With gusts of smoke and a shower of sparks it swept from one point to another, burning the dry brushwood. Already in the East there were skirmishes as the prelude to the great war of the nations. All Europe, Europe that only yesterday was sceptical and apathetic, like a dead wood, was swept by the flames. All men were possessed by the desire for battle. War was ever on the point of breaking out. It was stamped out, but it sprang to life again. The world felt that it was at the mercy of an accident that might let loose the dogs of war. The world lay in wait. The feeling of inevitability weighed heavily even upon the most pacifically minded.[72]

In the years before the war, European nations stumbled from one crisis to another, from Austria-Hungary's 1908 annexation of Bosnia and Herzegovina, which caused deep resentment in Serbia; the two Moroccan crises, in which Germany tried unsuccessfully to sever relationships between England and France; and the two Balkan wars of 1911 and 1913, when Germany restrained Austria-Hungary from participating. In each case, a larger war was averted through skillful diplomacy.

Otto von Bismarck, often called the Iron Chancellor, had remarked that the next war in Europe would probably occur as the result of a flare-up in one of the Balkan states. He was remarkably prescient, since it was in Sarajevo that the assassination of Archduke Franz Ferdinand and his wife Sophie sparked the Great War. Negotiations had settled the previous crises, but in this case there was an unwillingness on the part of some of the leaders to negotiate.

Multiple institutions failed to prevent the war, as Barth himself noted in his August 23 sermon. First, there was a failure of diplomacy, as diplomats had their hands tied behind their backs, so that they were unable to extend them in gestures of peace. Secondly, there was the failure of socialism. In 1912, the Third International had met in the Münster church in Basel and passed noble resolutions that, in the event of war, European workers would go on strike and refuse to fight. When war actually came, however, national loyalties trumped socialist policies, as in Germany, when the Social Democratic Party voted to give Kaiser Wilhelm II war credits.

Next is the failure of the churches to prevent a war. In his October 18 sermon (p. 145), Barth mentions the French archbishop speaking in Notre Dame, Paris, and shouting, "Vive la France!" He relates that a French Reformed pastor wrote to Kaiser Wilhelm's chaplain, suggesting that they might draft a resolution regarding legitimate war action, and the chaplain replied that Germans did not need to learn lessons from others regarding proper military behavior. Barth also reports that at a mission meeting held in Berlin, the members of the missionary society castigated Britain for entering the war. There had been considerable resentment in Germany about Britain's entry into the war to defend Belgian neutrality. An Austrian Jew, Ernst Lissauer, had written a poem entitled "*Gott strafe England*" ("God Punish England"), which then was set to music and used in public schools.

The fourth failure was that of the intellectuals. In his 1967 "Concluding Unscientific Postscript" to his essays on Schleiermacher, Barth stated that the Appeal and Manifesto of the ninety-three German intellectuals signed by his teachers Adolf von Harnack and Wilhelm Herrmann prompted his breakaway from liberal theology. Either through a lapse of memory, or more probably the confusion of this appeal with similar appeals in September 1914, Barth had mistakenly identified this manifesto as having been drafted at the beginning of the war in his "Concluding Unscientific Postscript" as well as in his essay collection *The Humanity of God*: "One day in early August 1914 stands out in my personal memory as a black day. Ninety-three German intellectuals impressed public opinion by their proclamation in support of the war policy of Wilhelm II and his counselors. Among these intellectuals I discovered to my horror almost all of my theological teachers whom I had greatly venerated."[73]

In his October 18, 1914, sermon, recorded here, he mentions the appeal "To Evangelical Christians Abroad," a similar but less widely known defense of Germany's actions from a Christian perspective. Interestingly, he does not mention the October 3 manifesto at all, though it was the subject of his letter to Herrmann. This later and more prominent manifesto, which sought to justify Germany's violation of Belgian neutrality, gathered over four thousand other signatures. Germany, the intellectuals argued, was simply defending itself; it was concerned about preserving its culture against "Asiatic" barbarism. As well, they dismissed reports of atrocities in Belgium. The scientist Albert Einstein drafted a counterappeal and manifesto, but it did not receive many signatures.

This countermanifesto illustrates the fifth failure—the failure of the peace movements. Peace was simply not loved and pursued with the same energy and vigor as war.

Barth was aware of the deep contradictions that existed in European society and life, particularly the use of brutal force disguised as a defense of civilization. Europe on the eve of the Great War calls to mind Hamlet's words:

> Fie on 't, ah fie! 'Tis an unweeded garden
> That grows to seed. Things rank and gross in nature
> Possess it merely.[74]

Shakespeare's analogy is apropos. On the one hand, Europe boasted of its intellectual and cultural accomplishments, and Germany in particular was noted for its high achievements in biblical and theological studies, archaeology, and *Wissenschaft*, in both the physical and social sciences, as well as in literature, art, and music. On the other hand, this high flowering of European culture was being overrun and choked by the weeds of racial hatred, lust for power, and quest for the mastery of Europe. It was also marked by vicious anti-Semitism, which was rampant in Europe and rife in Russia. For example, thousands of Jews lost their lives in Russia during the pogroms that took place during the Revolution of 1905.

Surprisingly, Barth does not mention the subjection of African, Arab, Asiatic, and Indian peoples in the colonies that the various nations of Europe possessed. For instance, the Belgians killed thousands upon thousands of Congolese. Winston Churchill readily admitted that the British Empire was gained and maintained by violence. It was shameful and hardly conceivable that the Christian nations of Europe should treat these fellow Christian brothers and sisters in the colonies in this way. At that time, Europe was seen to be the undisputed master of the world. As a result of the Great War, however, it was demoted to secondary status, and power was shifted to such nations as the United States and Japan.

There was little or no willingness on the part of Austria-Hungary and Germany its supporter to treat lightly the assassination of the heir apparent to the dual monarchy throne. Strangely, Barth makes no reference to the assassination of Archduke Ferdinand and his wife in his July 5, 1914, sermon. Seemingly Barth and other Europeans were completely oblivious to the crisis that had been caused. The assassination of royal personages was fairly common, and people took it in stride. Despite this, Barth was keenly attuned to contemporary events and movements; for example, he made the sinking of the *Titanic* the subject of a sermon, as he did also the Swiss Exhibition that was held in Bern, and he made reference in his 1913 sermons to the Balkan war that threatened Europe's peace. Later, in his October 18 sermon, Barth mentioned Gavrilo Princip, the assassin of the royal couple, and said sympathetically, perhaps too sympathetically, "The ill-fated murderer, Princip, committed his disastrous deed out of love for his country. We can and shall condemn him for his action but who can condemn him for his patriotism."[75] It was this action that led to the war. It was strange that Barth praised Princip's nationalism while at the same time he condemned German nationalism.

The summer of 1914 was unusually warm and bright throughout Europe, as Stefan Zweig noted in his autobiography and as others have remarked.[76] So was Sunday, July 26. But it was with heavy hearts and a measure of apprehension as the Safenwil worshipers made their way up the hill past the manse, where the young Swiss pastor lived with his wife and family, to the Safenwil Reformed Church. If Europeans in general had wrongly dismissed the danger caused by the recent assassination, they were shaken out of their complacency by Austria-Hungary's announcement on July 23 of its forty-eight-hour ultimatum. Barth was now aware of the threat to Europe's peace. At the top of his sermon manuscript, he wrote, "Austria-Hungary's 48-hour ultimatum to Serbia," the first such notation that he had made on his sermon manuscript.

Three days earlier, Austria-Hungary had delivered the ultimatum to Serbia. This list of draconian demands, that, if accepted, would threaten Serbia's sovereignty, came as the fearful climax to four weeks of inept and failed diplomacy that followed the assassination on June 28. Gavrilo Princip, a Bosnian student with Serbian sympathies and a Serbian-supplied military revolver, had gunned down the royal couple while they were on a state visit in Sarajevo, Bosnia. Austria-Hungary was determined to punish Serbia and to punish it painfully.[77]

Aware of the need to alleviate people's fears, the young Swiss Reformed pastor took his sermon text from Ephesians 2:4–6, on the theme "God has set us in the heavenly realm." At first sight, it strikes us as a strange choice of text for this particular occasion, but in Barth's deft hands, it turned out to be the appropriate one. He assured the congregation that God's heavenly realm is neither removed nor remote from the world but embraces it. Indeed, its freedom, peace, happiness, and order impinge upon and affect the earthly realm. Then, with pointed yet measured candor and what proved to be prescience, he warned: "And possibly we stand today on the eve of a *war* that could set all of Europe ablaze. The rubble heaps of the last war still smolder, the tears of thousands of widows and orphans still flow and now, barring a miracle, we shall unleash anew, like wild beasts, hundreds of thousands of men to attack one another."[78]

If the Safenwil worshipers were apprehensive about a limited Austro-Serbian war, the young preacher had alerted them to the frightening possibility of a total European conflagration. At the same time, Barth deplored the needless folly of even an Austro-Serbian war. "What possible reason do Austrian and Serbian farmers and workers have to hate and kill one another?" Barth asked. "There is no necessity for it other than the compulsion of primitive human passion, except the old principle of retaliation: eye for eye, tooth for tooth (Exod. 21:24)!"[79]

In the ensuing week the crisis escalated. Given a blank check, and not curbed but prodded by Germany, Austria-Hungary dismissed Serbia's response to its "formidable terms" as inadequate, broke off diplomatic relations, declared war on July 28, and bombarded Belgrade the following day. Austrian and German leaders counted on a sharp, swift, localized war. But alas, this was not to be. Russia, Austria-Hungary's long-time rival for influence in the Balkans, announced its intention to intervene. Not only were the Serbians fellow Slavs and Eastern Orthodox in faith, but Russia was simply unwilling to have the dual monarchy dominate the Balkan states and, worse, prevent Russian access to the Aegean Sea through the Bosporus. On July 29, Russia mobilized its armies along the Austro-Hungarian frontier, and on the following day both nations ordered general mobilization.

Russia's entry into the Austro-Serbian conflict set off a chain reaction in the two rival alliances of the six most powerful European nations: the Triple Central Alliance of Germany, Austria-Hungary, and Italy against the Entente Alliance of France, Russia, and Britain, drawing all of them except Italy in a matter of a few days into a calamitous European war. Thus on July 31, fearing encirclement by Russia and France, Germany issued a double ultimatum: one to Russia to demobilize within twelve hours, and one to France to stay out of a Russo-German war. When this ultimatum expired on Saturday, August 1, without a diplomatic response, Germany mobilized and declared war on Russia. At the same time, it also demanded that France give a guarantee of its neutrality in the form of a temporary surrender of its fortresses at Verdun and Toulon. France replied that it would act in accordance with its own interests instead.

"AN AUGUST 1 AS NEVER BEFORE"

Saturday, August 1, 1914, would long be remembered as one of Europe's most tragic days. By coincidence, August 1 was also Switzerland's annual Independence Day, but the customary festivities in 1914 were completely overshadowed by the specter of war. On the Saturday evening, church bells tolled throughout Europe to announce the start of the war between Germany and Russia. For the August 2 services in Safenwil and Ürkheim, where he was filling in for the vacationing pastor, Karl Barth had selected four hymns of confidence and courage, including Paul Gerhardt's "Commit Your Way" and A. Morath's "I Abide with You."[80] His sermon text was, appropriately, Jesus' admonition: "When you hear of war and rumors of war, do not be alarmed; this must take place, but the end is not yet" (Mark 13:7).

Barth had intended to begin his sermon by holding out the hope that a general European war might still be averted. The original opening sentence was: "In the past week we heard a good deal about war and rumors of war, and yet it is indeed not out of the question that we could still get to hear and see something rather different."[81] Along with many other Europeans, he had hoped for a last-minute diplomatic solution. That hope, however, evaporated on Saturday evening. So Barth struck out the opening sentence. The new sentence was dramatic: "Yesterday, we experienced an August 1 as never before." In the few hours between the time he penned the opening part, probably on Saturday morning, as was his usual practice, and when he mounted the pulpit steps on Sunday to deliver it, any remaining hope of peace in Europe had completely vanished.

In a somber, resigned mood, Barth included two more opening sentences to reflect the frightful new reality: "Wasn't it indeed just last evening—without all the usual national festivities but only the solemn sound of church bells as though one could sense our whole nation in all of its thousands of towns and villages holding its breath—that our nation, following the example of our ancestors, readied itself to summon all its strength to secure, at cost of life and property, Switzerland's freedom and independence? We now know the significance of the words: 'when you hear of war and of rumors of war'!"

It seems, although it is by no means certain, that at least the latter half of the sermon and the concluding prayer were written on Saturday night after Germany had declared war on Russia. This may be inferred from the sermon's contents that appear to presuppose Germany's announcement of general mobilization and its declaration of war on Russia. Switzerland's decision to mobilize its army at its frontiers followed upon Germany's action.

Barth's August 2 sermon focused on Jesus' injunction, "Do not be alarmed!" Only a heartfelt trust in God, Barth said, can give one a solid footing in difficult days and can facilitate fearlessness in perilous times. Switzerland's neutrality would not automatically guarantee it immunity from enemy attack. Encircled by Austria, Germany, France, and Italy, Switzerland could easily become a theater of war as in 1798, when it was overrun by French troops. Even if it escaped invasion, it would not be exempted from the effects of a European war.

In this sermon, Barth counseled the Safenwil and Ürkheim churchgoers on several mundane matters. He spoke about the folly of withdrawing money from banks and keeping it in a chest at home, since money was safer in a savings bank. Moreover, if this thoughtless practice persisted, it would have a disastrous effect on the economy. A more serious concern was Switzerland's order to mobilize its army of 250,000 soldiers at its frontiers. Since military service was compulsory for every able-bodied Swiss man, soldiers from towns and villages, including Safenwil and Ürkheim, would be required to leave next day to defend the Swiss frontier. Barth expressed the hope that all who were called would respond "unfalteringly and without hesitation"; moreover, that their wives would not make their departure more difficult than it already was by complaining and worrying. The responsibility of raising children would now be thrust wholly upon mothers, without the help of fathers, who would be at the frontiers. Mothers would need to double their efforts to discharge this all-important task.

In these and other respects, Barth's sermon was not too different from most sermons preached in Germany, Austria, and Russia on that August 2 Sunday. Clergy called on soldiers to rally to the defense of their homeland and enjoined those who stayed at home to support those who went out to fight. In every European belligerent nation, as might be expected, the war was presented to the public as strictly defensive. The German government had carefully manipulated the news during the July crisis and on August 1 to make it seem that it was forced into a defensive war because of the aggression of Russia and its allies. Germany had been attacked, and it was defending itself and its high culture. The propaganda weapon *Feinde ringsum* (enemies all around us) became the moral basis for Germany's war effort on both its eastern and western fronts. In view of the close ties that existed between throne and altar in Germany, most Protestant Lutheran pastors and Roman Catholic priests on that Sunday and the following ones ardently supported and promoted Germany's war policy.[82]

Yet Barth's August 2 sermon was also unlike many other sermons preached that Sunday in central Europe. It was a powerful protest against the war, and as such it might not have resonated with Barth's audience. Generally speaking, Swiss Germans tended to support Germany's cause, while Barth was intent that Switzerland maintain its neutral position. Barth was especially concerned with countering the claim that a European war was inevitable. Yet did not Jesus's words in that Markan passage give some currency to the thought that wars "must happen"? Barth admitted that on the first hearing they gave that impression, but not upon probing deeper. To show this, Barth raised two questions: "Did Jesus intend to say that war was an evil that simply must be endured? Is it a fate, that from time to time, human beings must mutually slaughter and murder one another and that fact has to be accepted with silence and suffering, because it cannot be otherwise on this earth? The obvious answer to both questions is: 'No!' a thousand times 'No!'"[83]

War belongs to the moral realm of responsible choice and not to the realm of nature, where phenomena, for example, the sun and the rain, are subject to unalterable, necessary laws. War is an outcome of wrong attitudes, which, in turn, are based on sinful actions. Therefore, when Jesus said that wars "must happen" he did not mean that they are caused by any necessity of nature, by an unalterable law beyond human control, or by a fate to which nations and individuals must passively submit. War is an act and deed of the human will. Barth thus declared: "War is wrong, war is sinful, war is no necessity but rather stems from the evil of human nature."[84] God's will regarding war is clear: Jesus taught that "God does not will wrong, suffering, misery; God does not will war. God is only love, salvation, peace."[85] Yet, as Barth explained in a letter to his friend Eduard Thurneysen: "The formula 'God does not will the war' is perhaps misleading. God does not will egotism. But God does will that egotism should reveal itself in war and become itself the judgment. Thus the will of God to judge is nothing other than love, the revelation of the divine righteousness."[86] Jesus' statement "It must therefore be" means that sin must ripen through much blood and tears in order to be universally recognized and rejected as sin.

By the following Sunday the war was in full swing. On August 3, Germany declared war on the French nation and invaded Luxembourg and Belgium in order to attack France in a counterclockwise sweeping movement from the north, outflanking the French fortresses on the French-German frontiers. It followed a plan devised by Alfred von Schlieffen, chief of the German general staff 1891–1906. Von Schlieffen sought to guard against the danger of a two-front war posed by the Russian-Franco alliance by delivering a preemptive strike against France before Russia was able to attack in the east. A timetable was part of the plan. Forty-two days after mobilization, the German armies would reach the French frontier. On the thirty-first day the German line would stretch along the Somme and Meuse rivers. From that position the right wing would move southward to envelop Paris from the west and south.[87] Six weeks after the outbreak of the war, Paris would be in German hands. Germany would go on to defeat Russia and then dictate the terms of peace. "The shortest road to St. Petersburg was via Paris," was how Henry Pachter, an American historian, cleverly summed up this plan.[88] The Schlieffen Plan's timetable gave Kaiser Wilhelm the confidence to promise soldiers as they left Berlin on August 2: "You will be home again before the leaves fall."

The other member of the Triple Alliance was England, which Germany hoped would remain neutral. England was a guarantor of Belgian neutrality. Admittedly, while this played an important role in Prime Minister Asquith's government's decision to go to war, Britain's fears of German hegemony in Europe and of German control of Belgian seaports proved to be equally or more important. Britain went to war on August 4, after its ultimatum to Germany to respect Belgian independence was ignored. Britain's declaration of war was binding on all the dominions within the empire, including Australia, Canada, India, New Zealand, and South Africa. As a result, the European war escalated into a world war. The United States declared its neutrality (and did not enter the war until 1917, in response to the sinking of the *Lusitania* in 1915 and the continued torpedo attacks on American merchant ships). Italy did not enter the war until 1915, and then, contrary to its supposed entanglement in the Central Triple Entente, took the side of Russia, France, and Britain.[89]

On the occasion of Italy's joining the Triple Entente, Eduard Thurneysen wrote to Karl Barth and in chagrin said that politics is politics and that he still wished that Germany would win the Great War. Karl Barth replied and agreed that politics is politics but went on to say that he did not want Germany to win, for two reasons: first, Germany's attack on neutral Belgium and its atrocities and, second, Germany's sinking of the *Lusitania*. With regard to Belgium, Barth particularly deplored the atrocities that resulted in the burning of the Louvain library. The Germans burnt the library and 200,000 ancient volumes that were irreplaceable. They also shot the rector of the University of Louvain, the mayor, and two priests.

Edward Gibbon wrote in the second volume of his *Decline and Fall of the Roman Empire* that the Goths sailed by ship through the Bosporus and Dardanelles to Greece and attacked Athens. The soldiers gathered the books from the philosophical academies and were about to burn them. One of the wise officials told him not to go ahead. He said as long as the Greeks busied themselves with books, they will not learn the arts of war. It seems there was no wise descendant of these barbarians who tried to stop the German soldiers.

The case of the sinking of the Cunard passenger liner *Lusitania* is more complex. The liner left New York City transporting over two thousand passengers and carrying weapons. It was promised the protection of British destroyers who would accompany it to its Liverpool port. This destroyer convoy was withdrawn, and the *Lusitania* was torpedoed by a German U-boat. Eric Larson has written a fascinating book on the sinking of the *Lusitania* and has speculated that Churchill deliberately withdrew the convoy in order to have it sunk and bring the Americans into the First World War.

Barth also expressed to Thurneysen his wish that neither the Triple Entente nor the central powers would win the war but would sign an armistice. Barth was naïve. He did not see that imperial powers are loath to talk about peace without there being a clear victor to dictate the terms of peace. The Germans refused to give up their claim on Belgium, and both sides went on to continue the war.

On the manuscript of his August 9 sermon, Barth had written: "*War between Germany, Austria-Hungary, Russia, France, England.*" The apostle Paul's advice to the Philippian Christians, "Do not worry about anything! But in everything by prayer and supplication with thanksgiving let your requests be made known to God (Phil. 4:6)," was Barth's text for the first Sunday of the Great War. In his brief introduction, he noted that in grave times people expected their pastors to be able to speak "with the tongues of men and angels." Understandably, they sought a word of comfort, encouragement, and spiritual uplift. But even more, in a time that resembled the prophet Amos's day, when there was "a famine of the hearing of the word of the LORD" (Amos 8:11), people longed for a prophet who could interpret the signs of the times for them.

We may not have a prophet like Isaiah or Jeremiah in our midst, Barth said, but we do have the Bible and the light of the prophetic word shining so brightly from its pages. "There is something wonderful about this ancient book," Barth told his people. "Particularly in these troubled times, yet at all times, we need to go to this source and to drink deeply from it." He reminded them of a few of its majestic passages: "Out of the depths I cry to you, O LORD! LORD, hear my voice!" (Ps. 130:1). "When you hear of wars and rumors of war, do not be alarmed" (Mark 13:7). "I know the plans I have for you . . . plans for welfare and not for evil, to give you a future and a hope" (Jer. 29:11).

The existential predicament caused by the outbreak of the war, and the pastoral situation of his parishioners seeking something higher than a worldly reality to hold on to, drove Barth to dig more deeply into the Bible. His rediscovery of the prophetic word reflected in his August 9 sermon was a harbinger of the theological direction that he and his friend Eduard Thurneysen would eventually take in a year or two. When these two young pastors discussed where they should start in finding a new beginning for Protestant theology, they decided to begin with the Bible.[90]

As well, Barth spoke to the Safenwil congregation about Switzerland's neutrality in the war. Germany's and France's diplomatic promises that they would respect Switzerland's neutrality, Barth said, provided a measure of security. Yet circumstances could quickly change as a consequence of the necessities of war. Switzerland must find and place its trust not in these assurances but in God. At any rate, the Swiss ought to be grateful that up to this point God had dealt more mercifully with them than they really deserved. He counseled the many Swiss wives who were worried and distressed by the question, "Will my husband return home safely?" He assured them how much more certainly and confidently they might regard the future of Swiss soldiers compared to those of other European nations: "I would like them to think for a moment of the millions of women whose husbands are now in Alsace, in Belgium, in Poland, in Galicia, on the Danube or somewhere on the high seas encountering a bloody battle or those who possibly on this beautiful Sunday morning are right in the thick of battle or have already fallen for their country on foreign soil."[91]

BARTH, RADE, AND HERRMANN

Karl Barth came into conflict with his former Marburg teachers Martin Rade and Wilhelm Herrmann over their enthusiastic support of Kaiser Wilhelm II's war policies. The "chaos" of the outbreak of war delayed the delivery of the first few August issues of *Die Christliche Welt*.[92] When Barth read these at the end of August, he was appalled by the content of Rade's editorials, an article by the neo-Kantian Natorp (to whom Barth refers in an October sermon) writing a letter to a friend in the Netherlands defending the war, and other articles seeking to justify the war. He regarded as especially objectionable Rade's decision to publish Luther's famous treatise *Whether Soldiers, Too, Can Be Saved* (1526) over three subsequent issues. In Barth's view, this was a brazen but rather clumsy attempt to enlist the sanction and support of the great German reformer for Kaiser Wilhelm's war. He wrote immediately to Rade stating that everything written lately in the journal seemed to presuppose that Germany was in the right in the war.[93] Barth went on to say, "For me, the saddest thing in these sad times is to see how in all of Germany now, love for the Fatherland, delight in war, and Christian faith are brought together in hopeless confusion."[94] On September 4 Barth wrote to his friend Thurneysen, stating that "[t]he unconditional truths of the gospel are simply suspended for the time being and in the meantime a German war-theology is put to work, its Christian trimming consisting of a lot of talk about sacrifice and the like. . . . Marburg and German civilization have lost something in my eyes by this breakdown, and indeed forever."[95]

Barth was scandalized that the articles published in *Die Christliche Welt* tried to "enlist" God for the German cause—an attempt to identify God with sin-tainted human actions. After Rade responded and asked for their debate to be published in the Swiss journal *Neue Wege*, Barth replied that he would prefer a more widely read German publication such as *Zeitschrift für Theologie und Kirche* or *Die Christliche Welt* itself, but Rade insisted on his first choice. Readership was thus limited compared to what it would have been, had it been published in Germany.

At the beginning of November, Barth wrote to his former and favorite teacher Wilhelm Herrmann after he had seen Herrmann's signature on the October 3 appeal and manifesto of the ninety-three German intellectuals. Among the other things that he had to say to Herrmann, Barth wondered whether Herrmann had read any of the French pacifist Romain Rolland's articles written against the Great War—with the implication that, had he not, he ought to. Above all, he was concerned with asking Herrmann where he stood in regard to the German "war theology," since Herrmann had taught him to value religious experience so highly.[96]

It seemed to Barth that the German experience of their war as a righteous and even holy war was not consistent with God's word. Barth began to question the doctrine of the centrality of religious experience, since it could be so easily misapplied. It is worth mentioning that, at the end of the war, Wilhelm Herrmann requested that his name be withdrawn from that appeal and manifesto. It seems that Barth's letter to Herrmann was not without its effects. On the other hand, Barth did not write to Adolf von Harnack, knowing that this staunch German nationalist would not be moved from his position by appeal or argument.[97]

REVOLUTIONARY THEOLOGY IN THE MAKING

On September 4, 1914, Barth sent Thurneysen a copy of his August 23 and August 30 sermons. He explained that they were not finished products but were to be regarded as experiments. He added that along with others he was experimenting every Sunday in different ways, "both for our own sake and for the sake of our churchgoers who have now become extremely eager." Barth then referred to the tension that existed in speaking of "God's order and human disorder," which in the 1932–33 seminars he had described as the tension between closeness to the biblical text and closeness to life: "*Dei providentia—hominum confusio*; round and round that center do we turn now Sunday by Sunday and have no other choice. I want more and more to hold them both together. Sometimes I have more success, sometimes less."[98]

Barth's sermons have not always received the attention they merit or been accorded the theological importance they deserve by commentators on Barth's theology. A notable exception is Bruce McCormack's fine study, *Karl Barth's Critically Realistic Dialectical Theology*, in which he quotes at some length from the 1913 and 1914 volumes of Barth's sermons.[99] That is salutary. It is a recognition of the importance that Barth attached to proclamation as a form of the Word of God. Moreover, these sermons constitute what Barth later described as irregular dogmatics (*irreguläre Dogmatik*), or unsystematic theology.

Barth made a helpful distinction between regular and irregular dogmatics. The former is an activity mainly of the schools but can take place outside the academy. It aims at inquiry, instruction, and comprehensiveness. Examples of regular dogmatics are such works as Origen's *On First Principles*, Thomas Aquinas's *Summa Theologiae*, Calvin's *Institutes of the Christian Religion*, and Schleiermacher's *The Christian Faith*. Irregular dogmatics, on the other hand, is occasional and fragmentary. The examples Barth gives include Athanasius, Martin Luther, Hermann Kutter, and J. Christoph Blumhardt. Barth commented: "And it must be noted that regular dogmatics has always proceeded from irregular, and without its stimulus and co-operation could never have existed."[100] This statement could well be applied to Barth's 1914 sermons, for from them and the *Romans* commentary, Barth's regular dogmatics flowed. These sermons, including the some five hundred other sermons he preached, cannot be separated from his later theology, any more than Schleiermacher's sermons, as Barth pointed out, can be separated from Schleiermacher's later theology.

We can now cast a first glance into the 1914 war sermons, which until recently were almost completely unknown in English. For four months of Sundays, from the end of July to the end of November 1914, Karl Barth not only let the war rage on in his sermons, but also raged against it by declaring his unremitting opposition to its folly and wickedness.[101] His war sermons are significant not only from a social, political, and cultural standpoint, as we shall discuss later, but also for their theological direction. G. C. Berkouwer, an early Dutch critic of Barth's theology, was the first to note the importance of Barth's sermons for the development of his theology. They show the initial phase of the theological revolution that was gradually taking shape.

Fifty years ago my former teacher, colleague, and friend James D. Smart translated the 1914–1925 Barth-Thurneysen correspondence and gave it the title *Revolutionary Theology in the Making*. Properly speaking, the title is more applicable to the 1914 war sermons than it is to the letters. Indeed, the sermons embody a theological revolution in progress; the letters are a commentary on it. The irregular dogmatics of these sermons is the basis of much of Barth's regular dogmatics, such as the famous multivolume *Church Dogmatics*. It will be our task to explore these sermons' themes of this irregular dogmatics, noting where Barth retains elements of his liberal teachings learned at Bern, Berlin, and Marburg, and where he has shed some of his liberal presuppositions.

BARTH'S THEOLOGICAL THEMES

Jochen Fähler, an editor of Barth's 1913–1915 sermons, also wrote an early dissertation on "The Outbreak of World War 1 in Barth's Sermons" (*Der Ausbruch des 1. Weltkrieges in Karl Barths Predigten*, published 1979). Only a limited use has been made of Fähler's dissertation, for two reasons: first, Friedrich-Wilhelm Marquardt, who reviewed the 1914 volume in *Evangelische Theologie*, has faulted Fähler for minimizing Barth's Swiss Religious Socialism; second, Bruce McCormack has criticized Fähler's work for its "limited . . . scope" and lack of context concerning Barth's theological development.[102] Fähler is particularly helpful, however, in tracing the theological themes, and I have followed him as a guide in this respect. In discussing these themes, it is appropriate to begin where Barth himself began, with his understanding of the Bible as the Word of God.

In his August 9 sermon, Barth stated that he had heard many express a wish that there would be an Isaiah or Jeremiah in their midst to interpret the

Great War to them. While an Isaiah or Jeremiah was not available, Barth said, "We have the prophetic word, which shines as a bright light in a dark place." Here for the first time, Barth made reference to the new world of the Bible, a world of God, as he wrote in his 1916 essay "The Strange New World within the Bible": "A new world projects itself into our old ordinary world. We may reject it. We may say, It is nothing; this is imagination, madness, this 'God.' But we may not deny nor prevent our being led by Bible 'history' far out beyond what is elsewhere called history—into a new world, into the world of God."[103] Revelation, not just religion, is found in the Bible.

Thus Barth asserted the supremacy of the Word of God and took his theological lead from God's revelation by the power of the Holy Spirit in the Scriptures of the Old and New Testaments. Barth's emphasis on the Word of God sounded strongly in the September 20 National Day of Penitence sermon on the text of Jeremiah 22:29: "O land, land, land, hear the word of the Lord!" It is customary on such occasions, Barth said, for the preacher to express his political opinions, but this year, the year of the Great War, would necessarily be different. We must, he argued, hear the Word of God and not listen to the political views of the parson. God speaks, and we human beings must hear and heed God's word.

It is said that a sermon should be about God and about twenty minutes. While Barth exceeded the time limit by at least another twenty minutes, his sermons were always about God. For Barth, the war had raised the "life and death" questions of God: Who is God, and what are God's ways? The transcendent, eternal God, clothed in majesty and splendor, is the constant subject of each of these sermons. From Hermann Kutter, the Swiss Religious Socialist, Barth had learned that God is a living God, and this emphasis on God's activity is found throughout the war sermons. God is basically a God of love, of peace, and of justice. God's eternal righteousness is set over and against all human righteousness, which is subject to the deception of "necessity knows no law," as Chancellor Bethmann-Hollweg claimed in his August 4 speech to the Reichstag.

As Barth stated in his August 9 sermon, "This God is the infinite power behind all things. In and through God everything that is exists and is held together. God imparts life and movement to everything." God is "wholly other"—by which Barth did not mean that God is distant and remote but that God's thoughts are not our thoughts, and God's ways are not our ways (Isa. 55:8). In his September 6 sermon he emphasized, "Everything comes from this God who is a God of justice and order, to whom oppression and conflict are a horror precisely because in God there is essentially only love and freedom. Everything is from God, heaven and earth, present as well as past and future, all that is greatest and least." As a result, Barth continued, the war is under God's control, but to say God supports one side over another is limiting and even blasphemous.

A constant refrain in these sermons is Galatians 6:7 (NRSV): "Do not be deceived; God is not mocked, for you reap whatever you sow." Barth saw the war as a punishment that the European nations in many ways inflicted upon themselves. The war was not inevitable but was an outcome of sinful attitudes and actions. Europe, despite its boasted high culture, received through the war a rebuke from God, a message that it was on the wrong path. Europe was ripe for judgment: "We stood in envy next to one another, all of us greedily working our way up, wickedly piling up tinder for the conflagration between the selfish masses that we call nations, always producing more, always wanting to become stronger—until now finally this explosion of evil had to occur" (Aug. 23 sermon, p. 85). As mentioned earlier, Barth, unlike his liberal teachers, usually spoke of God's love alongside God's judgment. God's love is a holy love and is set over and against human unrighteousness. For Barth, judgment was not the last word; God's final word was the grace that abounds over judgment. This is seen in Barth's October 18 sermon, where he noted that the war, however destructive and sinful, also has redemptive potential. This "unique time of God" was also a unique time of God's manifested grace.

It is not known whether Barth owed a debt to Johann Sebastian Bach for the cognate German word *Gotteszeit* in his hymn *Gottes Zeit ist die allerbeste Zeit* (God's time is the best time). Doris Day often sang an English version of this German song. Barth used the term *Gotteszeit* more than twenty times in his dogmatic works. Prima facie, the term *Gotteszeit* suggests natural theology. The German people flocked to the churches in the belief that the war was a *Gotteszeit* and that soon Germany's hegemony would be established in Europe, but Barth meant by *Gotteszeit* both God's judgment and the offer of God's grace.

At any rate, by using the term *Gotteszeit*, Barth connected the war with the mysterious action of God. The war was not something totally negative, the work and triumph of Satan; it occurred under the watchful eye of a sovereign God. Another way of stating this would be to employ the language of Martin Luther, who spoke of both the "strange" and "proper" work of God. God's "strange work" was his condemnation and judgment of the sinner; his "proper work" was his offer of grace. In Luther's Christology, the cross represented the former, and the resurrection the latter.[104] Barth followed Luther's dialectical method: God had drawn near, in both mercy and judgment, to the people of Europe. Furthermore, Barth had the rare ability to see both sides of a question or an issue, and to give each side its due. He saw both the negative and the positive aspects of the Great War. He recognized that the war brought out the worst qualities of humanity—hatred, death, and destruction.

But he recognized, as he elaborated in his October 18 sermon, that the war also brought out many admirable qualities, such as comradeship and willingness to sacrifice.

For Barth, God's love is revealed not only in imperfect human actions, but also and most importantly in his Son, Jesus Christ. Barth held that for the apostle Paul, "God is primary, absolutely primary. God became the primary reality for him through Jesus Christ" (July 26, p. 49). We can experience God certainly and fully only through Christ Jesus, as Paul did. In finding God through Jesus, we "immediately" enter God's kingdom (July 26, p. 49). Barth expanded on this idea in the next week's sermon: this introduction to God through Jesus, as long as we can feel in ourselves Jesus' love and trust for the Father, allows us to be fearless, even in the midst of war and grief. Such is God's kingdom on earth (Aug. 2, p. 59).

Besides Jesus' impact on the believing individual, if whole nations had taken Jesus seriously, Barth argued, the war would not have occurred but been "nipped in the bud" (Sept. 20, p. 125) He stressed the humanity of Jesus: "Jesus was a man of flesh and bone as we are. He also had to eat and drink and live as we do. He lived in the midst of circumstances, in the conditions of this imperfect, limited world" (Oct. 25, p. 155).

If Barth believed that the war had raised the life-and-death question of "Who is God?" it also raised the question of eternal life as never before. The Christian hope occupies a large part of these war sermons. In his July 26 sermon, Barth defined the Christian hope against worldly hope, which merely wishes for something better; by contrast, biblical hope offers "infinitely more," including present certainty in the future. He went even further to say, "It is 'a sure and certain hope,' for it already possesses what it expects" (July 26, p. 49)—meaning that eternal life in the kingdom of God has already begun, and the fulfillment of all things is near. Especially during the war's outset, he assured his parishioners that this hope transcends all earthly difficulties.

Though Barth often emphasized the sovereignty of God rather than humankind's actions, he also highlighted the role of faith in reaching the "goal" of assurance: "That goal is an unshakable hope. And it's no small, self-seeking hope. It's a hope that 'does not make us ashamed'" (Rom. 5:5). (Aug. 9, p. 69). In his August 23 sermon, Barth similarly argued that if the congregation had a solid faith, their hope would be firmer and less dependent on the ups and downs of life—in this case, the rapidly changing news of the war (Aug. 23, p. 85). This Christian hope makes us dissatisfied with things as they are and inspires renewal and change. It is often thought that Barth's eschatology was so extreme that it led to political quietism. Was it then the case that Barth, like some people, was so heavenly minded that he was of absolutely no earthly use? On the contrary, he encouraged Christian social and political responsibility by emphasizing the example of the kingdom of God. Barth's eschatological views continue to exercise considerable influence, as is evidenced by Jürgen Moltmann's *Theology of Hope*.

At the same time, some of the philosophical views expressed in his 1914 sermons can be interpreted as Gnosticism, if not political quietism per se. In his July 26 sermon, Barth included strong Platonic and Neoplatonic statements calling into question the external reality of the world. Perhaps due to the influence of German idealism, he used the language of "shadows and appearances" and left the impression that suffering and evil belong to an illusory world, a view that potentially minimizes the reality of suffering. Though Barth realized the horrific loss of life the war would cause, his language at times seems distant and ungrounded. Nevertheless, Barth would later shed these Neoplatonic ideas and adopt a more realist philosophical view. In these early sermons, he also retained the liberal view that Jesus' teaching was confirmed by the urgings of conscience, presumably the urgings of a Christian conscience. This line of thought he inherited from his liberal teachers at university, and he would later give it up in order to abandon any semblance of natural theology.

BARTH AS A SOCIAL AND POLITICAL COMMENTATOR

Toward the end of his life, Barth established a friendship with Carl Zuckmayer, the German dramatist who wrote *The Captain of Köpenick*. Zuckmayer had retired to live in Switzerland and had written his autobiography, entitled *A Piece of Myself*. Barth had written to Zuckmayer appreciatively about the book, and so began an exchange of visits, letters, and conversations. Zuckmayer related that during the summer of 1914, when he and his family vacationed in the Netherlands, a Dutch woman asked him if he would fight if there were a war, and he answered no. Upon his return home, however, he was caught up in the enthusiasm that the war had created; before completing high school, he enlisted in the German army. This was not unlike the experience of the adventurous youth and stormtrooper Ernst Jünger, who similarly was inspired by the spirit of 1870–71, the years of the Franco-Prussian war. He spent the most of the next four years at the front. Zuckmayer states in his book that he and his contemporaries were not sufficiently political to counter the German spirit that inspired many to go to war.

Unlike Zuckmayer, Karl Barth was more than sufficiently political and had the advantage of living in neutral Switzerland. He had honed his political skills at an early age, as can be seen from the 1906 lecture he gave to the

Zofingia student organization, "Zofingia and the Social Question."[105] He was an avid reader of Swiss and foreign newspapers and journals. As he boasted later, his basement was full of books and articles on contemporary social, political, and cultural events. After he had met Chancellor Georg Michaelis, Bethmann-Hollweg's successor, Barth speculated that, had he himself been appointed, he would have proved to be a better chancellor.[106] This was no vain boast but a just assessment. Clearly he knew more and would have been far abler to carry out the duties of a chancellor. Given his sharp mind, powers of observation, and vast store of social, economic, and political information, Barth was uniquely qualified to comment on the events of the war. As early as August 23, Barth perceived that Europe was only at the beginning of the war, contrary to the German belief that it would overcome France in a matter of six weeks. Barth predicted that millions upon millions would die and that the carnage and destruction would be indescribable.

In his August 23 sermon, Barth proclaimed, "[T]his time is one of the most serious of all world history. . . . What are all the wars we have known compared with the war that has now blazed up? What are even the Napoleonic campaigns and the Thirty Years' War in Germany, compared with the colossal clash of nations that is now being prepared?" (Aug. 23, p. 85). While Barth took into account the Thirty Years' War and the Napoleonic wars, he did not mention the American Civil War, with which he was probably rather unfamiliar until his 1962 visit to the United States. Moreover, he did not accept the sanitized view of the war as a matter of justice or injustice but was convinced that it was a power struggle among the European nations to have a "place in the sun" (Aug. 30, p. 95).

Barth also viewed it as a racial conflict: "The ancient antagonism between the German and the French way has broken out openly once more. . . . And on the other side, in Eastern Europe, German civilization is opposed to Slavic civilization. This racial hatred and racial conflict, my friends, do not concern us" (Aug. 30, p. 95). Who was just and who was unjust? All were culpable, even though some were more responsible than others for the instigation of the war. Barth held that historians would argue for decades to come concerning responsibility for the war (Sept. 6, p. 105). At the same time, God was working despite and through humanity's wickedness: the war, to Barth, was "a unique time of God; a time of judgment without equal. And for that very reason, it [was] also a wholly special time of grace" (Aug. 23, p. 85).

Barth counseled that Switzerland ought to pursue neutrality as its policy and refuse to take sides either openly or inwardly. He commended neutrality not simply for practical reasons but as a demonstration of God's coming kingdom, a higher ideal than a "fatherland": "We believe that humankind, in spite of different origins and competing interests, will live on the earth as brothers and sisters, as one united people, as we Swiss want to and now already can live as brothers and sisters in our small land" (Aug. 30, p. 95). It is not up to the Swiss to judge the rightness of either side. The "God of love, freedom and justice" is not a God who takes sides (Aug. 30, p. 95).

Barth was arguing against those who agreed that the war was horrible but still regarded it as a just cause. He himself did not attribute just causes to the war but, rather, more selfish causes, such as greed, racial hatred, and the quest for power. He referred to Luther's 1526 treatise *Whether Soldiers, Too, Can Be Saved*, which argues that soldiers may fight in a war with a clear conscience—the same essay Rade reprinted in *Die Christliche Welt*—but suggested that Luther himself was misguided, since, even for one so close to God, it is tempting to make excuses for human behavior (Sept. 6, p. 105).

Barth realized that, as a result of the war, world power would shift:

> What about the things that will be destroyed, the means of livelihood and works of art, what Europe will forfeit economically through American competition, which now all of a sudden and for a long time can develop freely at our expense? And how much can the European nations lose with regard to power and respect in the eyes of other nations in Africa and, above all, in Asia, with all the uncivilized and half-civilized peoples, who have long waited to free themselves from a hated Europe? All this can scarcely be predicted. (Aug. 30, p. 95)

Barth saw clearly that that political power was being shifted to such comparatively new nations as the United States and soon-to-be-independent colonies in Africa and Asia.

Philip Jenkins's comments that the Great War redrew the religious map of the world, with Christianity beginning to penetrate more deeply into Asia and Africa. In 1900, there were three European Christians for every one African Christian. By the year 2050, that figure will be reversed.[107] Despite Barth's early view of these less-developed nations as "uncivilized," he regarded the fall of European supremacy as a necessary judgment for and result of the war. Barth first acknowledged the appellation of the war as a world war on September 6; as an aside, he remarked that it was more of a European war than a world war. As the war progressed, however, it did involve many Asian and Middle Eastern nations, and only a few smaller nations remained unaffected.

Barth was impressed by the "German war machine" and its success. The German nation had told itself that it would win or perish. By September 6, the date of his sixth war sermon, the German armies had advanced far into France, but Barth stated that the contest had not yet been decided—in contrast to Germany's assurance of conquering Paris within a week. In 1961, historian Fritz Fischer wrote a book, entitled *Germany's Aims in the First World War*, that created considerable controversy among German historians. It posited a fundamental continuity between the First and Second World Wars, in that both were instigated by Germany and expansionist in aim—a search for *lebensraum*. The term *lebensraum*, meaning room to live, was formulated during the First World War, not the Second. Fischer's thesis is still being debated by historians. Barth, as far as I know, did not comment on Fischer's work, written late in Barth's life, but he probably would agree with its thesis. Friedrich Naumann, in Barth's view, represented many German intellectuals and politicians who held to this imperialist, expansionist view, a view that Barth himself rejected.

As to the question of a "just war," Barth argued that nations who had justice on their side would not need to go to war in the first place. To him, nations praying for war victory were analogous to street thieves who pray before and after stealing (Sept. 6, p. 105). It is God's grace rather than Switzerland's virtue that allows the country's neutrality; furthermore, its neutrality is a blessing, because it allows it to discern the right and wrong in different points of view without having to take sides (Sept. 20, p. 125). Indeed, Barth exercised his right to criticize the failings of most of the warring nations. In his October 11 sermon, Barth spoke of "the hunger for power of the Russians, the self-righteousness of the Germans, the revenge-seeking of the French, the cold commercial spirit of the English, and the brutish cruelty of the Belgians . . . and the petty meanness of us Swiss" (Oct. 11, p. 135). Yes, even the neutral Switzerland was not exempt; true peace, Barth insisted, comes from God, and it should not be confused with complacency and worldly concerns.

One cannot go away from these war sermons without the clear and distinct knowledge that Barth was passionately devoted to the cause of peace. In his view, God was a God of peace rather than of war. He lamented that, during more tranquil times, the Swiss trusted blindly in politicians and did not "let the forces of peace become stronger" while they still had the chance (Aug. 23, p. 85). Earlier, Barth had envisaged a moment to come when millions of people and entire nations would refuse to engage in war.

At the same time he recognized that, despite this utopic vision, those opposing the war were small in number (Aug. 2, p. 59). Barth commended Pope Pius X for speaking out against the war in 1914. His was the only sane voice among world and church leaders, but it was like "the voice of a child in the storm, so helpless and ineffective, and yet I'm sorry to say the only luminous point; here at least was a voice that was not the voice of a combatant, that pointed to something higher from a position *above* the fray" (Aug. 23, p. 85).

It is told that Sir Edmund Hillary, the mountaineer, was once asked why he persisted in seeking to scale Mount Everest when so many had failed, dying before they reached the summit. Sir Edmund replied that he pursued his goal on their account, to make their sacrifice worthwhile. Karl Barth would probably have agreed with this sentiment as applicable to the Great War. Millions of lives had been sacrificed on the battlefields to secure peace in Europe, and it was necessary to pursue the goal of peace to make these sacrifices worthwhile. The Christian gospel, Barth believed, is a gospel of peace, and Christ the Prince of Peace causes people to be reconciled to one another and to live together in peace and justice.

The pursuit of peace is the perpetual task of each new generation. In the unforgettable words of the last stanza of John McCrae's "In Flanders Fields":

> Take up our quarrel with the foe:
> To you from failing hands we throw
> The torch; be yours to hold it high.
> If ye break faith with us who die
> We shall not sleep, though poppies grow
> In Flanders fields.

BARTH AS A PREACHER

The worship of God, including the celebration of the sacraments, is the central practice and activity of the Christian religion. The sermon or homily continues to be the staple of Sunday services. Even in 1915, however, the doctor and social commentator Arthur Shadwell wrote that the contemporary mind dismisses the sermon as either obsolete or so ordinary as not to merit mention in assessing the mood of a nation. Yet this failure has the effect of impoverishing the moral and spiritual life of the nation. In his article on "German War Sermons" Shadwell argued that there is "always something to be learnt" from the religious element in society, and "in judging national character it should never be left out of account."[108] High ideals and noble thoughts are often set forth in sermons, and their purpose is to inculcate the Christian virtues of love, faith, and hope. To be sure, like the news media, sermons may appeal to people's prejudices and inflame passions and hatreds. Yet the responsible preacher will strive to offer a balanced view of the situation and to instill a readiness for peace and justice. Particularly in times of crisis, sermons play an important role, as, for example, Martin Luther King Jr.'s famous sermon "I Have a Dream." War is one of the great crises, and sermons preached during it are important to take into account.

A war sermon is one preached during war in which there is a direct or indirect reference to the war.[109] Roland Bainton, the former Yale historian, in his book *Christian Attitudes to War and Peace*, spoke of three possible approaches to the issues of war and peace: pacifism, just war, and holy war or crusade. In these 1914 sermons, Barth—like Romain Rolland, Stefan Zweig, Bertrand

Russell, and Albert Einstein—took a pacifist position and spoke of war as "wrong" and "sinful."[110] He was not always a strict pacifist, as seen from his later life, when he counseled the Allied nations to defeat Nazism during the Second World War.

In any case, Barth found much of the jingoistic preaching that emanated from German pulpits in World War I not only crass but bordering on the blasphemous: preachers identified the nation's cause with God's cause and slipped into the view that this war was a holy war or crusade. Frank J. Gordon writes that "[o]nce in church, worshippers generally heard ringing calls to battle and impassioned identifications of the German cause with that of Christ."[111] Gordon quotes Leipzig's Professor Franz Rendtorff as saying, "Arise then, my people, in the name of God to the holy conflict, in unity and joy and piety . . . with God for king and country, for kaiser and reich, for honor and freedom."[112]

However, this was not only a German failing. Barth refers to the French cardinal and archbishop of Paris, Léon-Adolphe Amette, standing at the door of the Notre Dame Cathedral and delivering an address calling for war against the nations opposing France. A similar identification of God's cause with the nations was made by the bishop of London, Arthur F. Winnington-Ingram, in his letter to the *Guardian*: "I think the Church can best help the nation first of all by making it realize that it is engaged in a Holy War, and not be afraid of saying so. Christ died on Good Friday for Freedom, Honor and Chivalry, and our boys are dying for the same thing."[113] The American Congregationalist minister Lyman Abbott likewise wrote that "a crusade to make this world a home in which God's children can live in peace and safety is more Christian than a crusade to recover from pagans the tomb in which the body of Christ was buried."[114]

Barth's choice of biblical texts for his war sermons is intriguing. Some of the choices are obvious ones, such as the Mark 13:7 text, "But when you hear of war and rumors of war, do not be alarmed" (Aug. 2), and the Revelation 6:4 passage, "And out came another horse, bright red; its rider was permitted to take peace from the earth, so that people should slay one another, and he was given a great sword" (Aug. 23). Particularly appropriate is the text "O land, land, land, hear the word of the Lord!" from Jeremiah 22:29, preached on the Swiss National Day of Penance (Sept. 20). The Psalm text "Your righteousness is an everlasting righteousness" (Ps. 119:142) strikes one as a peg on which Barth hangs his sermon devoted to the theme "Necessity knows no law." To be sure, the passage speaks of God's eternal righteousness, which Barth contrasts with human righteousness, though a more appropriate text might have been found. John 17:20–21—in which Jesus prays that his disciples "may be one," as he is one with the Father—is a fitting text for that Reformation Sunday's sermon that stresses the importance of unity between Protestants and Roman Catholics. It is difficult to know why he chose some of the texts, since it does not appear that he followed any kind of liturgical calendar.

Barth's later assessment of these sermons, as indicated earlier, is not particularly favorable. In his 1932 and 1933 Bonn seminars on homiletics, the same seminars in which he spoke of letting the "war rage in all [his] sermons," he described his 1914 preaching as disgracefully forgetting "the importance of submission to the text."[115] This severe judgment was made in the context of setting forth his twofold criteria of the sermon—closeness to life and closeness to the text—and also noting that no principle can resolve the tension that always obtains between the two. To illustrate, Barth gave two examples: first, concerning his 1912 sermon on the sinking of the *Titanic*, he felt that by making it the main theme, "a monster of a full-scale *Titanic* sermon resulted."[116] His second example was his 1914 war sermons; he thought that they were not sufficiently close to the text but too much in keeping with the *Zeitgeist*. He added this piece of advice to preachers: "All honor to relevance, but pastors should be good marksmen who aim their guns beyond the hills of relevance."[117]

What are we to make of this assessment by Barth of his war sermons? Had Barth's 1914 preaching been so thin, biblically and theologically, that Barth, now looking back, thought that in 1914 he had resembled a Swiss version of Reinhold Niebuhr, the astute American critic and theologian?[118] This question is left to the reader to decide. On the one side is the consideration that Barth believed his political views were rooted in the Bible and theology. On the other side, it has to be granted that he had misgivings about his preaching and that in a number of the sermons, the social and political commentary overwhelms the biblical and theological content. If a deficiency existed, certainly Barth corrected it in the years that followed at Göttingen, Münster, Bonn, and Basel, where his work became determinedly biblical and theological.

In his introduction to the English translation of the *Homiletics*, David Buttrick makes two comments that require correction. First, he criticizes Barth's remarks about relevance, under the impression that Barth spurned relevance. This is not so. Barth believed that we do not need to *try* to make the Bible relevant, because of its closeness to life. Its relevance was axiomatic. To be effective, cultural and political references should be wedded to a higher aim, that of biblical truth. Second, Buttrick holds that Barth rejected correlation between religion and culture. Again, this is not so. Though Barth rejected the doctrine of the *analogia entis*, which states that the human being is an analogue of God's being, he believed that faith, itself given by God, allows humans to discern God's voice in the fallen word.[119]

Even before Barth expanded this view in his *Church Dogmatics*, he indicated in the "irregular dogmatics" of his sermons that God, though transcendent over human attempts to "enlist" God's favor, speaks to God's children in a special way at certain historical points—particularly here through the judgment and privations of war. Even in his *Homiletics*, as stated above, he cited "closeness to life" as an important element of the sermon. Barth was generally correct in stating that on Sunday "people do not want to remain stuck in everyday problems; they want to go beyond them and rise above them."[120] Nevertheless, to overcome them, they need to face their reality, in order to go beyond it by seeing it sub specie aeternitatis.

Barth worked on his sermon preparation during the week, and wrote his sermon on the Saturday, sometimes working late into the evening, as for example he did on August 1, the day of the outbreak of the war. His sermons were about forty to forty-five minutes in length. In terms of structure, Barth exercised remarkable freedom in the way that he began his sermon. He was more inclined to start his sermons with a strong, attention-getting statement than with a formal introduction. For example, his August 2 sermon begins with a clear reference to the outbreak of the war on Saturday, August 1, and his October 25 sermon begins with a quotation from Chancellor Bethmann-Hollweg: "*Not kennt kein Gebot*" (Necessity knows no law). Other such openings lead into the sermon's theme rather than its application. The July 26 sermon begins, "God has set us in the heavenly realm!" and the August 16 sermon, "All men and women stand under God's will."

Barth's August 9 sermon combines this type of theological statement with a direct reference to himself and his congregation: "In times such as ours, we pastors should be able to speak to you 'with the tongues of men and of angels' (1 Cor. 13:1). We know, indeed, how many are counting on us for a word of comfort, encouragement and support." After comparing the present time with similar times of trial in Old Testament prophecy, Barth follows with his thesis: despite the lack of prophets today, we do have the prophetic word of God. By highlighting the relationship between pastor and congregation, the first lines serve as an entry point for the congregation, without necessitating a formal introduction. Similarly, he uses strong statements to conclude his sermons rather than employing a summary of what was preached.[121] Often the sermons build up to a particular realization or insight. In the above sermon, the "necessity" of "Necessity knows no law" is argued to be a human construct arising out of humanity's sinful nature, rather than a genuine need formed by external circumstances.

For Barth, submission to the text was essential. Closeness to life and closeness to the text ought to be the criteria of every sermon. Barth was very sparing in his use of illustrations. There are only two illustrations in these thirteen sermons: the anecdote about the woman who throws her walking stick into the air to determine God's will for the direction of her walk, and keeps throwing until God's will aligns with her own (Aug. 9, p. 69), and the comparison between pious warmongers and Italian street thieves who pray to the Madonna before and after their robberies (Aug. 30, p. 95). On the whole he regarded illustrations as unhelpful.[122] Instead, he made frequent use of the technique of repetition, particularly in his October 18 sermon, where after each of the failures of institutions to prevent the war, he sounded the refrain, "How you are fallen from heaven, O Day Star, son of Dawn!" (Isa. 14:12 NRSV).

Normally quite sure of himself and his abilities, Barth had misgivings about his aptness as a village pastor. When he compared himself to his friend Eduard Thurneysen, in his view the ideal pastor, he found himself to be wanting. Yet he was no slouch or misfit in the ministry. It was simply that he was more suited to the academic than to the pastoral role, though he was a vigorous and robust preacher and a caring pastor. As mentioned before, in a television broadcast about Barth's Safenwil ministry, a member of the Safenwil congregation expressed the opinion that Barth spoke above the heads of the church members, but this is probably an exaggeration. During the first few months of the war, church attendance had markedly improved. At the same time this parishioner expressed appreciation for Barth's work as a union organizer among the village workers. Barth was known by the villagers as the "red pastor" because of his strong socialist views.

There are lessons to be learned from Barth's work as a pastor and preacher. There are lessons for budding preachers from Barth's example: the pulpit is the real arena of the kingdom of God and should be the minister's priority; daily Bible reading and study are essential; the pastor must live in love and solidarity with the congregation and understand their struggles; biblical knowledge should go along with an awareness of current news; and the pastor should always be reading a theological book.

The ecumenical character of Barth's preaching must also be emphasized. In a remarkable Reformation Day sermon that was unusual for its time, Barth emphasized what Roman Catholics and Protestants have in common rather than what separates them. The war had changed everything, bringing these commonalities to the forefront. Barth lists Protestants' and Catholics' common guilt (particularly in failing to prevent the current war), their belief in the power of prayer (as both the saints of the Catholic church and the reformers were great people of prayer), and their shared hope in the kingdom of God (Pope Pius X's motto was similar to Calvin's wish to build the city of God on earth). His sermon's text was Jesus' prayer in John 17:20–21, in which Jesus is urging the disciples to be "one"; Barth uses this as a call to his congregation to recognize the shared elements of the Protestant and Catholic faiths.

This kind of openness to Roman Catholicism marked the beginning of Barth's openness to the whole Christian tradition, Eastern as well as Western. It was a harbinger of the ecumenical activity that would occur during the Weimar Republic and the first few years of the Third Reich. In the 1930s, Lutheran, Reformed, and United Churches came together to draft the Barmen Declaration, which took a stand against the Nazi state and its autocratic power. This ecumenical ferment led to Barth's vigorous involvement in the modern movement that was initiated by the founding of the World Council of Churches in 1948 by Barth's friend Willem Visser 't Hooft.

CONCLUSION

The impact of the war on Karl Barth and his contemporaries can hardly be overstated. Yet it would be a mistake to claim that the social, political, cultural, and religious crises that produced the cataclysm of the Great War and its aftermath also fathered the "theology of crisis." Barth admitted that his theology had its beginnings during the war years. "We were not asleep but were taught some things by the events that took place," Barth wrote in 1940. "I neither can nor want to prove that without the World War we would be standing where we are standing today. But who can prove that we have been brought to our present positions by the World War?"[123] In fact, a number of factors, particularly his involvement in the Swiss Religious Socialist movement and his trade union activities on behalf of the Safenwil textile workers, played an important role, along with the calamity of the war. But they served mainly as catalysts. They made Barth question the liberal theology he had learned from his revered teachers, Adolf von Harnack and Wilhelm Herrmann.

More and more, his involvement in Religious Socialism and the shock of the outbreak of the war drove him to "the strange, new world within the Bible," which he believed to be "the world of God."[124] Like Martin Luther before him, he rested his confidence in God's Word, which sounded forth from God's realm. Luther, as is well known, claimed that the German Reformation was solely the work of God's Word: "I simply taught, preached, and wrote God's Word; otherwise I did nothing. And while I slept, or drank Wittenberg beer with my friends Philip and Amsdorf, the Word so greatly weakened the papacy that no prince or emperor ever inflicted such losses upon it. I did nothing; the Word did everything." (cf. Mark 4: 26–29). Similarly, Barth attributed the theological revolution that he and Thurneysen had launched to the power and efficacy of God's Word. This focus on the Word of God is evident in the title that Barth gave to his first collection of essays, *The Word of God and Theology*,[125] and of course the title of the first volume of the *Church Dogmatics*, *The Word of God*, where the Word is the revelation of God, the event in which "God speaks."[126]

If it may be rightly said that the First World War decisively shaped the twentieth century,[127] it may be equally claimed that it formed Karl Barth as a theological, social, and political thinker. Under its impact he broke with the liberal Protestant theology he had imbibed in Berlin and Marburg. The break was not sudden but gradual. He began to set off in a new theological direction, starting with the Bible and the biblical theology of the Reformers, Martin Luther and John Calvin, later mining the rich sources of the Christian theological tradition, both Eastern and Western. Barth produced a classical theology of ecumenical significance and became not only the theologian par excellence but also one of the twentieth century's leading social and political thinkers.[128]

Sermons

July 26, 1914

Sermon at Safenwil and Ürkheim[1]

Austria's Ultimatum to Serbia[2]

Ephesians 2:4–7: But God, who is rich in mercy, out of the great love with which he loved us, even when we were dead through our trespasses, made us alive together with Christ—by grace you have been saved—and raised us up with him and seated us with him in the heavenly places in Christ Jesus, so that in the ages to come he might show the immeasurable riches of his grace in kindness toward us in Christ Jesus. (NRSV)

Dear Friends!
God has set us in the heavenly realm! Isn't that an utterly astonishing, indeed incredible thing to say? It's something that may make us shake our heads in disbelief and say quietly, "No, it can't be so; there is little sign of it!" To be sure, it's the right thing to believe in church, but only there, when the pastor is preaching or the organ is sounding forth, something to shelve as soon as we get back outside again to our familiar life in our homes or at the factory tomorrow. Perhaps, we may even sigh and say, "Wouldn't it be wonderful if it were actually true: 'God has set us in the heavenly realm'!"

Indeed, the words are there, and they were written by a real man, a man of perceptive vision who knew the world and humankind rather well, both of which were just the same as today—but still, he wrote this without shaking his head in dismay: "God has set us in the heavenly realm!"

"*Heavenly realm!*" What precisely is that? Actually, it is a multiplicity of things, and that is precisely why it truly defies description with dry-as-dust words. It's something majestic like the sun shining on the leaves of a beech tree, joyful like the laughter of children, serious like the eternal calm with which the stars follow their eternal course, kind like the glance of a mother.

The "heavenly realm" is all these things and hence cannot be reduced to a single blissful idea, but rather is an abiding, enduring condition much like the surrounding air we breathe.

We can call it freedom, because all chains and constraints, all anxiety and cowardice, vanish in the heavenly realm. We can call it happiness, since here joy, beauty, and peace have triumphed. We can name it orderliness, because injustice and tyranny do not exist there but only a righteous will in the form of *one* sacred law in all things and governing all things and everyone. And we can also call it eternal bliss, because here need and want are no more, and therefore disquiet and worry have ended. Everything petty is taken up into what is important, every calamity into the calm of an inexhaustible fountain of life.

We no longer harm ourselves through indolence and passion. Instead, we try to understand one another, and we are able to do so. We have no reason to get agitated about our personal reputation and income level. There is no reason to deceive and to sever relations with one another. We can look each other directly in the eye, extend a friendly hand, and do it without regret or an ulterior motive. We no longer focus on ourselves and what is ours, but focus on what is God's and on that which from the very beginning effects harmony among one another. We know why we are placed in the world and therefore have no time to gossip about one another, to blame others for all sorts of things, and to carry out this or that grudge against one another. That's hopelessly childish behavior. The one thing needful is that we understand this one truth: that God is and that God is love. This leaves us with no time, desire, or appreciation for anything else. All that we think and say and do comes from one source alone: "God is love" (1 John 4:8, 16).

But now we ask: Where does there exist anything like this wonderful state of affairs? Are we speaking of a beautiful distant land? Are we talking about a star in the universe on which blessed beings lead a kind of heavenly life? That is what some have often imagined, but it's a totally absurd assumption. In no respect is this how the apostle Paul is to be understood. Paul didn't think it was worth asking, where is this blessed heavenly life? Undeniably, he speaks of a "heavenly" realm, but he has no intention of saying that it is only "in heaven," any more than Jesus wished to say that God is only in heaven whenever he addressed God as our "Father in heaven."

In fact, Jesus meant the very opposite. To be sure, heaven is elevated *above* us, but we are always and everywhere under it, just as we are always and everywhere under God. Similarly, the heavenly realm is present always and everywhere. It is not a distant land; it is not a "better star," as some may perhaps say. It is not made up of wishes and dreams but is something present and very real. Paul doesn't even think of asking whether there is such a heavenly realm and life, and where this could be located. He takes it as true that it's there, actually there, as present and real as the sun that shines, the air we breathe, and the water we drink. He doesn't doubt for a moment that there is something higher than our low human nature, something greater than our inferior, modest thoughts, customs, occupations, and institutions, something eternal above our temporal realm, something perfect above our imperfections: in brief, something heavenly above our earthly realm.

And we have to agree that Paul spoke of what he rightly knew. It's quite impossible to claim that he dreamed or imagined it. Our conscience and the deepest longings of our hearts confirm that he is right. Our struggles, sufferings, sins, and recoveries, the most hidden and precious things in our souls, tell us, yes, he is right: there is a heavenly realm and life, a higher and better state of being. And we do not need to spend time asking: Where is it? We know as well as Paul that it is simply there, and that it makes itself known. Do not all the finer things in us, all the faint urgings of love and seriousness and truth, aim at this heavenly realm? Do we not feel that we must seek it, whether we want to or not? Is there not in every one of us an innate sense that tells us: I am not really at home here in this world of wickedness, narrow-mindedness, pettiness, and sin? My true home is above in the heavenly world of freedom, happiness, order, and bliss. Oh yes, we know about this heavenly world. So we cannot deny our origin and say, "I know nothing of it." No, it really is, and it is there. But the basic question is whether it is there for us, whether we belong to it, whether we have a living experience of it. That is the question: whether we are really in the heavenly realm.

Paul answers and says, "God has *transferred us*." Yes, he says, we are set in the very midst of this heavenly world. He tells the Ephesian Christians to whom he is writing his letter: God is rich in mercy and through his love, with which God has loved us, God has set us in the heavenly realm. It sounds so certain and joyful and complete when he says it, that we can scarcely doubt it. And yet we have to doubt it. Is this supposed to apply to us, to you and to me, to the individual Christian, to Christian people? Surely that isn't true. We can't really be inside the heavenly realm.

We work hard, and we worry so wretchedly from day to day about where our next mere crust of bread is coming from. This leaves us little time to reflect about higher things. Moreover, there is so much discord among us. There are also bad people out there with whom the most devout cannot live at peace.[3] Then, there is cowardice; yes, much cowardice is to be found among us. Of course, we have to be careful and to respect those who wield power and have money; otherwise it could prove to be just too uncomfortable for us. Who of us can claim to be totally honest and have nothing to hide from a neighbor? Who of us has never had something nasty to say about those with whom we have conversed in such a friendly way today on the road to the church?

That's the way things are. Isn't it so? We have to attend to our own affairs. We can't expect others to help us. Hence our life is like a race and from time to time, a sheer struggle. Without envious, grudging glances to the left and right, without a dig in the ribs, we don't manage it all that well. Are we not told, more or less brutally, to make sure that we save our own skin in this life? Must we not also simply put up with all those bitter and unpleasant things that are a part of life? We remind ourselves once more of all those things that afflict us, all the reversals of fortune that perplex us, all the human weaknesses and mean tricks that poisoned our life. There is so much coercion, so much that gets us off track, so that it is difficult to get back on again. There is so much that is sad and even fearful. And now it is asserted, "God has transferred us to the heavenly realm!" Surely, that cannot be true!

We look at the state of our contemporary world, and we see a number of deep, devouring, ineradicable evils—for example, tuberculosis, which is incessantly transmitted to new households, always claiming more victims, in spite of all efforts to combat it. And then there is alcoholism, the mention of which causes embarrassment but which is so widespread that almost every few days a tragedy occurs in some family in our nation. Similarly, there is capitalism, the money-hungry, acquisitive spirit of the last hundred years that has fed off the masses, driving them to exhaustion and illness, and that is guilty of exploiting their labor. Yet there in the Bible it says: "God has set us in the heavenly realm!" It just isn't true!

And possibly today we are on the eve of a *war* that could set the whole of Europe ablaze. The rubble heaps of the last war still smolder; the tears of thousands of widows and orphans still flow; and now, barring a miracle, we shall unleash anew hundreds of thousands of men like wild beasts on one another, hundreds of thousands who do not know one another and who have done nothing to harm one another. They will once again shoot and slaughter one another; they will kill one another with all the means of modern inventions. They will be told about the fatherland and of military honor—but what do they really know about what is said? What possible reason do Austrian and Serbian farmers and workers have to hate and kill one another? There is no law of necessity for it, no need for the compulsion of primitive passion, other than the ancient principle of retaliation: "eye for eye, tooth for tooth" (Exod. 21:24)! The spectacle that is being played out before our eyes is a bloody madness, a madness to be sure, even if does not take place to the extent that is feared, even if through an unexpected turn of events the war is avoided. Fierce and determined to the last, armed to the teeth, the European nations are ready for war, and these Christian nations stand against one another! The war hangs like a fearful thunderstorm over them all. If it does not come today, it will come tomorrow.

What then should we say about Paul's assertion that God, who is rich in mercy, through his love, has set us, us human beings, in the heavenly realm?! Doesn't every word almost sound like bitter mockery, particularly in our present critical situation?

We must not tone down the incomprehensible element in Paul's words by saying that his words do not apply to the present life but refer to a better, happier future life, possibly the survival of the soul after death or of the perfection of humanity in the span of thousands of years. Of course, Paul also believed in the future breakthrough and divine victory; it was wholly self-evident to him that magnificently good things flow from the heavenly realm for both time and eternity. He certainly believed that Christ will come again and perfect his kingdom on earth, and in such a way that, in every one of us, what is mortal must 'be swallowed up by life" (2 Cor. 5:4). He says it so explicitly: "God has set us in the heavenly realm" so "that in the ages to come [God] might show the immeasurable riches of his grace in kindness toward us in Christ Jesus."

Yet this peering into the future in no way whatever inhibits Paul from accepting the heavenly realm with all its light and strength as something wholly present. We are now in its presence! You see, what the Bible calls hope differs radically from everything that is usually associated with this word. Ordinary hope is a surmise, a dream, or speculation concerning a better time to come. It suggests a happy circumstance or a coming better time. Biblical hope does the same. It also speaks of those things that will be. But it offers us infinitely more: namely, a present reality that gives us the courage and the will to hope in the future. It is "a sure and certain hope," for it already possesses what it expects. And that's how we need to understand Paul's "heavenly realm." He doesn't wish, "Oh, if we only possessed it!" He doesn't prophesy, "We will possess it one day!" But he assures us, "We possess it; it is here now!"

Yes, it's here, it's present now in the midst of our lives with all their sorrows and disappointments, in the midst of the uncouth, fierce world, with all its misfortunes and sins. That's actually Paul's meaning. We must try to understand him. For Paul there was *one* fact in the world that was more important to him than anything else. Next to this one fact he accepts absolutely nothing in the world as more significant—not sin, not need, not death. All else disappeared when he thought that such a man as Jesus once lived here on earth among us. This personality made a completely overpowering impression on him: namely, that God is truth. Paul had indeed known of God for a long time, but in Jesus he discovered for the first time that God is real and living. The deep, joyful peace with which this man, Jesus, endured everything; the lavish love with which he loved his fellow men and women; the majestic dignity with which he suffered, battled, and conquered even in death: this incomparable personality as a whole, and not simply any one virtue, was what now fascinated Paul, placing him directly before God, so that he could do nothing except fall to his knees in adoration and worship. The kingdom of God had come to him. Quite literally: he was under God's lordship and reign. Jesus had not only touched his life but had also awakened him.

From that point on, Paul could not think of Jesus without immediately thinking of the other fundamental reality: God lives and God reigns. This God-consciousness was now so strong in him that meanwhile *everything else simply had to be silenced* and had to take a lesser place. To be sure, he still saw the evil of this world and its wickedness, human folly, bodily suffering, injustice, and violence. He was familiar with all these things. He suffered them in his own body, yet they could no longer have any significance for him; nor could he grant them any importance at all. With regard to all those things Paul simply thought, "Of course, that's how things are; nevertheless I still know something else. I know God and God's love. I have come to know God powerfully and luminously in my Lord Jesus. In every respect his love is stronger and greater than anything else that will oppose it. God's love transcends all things. It finally overcomes everything. In the end, compared to it, everything else is only provisional and temporal." He was far from simply acquiescing in the misery and wickedness present in life and from accepting the world's injustice and insanity merely as a fact and then perhaps asking timidly, is there a cure for it? That's what we do, and, of course, we end up shortchanged, finding only small comfort and meager, inadequate help in face of all the sorrow and evil that we see. But from the outset Paul takes a different approach. The primary thing for him was always the love of God manifested in Christ. That was the basic and decisive fact of life. And on account of that fact, all other facts were now submerged and had paled into insignificance. They could no longer exist as facts at all. They are now merely semblances, shadows, which are unavoidable because the light shines so brightly.

Paul also knew a different state of mind with its tendency to take the world's horrors with the utmost seriousness, where one with a sigh laments, "Indeed, I am a weak and imperfect individual, I sin every day," so that among people in general things necessarily get to be unpleasant and petty. But there is also all this sadness and evil, tuberculosis and alcoholism, capitalism and war. Paul was familiar with the situation where one sees such evils and powers, trembles before them, and is left without hope. He describes this state with this phrase: "we were dead in trespasses and sin." Paul believed that hopelessness in the face of the sad—and the conviction that it must be so!—is a form of hostility to God, a wretched state of mind. This he called hell, especially when one knows nothing other than the earthly realm, its principalities and powers with their evil designs and wicked works.

But Paul had certainly succeeded in finding a way out of this state of hopelessness. As he says, "while we're yet dead in our sins," it was through God's great love that God raised us and made us alive. "Ever since I found God," Paul wants to tell us, "I discovered that the sad and evil things are of no great consequence. Since God became my Master, I also know who is Master in this wicked world. Ever since I awakened from the sleep of godlessness and opened my eyes, I saw that the world and its evil things have lost their power over me."

Moreover, since for Paul all this had to be silenced and to retreat, so that the Other, the light of the divine reality, shone forth in triumph, he could boldly state, "Now, at this very moment God *transferred us into the heavenly realm*, and we are actually in its midst." Now perhaps we understand better what he meant. Had Paul thought first of the evil and sad things in the world and then alongside them set the good, the divine reality, as we are inclined to do, then he would have been left with only a tiny shoot of hope. He then would have been driven to think, maybe, one day in a better future in the beyond, and so on. Were that the case, Paul would not have said joyfully and confidently that we are now in fact transferred into the heavenly realm, and this isn't just a matter of wishful thinking and fantasy. There would have been no talk of joy and boldness. For him, God is primary, absolutely primary. God became the primary reality for him through Jesus Christ. But what immediately follows for him is that the desolate and dark things in the world could have the status only of being shadows and appearances. A space that had previously been barred is now opened. Now the good must no longer stand simply as a tiny sprig of hope alongside all that is wretched and sad. Paul now recognized that the good is the only truth. Only what comes from God is true.

Christ showed him what is from God: namely, faith, love, joy, a childlike spirit, peace, and strict obedience to God's good will. And what also belongs to this is complete freedom, complete happiness, complete order and bliss. After the other world faded, it was perfectly clear to him now that this is the true world. Accordingly, the other world faded away and disappeared from view. It is this true world that is important. It endures. It does not pass away. Thank God, that God has freed me from the world of shadows and appearances. Thank God that God has awakened me and given me eyes to see the real truth and power in the world. Thank God, that God has shown me in Christ what true life means: life does not mean suffering, sinning, and dying. Moreover, it does not mean pettiness and quarrelling and being the slave of one's passions. The evil and wretchedness of the world undoubtedly exist, but they are not necessary. They do not essentially belong to life. Life means freedom, happiness, and bliss. We actually *possess* this life of freedom, happiness, and bliss. We *are* transferred into the heavenly realm. I will repeat what I said, and therein lies the whole rationale for Paul's marvelous words. He could speak in this way because God was for him a living God. Thus he *had* to say, if God is a living God, then there is no other world than the heavenly world, and that's the only realm in which we can have our true existence.

Up to this point we have spoken of Paul and of his experience. I wish to goodness that each of us could say, yes, I understand that, because it has also been my experience. Only by also experiencing it can we completely understand it. We want to understand, don't we? But we don't really dare!? We also long to be able to say, I am in the other realm, removed from all that's mean and sad; I have moved into the resplendent realm of the beautiful and the good. Again we think, it's only a dream, just a fantasy, suitable for the Bible, suitable for church, but completely unsuitable for the rough-and-tumble of real life. It is perfectly natural that we should think like this. Yes, completely natural, so long as we are still dead in our sins, as Paul says, as long as God is still distant and alien and only an empty concept.

It's of no help at all either to reflect too much about this heavenly realm or to speak too often about it. At the same time, it doesn't help either to hear too many sermons on it or, because of zeal for the good, to do too much. Nothing is achieved thereby. Our greatest need is God, the living, true God, who says to our soul, "I AM!"—so that we will never forget it. We will find God, as Paul did, most certainly and most fully in Jesus. Once we have found God, we are immediately placed in the heavenly realm. The present world is submerged, and it no longer has any power over us.

But it's not as though it occurs in an instant with one decisive blow. The fog of the earthly, of the sad and of evil, lies thickly on our souls, and it lifts slowly. Yet the main thing is that we know it's *only* fog, not a mountain as we thought. The one thing needful is that we know the world of freedom, love, and peace exists, and that this is the real world, hidden yet nevertheless real. True, we must often grope for it in the darkness of our world, but it is there and must reveal itself more and more completely. Knowing this, we can make our journey, keeping to the high road and giving no credence to the fog, thick though it may be, but giving credence to the sun, whose rays are there piercing the fog, and so taking pleasure at the prospect that its brightness must soon break through fully.

What do you think? Could you live with this belief in the sun in the midst of the fog, with this belief in the heavenly world in the midst of our earthly realm? Could you live with it? How would it affect the way you conduct your life out there in the world? Take this question with you into the things that trouble you, into those things you dislike, into your business dealings, into your joy. Read the newspaper with this question in your heart, and speak with your neighbors and friends about what agitates you about this question—always making it a matter of the heart and not just of the tongue—the question whether it would not be redemptive for you, indeed for all of us, if we could believe that the sad and evil are not the final reality, that we are truly in the heavenly realm and life.

And then think once more about how Paul came to this saving certainty. Amen.

August 2, 1914

Sermon at Safenwil and Ürkheim[1]

War between Austria and Serbia.
Threat of a conflict between Germany, Russia, and France.
Mobilization of the entire Swiss army to defend the frontier.

Mark 13:7: When you hear of wars and rumors of wars, do not be alarmed; this must take place, but the end is not yet.

Dear Friends,

Yesterday, we experienced an August 1 (National Day) as never before.[2] Wasn't it indeed just last evening—without all the usual national festivities but only the solemn sound of church bells, as though one could sense our whole nation in all of its thousands of towns and villages holding its breath—that our nation, following the example of our ancestors, readied itself to summon all its strength to secure, at cost of life and property, Switzerland's freedom and independence? We now know the significance of the words "when you hear of wars and rumors of wars"![3] Regardless of how it may now turn out, we will not soon forget these days of stress, constant worry, calm, and new worry that we have experienced.

There is a kind of magical power in that little word *"war"*! None of us has experienced it at firsthand. A few rather elderly people in the village remember what their parents told them of the French army marching through this region in 1798.[4] In the old family album, next to a few names of young men, there is the note "killed in action in Russia along with 12,000 Swiss soldiers." So the great Napoleon's long shadow is cast from the distant past to the present generation. That was the last time that we actually experienced the misery of war in our land. What has occurred since cannot be called that. What *we* know of war, we know from books and newspapers and not from personal experience. And yet this word conveys to us a totally incomparable power. Have we possibly inherited from our ancestors, along with their genes, the horror of war, which through prolonged, severe suffering of the past hundreds and thousands of years became second nature to them? Or do we immediately suspect something of the frightening fact that the chains have been removed from the original savagery of human beings and that individual against individual, nation against nation, now face and oppose each other as enemy against enemy, as vulture against vulture?

That is certain, and we now experience again, in view of this fact, even if it seems a remote possibility, that *everything else*, the things that touch and inspire us, has become, in comparison, *small and insignificant*. What about our livelihood and possessions? In war, the most secure foundations of our existence are shaken and possibly destroyed. What about our future plans? In war, we have to be prepared in an unprecedented way to face the fact that everything will turn out differently from the way we envisioned or calculated it. What about our affections and hatreds? In war, every life is threatened; the dearest and the most disagreeable persons can be suddenly snatched away. Then what is the significance of our likes and dislikes? What importance do our little wishes and fancies, our peculiar characteristics and habits have? War can, all at once, switch our life on to another track, perhaps shattering our good fortune, possibly saddling us with sorrow in a way that we now hardly suspect. In any case, these experiences teach and lead us to thoughts that must be quite new, even to the oldest among us, and that may perhaps make us completely different men and women. Little wonder that the other things that now seem so significant to us must keep silent and be of secondary importance, before the enormous fact that war appears to have drawn nearer.

We also experience something of the incomparable power of war when we see how what usually remains *hidden* in individuals and in nations is suddenly *revealed* in war, as it rarely is otherwise. There is so much that individuals and nations are careful to hide from themselves and from one another during normal times. They hide these things under the thick cloak of what we like to call civilization and culture, but equally under the cloak of piety and Christianity. In wartime, it appears that this cloak has gaping holes, or rather it actually falls down completely. Humankind is forced to be honest. How much stupefying, passionate hatred we now suddenly see blazing up between the nations, and one wonders what kind of effort responsible state leaders are making to restrain the thousands who are burning to revert to the ferocious, bloody, primitive state of humankind, and to settle old scores, after decades of resentment toward long-hated foes. How much pugnacity and lust for adventure have been boiling and seething in countless brains and now all at once want to boil over! How does that tally with the human progress of our day?

And on the other hand, how much pathetic, quavering fear there is on the part of both the high and lowly for one's cherished life, particularly for one's precious money! You've read the warning in the newspapers that we ought not to lose our head and think that money is safer in the chest of drawers than in the savings bank, and you certainly know yourselves how necessary these warnings are. Yet isn't it sad that such warnings are necessary at all? There is so much twaddle about these things. By keeping their savings at home, people commit a folly (for even in wartime money is safer in the savings bank than at home) and a betrayal of one's country (for banks need ready cash; otherwise all commercial transactions are disrupted). How do this nervous disquiet and loss of composure tally with the clever domestic mind that people nowadays should possess? So the war discloses what is hidden.

In these days when such a new, frightening thing moves into our life, when so much unpleasantness and weakness that lie dormant in us want to emerge into the light, we really need more than ever to ask, what can give our life a *solid footing*? To be sure, those who do not already have this solid footing will hardly find it in our calamitous times. Those who have not brought a treasure trove of heartfelt trust in God and ardent love from quieter, reflective, and spiritually deepened times are not likely now to possess the light and strength to face difficult and dark experiences in the right frame of mind. "What we sow we must then reap" (see Gal. 6:7). It has always been so that in such perilous times much superficial and scanty Christian faith fails pitiably and collapses. But, my friends, we *have* such a solid footing, and we don't need to seek it first, even if we forget it often enough and have not made use of it or else despised it. We simply need to pay attention to what is given to us, to grasp it, and to find support in it. Penetrating below the surface into the depths, letting what is weak in us become strong is what we all must do and can do. What is given is the presence and love of the eternal, living God, who holds all things in his hand and guides us by his righteous, holy will and who has drawn near and revealed himself to us in Jesus Christ. Whoever finds a resting place in God will not break down and collapse in face of the sad and horrible things that we may have to face.

And now let us listen attentively to what comes forth from Jesus' mouth as he tells us what *God's thoughts* are of *the war* that has come into such uncanny proximity to us. "*When you hear of wars and rumors of wars*" he says to us, "*Do not be alarmed; this must take place, but the end is not yet.*" We all feel, isn't it true, that here is something higher, something superior that enters our thoughts. We are now quite distressed by the general misfortune that endangers us. Our troubled thoughts rush to the future. Many of us think of loved ones who will have to march out, no longer to harmless military exercises this time, but perhaps to bloody battle. Others wonder what is to become of trade and commerce in general, which until now has provided our livelihood. Still others think of the inflationary times we probably face. And if things get worse, if our land were to become a theater of war, with all the attendant horror, as at that time in 1798, what would that entail?

Once we have war, nothing and no one is altogether safe. Now we are prompted to call on God: Lord, have mercy on us and save us! Let the light of your kindness shine on our beloved Switzerland.[5] Let this cup pass from us (see Matt. 26:39)! Lord, graciously give us peace! Yes, so may and so will we pray and implore as long as we can, and God certainly hears us. But whether God grants, whether he does what we request—that we cannot discern, for it is entirely in God's hand. God does not say, "I will save you. There will be no war." But God definitely says, "*Do not be afraid*"!

My friends, we have to learn to understand that this is the greatest thing that God wants to give us and for which we must pray above all in these days: this fearlessness. Being able patiently to wait, from one hour to the next, faithfully and soberly doing our duty, bravely quelling useless worries and grievances about things that still lie in the distant future, yet if misfortune should occur, courageously taking hold and surmounting it: that is true fearlessness, and that is what we now all need. Our thoughts are with those who now have to move toward the frontiers to protect our country from enemy invasion. May they all respond unfalteringly and without hesitation to the call tomorrow, even if it may prove to be rather difficult for the majority of them. May it now be evident that our patriotism, which gives vent to so many very joyful August 1 celebrations, to so many rifle and gymnastic displays, means more than the noise of fireworks and empty shrieks! Fear not; you ought not to be afraid! But if what is feared should happen, then everything will depend on your composure, on the calm and the certainty of your sense of duty. Yet those of us who do not march out might need this fearlessness even more. The power and resistance of a nation in wartime lies not just with its soldiers at the frontiers but equally as much with all the men and women, both old and young, who support the soldiers. With thoughts of all that has happened and can come, it is difficult for us to stand by and remain calm; many of us may have the obvious thought, Oh, if I could only be there, where something can be done! But that does not really help; we have other obligations, we have our specific duties. Much will depend, for example, on the spirit and understanding with which you women will let your husbands leave for their duties tomorrow, whether in a spirit of ceaseless disquiet and worry, or in the spirit of confidence and faith. A great deal will depend on the kind of letters you will write to them, whether you will upset them through complaints and annoyances or strengthen their resolve through the feeling that you are calm and safe and that you are busy doing what is necessary without them.

And when the war is over, our daily work, our family life, will one way or another largely need to resume again, and the responsibility that it does so most satisfactorily and happily lies, more or less, with those of us who stay behind. Days of hard work are now in store for many; reluctantly, many fathers and sons will have to give up all that needs to be done and will have to entrust it to family members. Fear not! also means don't let yourself be rushed into pointless anxiety and agitation on account of all that needs to be done. Do what is necessary each day and complete what is possible; then the burdensome task will not be as formidable as you now think. Then you will make all those who march out, and who need all their wits about them for their task, calm and confident about their venture.

I also have in mind the important task of raising children, which now you mothers will be obliged for some time to do on your own. You will need to double your efforts and attention in this important task, now that the steady hand of fathers cannot help you any longer, so that a faultless, strong, industrious, and courageously truthful next generation grows up. Our youth is our future, and it is now placed in your hand. If we would now all be moved by the strong spirit of fearlessness, if we cast off everything that can now only disturb and hinder us and others, if we looked and thought of nothing except what is now my duty and my responsibility, which I must fulfill for the welfare of my loved ones and my whole nation, as well as I can! See, that is what God wants from us in these days, what he wishes to give us if we ask him for it, and this is what before all else we must ask. Should then the storm that we fear break loose, we do have this one thing. It will not break us; yes, there might even be a blessing hidden for us in this troubled time.

But how do we acquire this good and strong spirit of fearlessness by which we will be able to persevere through these times and circumstances? Fearlessness needs to have a foundation and a hope. God provides these also, if we are willing to hear what God has said to us through Jesus. Jesus says, "*It must therefore happen.*" On the first hearing that sounds rather harsh and discouraging. Did Jesus intend to say that war was an evil that simply must be endured? Is it a fate that from time to time human beings must mutually butcher and murder one another? Is this a fact that has to be accepted with silence and suffering, because it cannot be otherwise on this earth?

No, a thousand times no. We are not to accept war as a necessity. Especially now, when war occurs once more in the world, when the war threatens to submerge all other interests and ideas even now, all of us—and that means those who march out and those who stay at home—must be absolutely clear about the matter: the war is wrong, the war is sinful, the war is no necessity but, rather, stems from the evil of human nature. There will now again be more than enough people who talk as if war, so to speak, were a natural phenomenon like the sun and the rain, and like them unavoidable and insurmountable. Not lacking are weakhearted Christians who give credence to no other world than this world of war, who say to us, "Peace, eternal peace, is found only in the grave, only in a better beyond." You may decide for yourselves in the situation in which we now find ourselves whether these interpretations seem comforting and true.

Should we really accept the impending misfortune of war, with all its consequences, that now wants to break in over us, with the thought, it will always be so? Must we really think that our human life is now again, so to speak, walled in by such harsh necessities of nature that we cannot overcome and from which we cannot escape? In what kind of oppressive and stifling position would we be, were this the case? Yet the matter is wholly different. We may and ought to expect much, much more from God than that. When Jesus says, "It must therefore happen," he is heaven-high above such a view of nature, which knows nothing other than, it is just so! We need to ascend to his height; then we will discover how with his "it must," he gives us a foundation and hope for the fearlessness that is now so needful.

Jesus lived in the realm of the heavenly *Father*. He knew that the Father is *not cruel*. God does not will wrong, suffering, misery; God does not will war. God is only love, salvation, peace. The Father is also *not indifferent*. We belong to God, and God does not abandon us in the darkness of sin and guilt. God does not will that we mutually embitter one another's lives; God's heart aches when God sees how humankind causes hardship for itself; God desires to draw us to himself. And the Father is *not feeble*. God does not stand apart from or above his human family and abandon it to go its confused and miserable way; rather, God guides us and our destiny. God can and does actually turn all things around so that they correspond to his good and holy will. God alone is the mighty and powerful One, and aside from God there are no necessities. These thoughts ruled Jesus' life, and they were not simply ideas but facts: the holy, all-loving, sovereign God was for Jesus the most certain of certainties, the reality of life on which he based every thought, every word, and every action. He thought, said, and did everything on the basis of this certain presupposition: God is alive.

Compared with this, nothing else mattered to him. The evil and desolation in the world, injustice and suffering, sin and death, war and persecution and betrayal: he saw all that, of course, and he was deeply pained to see it. He suffered under it, but finally it could not have any force, any validity. He didn't say, such is life, because he considered everything from God's perspective and because he knew that God is greater than everything. He saw the *consummation* of everything that God has in mind for the world and humanity. This hope of consummation dominates the chapter from which our text is taken.

It describes how through everything that happens the goal of God's love is accomplished. Nothing of all the hostile and antidivine powers in the world can finally endure: misfortune, hunger, error, lies, and devastation. Everything shameful and sorrowful is only a stage. Over and above them passes the sure way of God until finally the Son of Man comes in his power and glory (Mark 13:26), and that means until finally the redeeming power of Jesus has transformed humankind, so that human beings truly reflect the image of God.

My friends, if we can let ourselves be gifted by Jesus, now so truly rich, with some—only a little—of his faith in the holy, gracious, and powerful God and in the consummation of all things in accordance with God's will, then we really are without fear in these difficult times. We *are* fearless; we don't need first to become fearless. It is then evident that the difficult and sorrowful things that now come up against us cannot be the last and final reality. We are liberated, at the outset, from everything that now occurs, looking away from the former larger fears and focusing on the love of God, which guides everything, and the consummation toward which all things move.

The misfortune that threatens us may indeed unsettle and frighten us, but it cannot knock us to the ground. It is nothing strange, it is nothing still shocking; but we know what it is and what it is supposed to do, even if we do not yet know its extent and end. It is a step on the way to God—indeed, a difficult and steep step that we now encounter—but a step that must bring us forward and upward. Can we really be anxious, can we let ourselves be given over to nervousness and trembling disquiet, if we know we are on God's way, if we know that this way has a goal, if we know that the war, indeed also *this* war, like everything that is difficult, must be a step on this way?

My friends, I am not saying we want and now ought to be fearless and trusting. That would be rather idle talk. How can we be so when our heart is so full of disquiet? But I do say this to you: if we let ourselves be introduced by Jesus into fellowship with God, in which he himself stands, if we feel only a little bit of his way, of his love and his trust in the Father, then there is no more need of "we should, we would"; we are then fearless, because we are with him in the realm of the heavenly Father, even if it has to be, in the middle of war, in tears and partings and perplexity. Indeed, we might be able to say also of this terrible European war, whose storm is now breaking loose on all sides: if it must be, *so must it therefore happen*, so is it a necessity, but a divine, gracious necessity, that we are now to be led on this dark road.

There is indeed something strange and, time and again, fundamentally incomprehensible about the truth that the way to the full lordship of God must pass through such evil, sin, and suffering, that such steep steps have to be ascended with so much bitter woe, until one day the full victory of the Son of Man in power and glory will be achieved. Who is able to peer into God's plan? We often witness how the victory of God always follows great evil and horror. So it was with the war, famine, and persecution that in our text Jesus first proclaimed to his disciples for their particular time. They went through everything, they suffered and endured; and finally God still triumphed. So it will turn out for us, if, fearlessly and with victorious certainty, with childlike believing hearts, we say, "Yes, it must be so!"—that is, if we let ourselves be led through it all with our eyes fixed on God, who holds the end in his hand.

We also note how all enormous and small evil, suffering, and unrighteousness in the world have had their day. They arose, they grew, they towered to an alarming size and strength; they lived and made themselves felt, and then, when they reached their high point, they collapsed: they became impossible in virtue of becoming so huge. It was so with the many lies and brute force on which world empires are built. It was so with slavery and alcoholism—God waited and waited—God still waits today with regard to many similar evils and sins. How much time do human beings need until they wake up, until strength is born out of necessity, the necessity that overcomes, until they learn to use their eyes and minds and hands, until they learn to pray that evil and sin be destroyed? These high-point moments and moments of collapse, of the gathering up of suffering, sinful humanity, are still happening. Will not such a moment simply come also one day for the evil and sin of war, a moment when the misfortune and injustice of war has become so great, that it cannot continue any more, and people's eyes are opened, and they act together, not only in small numbers as today but in their millions, in entire nations, and declare, "We cannot and do not want to engage in war anymore, and this war is definitely the last one"?

My friends, we gaze into a distant future that we will all probably not live to see; nevertheless we stand on firm ground. We can rely on our experience and the certain promise of God if we truly believe. We are given the courage to think and to say of the current events even as they unfold, "It must be so!" The evil and sin of war must ripen, ripen with much misery, blood, and tears; but when it has fully ripened, then God acts and the evil and sin are overcome. Are we not glad when we get a step closer toward this goal? Are we not willing to think that the anxiety and worry that we are now enduring belongs to the signs of the times, and the time belongs to God? See, we then have the moral stability that is now so necessary for us, for those who march out to the frontier and those who fulfill their duties at home. Then we are not afraid, and we do not surrender ourselves to small, disturbed natures in spite of the seriousness of our situation. Then we can wait on God, as God waits on us, until heaven becomes bright again and we are in a position to know that above everything the great day of God has drawn closer.

God gives richly to all of us what is now most needful for us: the fellowship of God's Spirit, who is a Spirit of power and of hope.
Amen.

> *O Lord our God, heavenly Father, in deep anxiety, we lift our eyes to you, from whence comes our help. You know how restless our hearts are at this time. You know how alarmed we are about the unexpected that has befallen us. Father, if it is your will, grant us your precious peace. Hinder the hatred of the nations, and prevent the conflagration that threatens to break out. Take our beloved land into your safekeeping. Preserve our independence, for which our forefathers struggled in fierce battles. Be with our soldiers, with all fathers, husbands, brothers, and sons who have to go out tomorrow to face an unknown fate. Bring them back to us safely. You know how much we need them. Be with us also who remain behind. Preserve us from hunger, need, and every disorder. Hear and answer us, if it is your holy will.*
>
> *But if it is your will that we should suffer, if war, anxiety, and misery lie ahead, then we say with our whole heart, Lord, your will be done! We are in your hands; do with us as it pleases you. Give us only the one thing we need, that we abide in fellowship with you, so that nothing may snatch from our hearts the trust and love in you, so that when the days are more difficult, we may surrender ourselves more affectionately and obediently to you. And then let your kingdom, the kingdom of peace, come nearer, through the midst of all sorrows and difficulties, and let us always be comforted with the knowledge that the end of all things is in your hand.*
>
> *Our Father . . .*

August 9, 1914

Sermon at Safenwil

War between Germany, Austria—Russia, France, England

Philippians 4:6: Do not worry about anything, but in everything by prayer and supplication with thanksgiving let your requests be made known to God. (NRSV)

Dear Friends!

In times such as ours, we pastors should be able to speak to you "with the tongues of men and angels" (1 Cor. 13:1). We know, indeed, how many are counting on us for a word of comfort, encouragement, and support.

An experience that an Old Testament prophet describes is what we are now going through: "The time is surely coming, says the Lord God, when I will send a famine on the land; not a famine of bread, or a thirst for water, but of hearing the words of the Lord" (Amos 8:11). We feel how dire the outlook would be, were there nothing higher to hold on to. We rejoice in every tiny ray of sunlight that breaks through in the dark, overcast sky. We look to the one who knows more and is able to know more than we ourselves. And oh, if only we now had a prophet in our very midst like Isaiah and Jeremiah, who knew how to interpret the signs of the time for us as they interpreted them for their people in their time—a prophet who knew how to show us with divine authority and inspiration the correct view of these events! But that is perhaps a foolish wish. We *do have* the prophetic word, of which it says, that it is "shining in a dark place, until the day dawns and the morning star rises in your hearts" (2 Pet. 1:19).

We *do have* our Bible. There is something wonderful about this ancient book. For years perhaps, we have not really known what to do with it, having read it only from time to time, more out of a sense of duty than out of an inner conviction. And now, all of a sudden, we have had to learn as well, to cry "out of the depths" to the Lord once again (Ps. 130:1). There are such words shining out from the pages of this ancient book as the passage we heard last Sunday: "When you hear of wars and rumors of wars, do not be alarmed" (Mark 13:7)! . . . and "For I know the plans I have for you, plans for welfare and not for evil, to give you a future and a hope" (Jer. 29:11)—words full of comfort and strength, as valid for us today as they were for the people a thousand years ago to whom they were addressed. How many such luminous words there are in the Bible, for example, just in the book of Psalms alone! With what different eyes we read the newspapers in these calamitous days if we have just a single one of these passages lodged in our minds and hearts, if through everything unexpected and alarming that we now hear coming from our world there rings out so powerfully the lines from Paul Gerhardt's hymn: "Everything lasts for its time, but God's love abides forever!"[1]

And then how completely different will be our understanding of our destiny and concerns, when such a biblical passage becomes a living word for us! We need to learn aright in these times, and not only for these but for all times, to go to this fountain and to drink from it. It is truly free to all. We will want to hold on to this more firmly than ever when we gather together here in church, ensuring that we have this prophetic word that has been given to us to be a light and a strength for this time and for all times. Then we will receive the greatest comfort and encouragement, even though no Isaiah or Jeremiah comes in person into our midst.

But, my friends, we have to *look up*, if we want to find comfort and encouragement from above. So many hearts now long for this but fail to obtain it, simply because we are constantly looking downward and backward instead of upward and forward. Also, so many now reach for their Bible and go to church yet do not find the comfort and courage they seek while preoccupied with their own thoughts and wishes. What about us, what are we searching for, when we open the Bible or go to friends and neighbors in these times and pour out our hearts to them? If we are totally honest with ourselves, isn't it true that we must admit, "What I really want is a guardian angel or a special message from the loving God that my husband or brother or friend will return safe and sound from the frontier. That would be true comfort, and I would be totally content!" To be sure, this is a reasonable and permissible wish for you to have, and we hope with all our hearts that it will be granted.

But look, if you really want to succeed in gaining comfort and taking hold of courage, you *ought* not to spend night and day turning only this one wish over and over again in your mind. If you earnestly desire to receive light and strength from God, you *ought* not to inundate God with this one wish only. Life is not at all like that, and our relationship to God is not such that we can pressure God with such questions and demand an answer. Whoever cannot let go of them, whoever knows nothing beyond such worries, will not find firm ground on which to stand. If we constantly raise the one question, "Will they return?" then we may find human comfort of a sort. Germany's and France's announcement this past week that they would respect our country's neutrality in the war at hand provided us with this kind of worldly comfort. Such comfort is no more than a feeling of relief that the thunderstorms are active presently in other locations than in our own immediate neighborhood. Yet this kind of human consolation, which most of us at this present time want so desperately, can one day suddenly come to an end. We already experienced something like that last Sunday evening, when, in response to a report that all danger was supposedly averted, we slept peacefully.

My friends, we cannot and do not want to be satisfied with this kind of comfort. For the lengthy period of hardship and heartache that confronts us, we cannot and do not want to make ourselves dependent on what today this one, and tomorrow that one, asserts and argues. If we would only be willing to give each other our word in this critical time, that from now on we would *no more* put our trust primarily in this human comfort, beautiful and true though it may be, and that above all we would *no longer* bring our heartfelt questions and concerns when we come before God, important and urgent they may be! We cannot and should not want to suppress them. We will certainly ask lovingly and anxiously, again and again, what will happen to him, and what will happen to us? And time and again we will eagerly latch on to anything that even hints of providing a satisfactory answer to our question, and that is natural and justifiable.

Still, now we should promise one another: stand back from these kinds of questions and answers. Away with them! For if they become our top priority and we continually brood over and examine them, we will certainly be unable to escape from the anxiety and despondency in which so many people now find themselves. Yes, and the longer this goes on, all the worse we will become, no matter how much we pray and read our Bibles. For our praying then is not real praying, no matter how eagerly we besiege God with our anxious requests; for then the Bible's light and strength remain shut to us, even if we pore over it night and day.

If we want to receive something from God, we must look up above our human questions and answers, no matter how much we have them at heart. Then we will understand that marvelous apostolic word, "*Do not worry about anything!*" which doesn't in any way correspond to our questions, doubts, and agitations. Those who direct their gaze downward or backward, and whose only desire is to have their human requests gratified, cannot understand advice such as "Do not worry about anything!" This is because they cling tenaciously to this kind of human comfort. How can one tell someone else who demands that God should tell him what precisely *he* would like to know—who demands of God that God should do exactly what *he* wants—how can one propose to say to such a person, "Do not worry about anything!"? This sort of person hears but hears not. The biblical injunction washes over him like water over a pane of glass. He thinks, of course I must worry, of course I must be perturbed and upset, I insist on it; in fact I have every reason to insist, and this advice "Do not worry about anything!" I will leave to those who have nothing to complain about. So he thinks, because he in no way knows God, or perhaps knows God no longer. In any event, such people do not experience the sense of God's presence—God doesn't dwell in their hearts—otherwise they wouldn't think this way. They don't know that God is our gracious and loving Father, who purposely and certainly directs all things for our good. They also don't know that our heavenly Father's will is absolute and unconditionally valid, unwavering and without contradiction, and that from the moment we act apart from or against God's will, we are poor, pitiable creatures. Moreover, they don't know that even in the most difficult times, our primary request in life should not be that God do what we want, but rather that we do God's will, that we perform God's purposes and carry out God's commandments to the best of our ability. Whoever does not know all that cannot possibly understand what "Do not worry about anything!" really means, and still less obey it.

An elderly peddler with a load on her back and an oak walking stick in her hand came to a crossroad and didn't know which road she should take. She threw the stick into the air seven times until finally she cheerfully carried on with her journey. Another traveler, walking behind her, wondered about this and asked the woman why she had thrown the stick into the air seven times. "Don't you see?" she replied, "If I don't know which direction to take at a crossroad, then I ask, 'What is God's will?' To find out, I throw my stick into the air, and wherever it falls, I go in that direction. This time I had to throw my stick seven times until God showed me the way that I wanted to go"—the way I myself wanted and was determined to go! *My* will is God's will; rather, God's will must conform to my will.

Dear friends, don't countless persons think exactly like this elderly woman who spoke so honestly and frankly? Similarly, don't innumerable individuals think precisely this way at this moment, when a greater sorrow lies heavily upon all of us? Are we surprised then that we have no receptive ears and heart for the joyful message, "Do not worry about anything!" which is so valid for us in our present situation? Are we really surprised that we don't know how to obtain this real comfort and courage that we should have at this time? Look! As long as we think and pray this way, as long as we secretly quarrel with and oppose God's will, even if we still invoke God's name so fervently—so long then will our whole life, particularly at times like these, be a game of chance even more foolish than the old woman's; so long then will we certainly never come to possess that inner composure, confidence, and purpose that are so necessary for us. Before everything else, we need to hear the words, "Raise your eyes; lift up your hearts!" And that is exactly also what the apostolic word, "Do not worry about anything!" really wishes to say to us. Look to God! For without God and against God there is no comfort and no courage. Look to God! Look for God's instruction, instead of sticking to what we know of God and desire to have from God.

Who then is this God to whom we must look to become free and strong? God is the infinite power who holds sway over all things and in all things. In and through God everything exists and is held together. God imparts life and movement to all things. There is no particle of matter that existed or would exist without God, and there is, was, and will be no second of time in which God does not rule and govern. No force of nature can oppose God, and no human heart can cut itself off from God. It is our salvation and joy to submit ourselves to God's power, yielding ourselves totally. Then we are saved, then we are secure and blessed, even in the deepest suffering! If we resist God, then we are wretched, lost, and condemned to live in eternal anxiety, uncertainty, and dependence on others, even if we first possessed all happiness and good fortune. It cannot be so hard for us to yield ourselves to God.

God's power is certainly not that of a capricious tyrant; God's power is God's grace. What God wills is holy, righteous, and altogether good, even if we don't always see God's purposes. The deepest, innermost longing of our hearts, the unequivocal stirring of our consciences, tell us, tell each one of us, Give yourself to God, depart from your own way; you belong to God, and God intends the very best for you. You are destined to submit your will to God's will. As long as you fail to do it, you will be sad, confused, and weary. God smooths the path for you so graciously; God shows you so clearly what you should think, say, and do, if you are only prepared to listen. Look! We come to know God when we truly lift up our eyes. God is present to us, just as Jesus Christ has shown us. This is God, the true God: our holy Father, who has eternal, victorious power.

Now we can ask, when we consider God as God truly is, what bearing does this have on our lives? More specifically, what bearing does it have on lives chock-full of worry and anxious thoughts? What bearing can it have, especially when we cease to interrupt every moment with selfish interjections: yes, but *I* . . . *I* would especially like this . . . I wish . . . I really need . . . ? If all this is reduced to silence in us and takes a secondary place where it belongs, then, yes, what bearing does it have on our lives? Just think, what we receive from it is the liberating, bold apostolic word: "Do not worry about anything!"

However odd this may seem to us at first glance, it is completely natural and self-evident advice. What then does this mean, this "Do not worry about anything!"?

Unsurprisingly, our worries and sorrows are still there. During many lonely hours they will make our hearts ache and oppress us with many tears. But we know that whatever can or will come, God is there guiding it all. God wills only what is good, and this God certainly accomplishes. What then do I want? Shall I simply resign myself to my agitation and disquiet? Am I simply to act as if something bad should befall me or my loved ones? God forbid! Should I make my burden even heavier than it is on account of my fleeting, petty thoughts, my struggling and complaining? Admittedly I cannot do better than God, and so I would only make things worse with my useless busyness. God indeed makes everything, and God makes everything good. I can do nothing, absolutely nothing, except be attentive to God's will and remain true to it, so that in no time or place, either in thought, word, or anything else, will I separate myself from God, mistrust God, or act against God. Always, above everything, stands the golden, simple yet powerful, rule: "Thy will be done" (Matt. 6:10)!

> This is the beginning of all rest,
> This is the end of all pain,
> That one does the will of God,
> For rest is in God alone.[2]

Yes, rest is in God alone. Those who don't know this, who in this time of testing don't seek their peace only in the power and grace of God, those who stubbornly continue to grope their way, stumbling over their human questions and answers, will never find comfort and courage. But those who have sincerely acknowledged God, who have also experienced that in God is rest, will safely go God's way, in spite of difficult worries and tears. They know they have a destination. They are freed from obstacles and afflictions breaking in upon them; these oppress yet do not overwhelm them. They know that something different comes from heaven above.

Before all else, they are freed from themselves, from the aching of their hearts and from their frayed nerves. They no longer need to be jittery slaves of their own weaknesses, for they have become God's servants, and God is the strength of their hearts. They can wait patiently; it is no longer terribly urgent to think—if they only knew this and that already! Why should that matter to them? What they don't know doesn't matter, but God knows, and all will be well. And they always have hope, a vastly greater hope than the hope that prevails currently that everything will soon blow over and end happily. Such hope could disappoint us.

I want to add that it is truly deplorable to hope in a self-seeking fashion—such as "Oh, if only it will fare well for us Swiss and in particular for me"—while all around us millions of people will suffer loss after loss. No, those who've found their rest in God—who have set their hope on God's kingdom and glory, which are finally revealed within all the sufferings of life and horrors of the world—those are the people who have a genuine hope. They rejoice that every step freely taken forward is a step toward this goal. That goal is an unshakable hope. And it's no small, self-seeking hope. It's a hope that "does not make us ashamed" (cf. Rom. 5:5).

See, *this* is what we receive when in these troubled times we look upward. In freedom, with strength and joy, we can face everything that may come our way. That means, "Do not worry about anything!" The whole world of suffering and worry, both present and future, exists and presses on and causes us pain, yet we remain calm and secure because we see beyond this. Even though we are only abject, frail creatures, we stand not under but above this world, just as the mighty, holy God is above it. Do we not prefer to have rest in God, rather than unrest in ourselves—that is, in the worry and agitation that are our lot when we abandon ourselves to our selfish inclinations?

My friends, if we respond to the apostle's injunction, "Do not worry about anything!" as he really suggested, then the other thing he says follows as a matter of course: *"but in everything by prayer and supplication with thanksgiving let your requests be made known to God."* This is precisely what we have described. This is what matters, whether we focus on our requests, both the great and small ones, circling around them, keeping them to ourselves, always rummaging around in our scruples and doubts (that suggests worrying!) or whether we make them known in prayer and supplication to God—truly to God, the mighty and holy God, and not to the self-made idols of our imagination.

With *thanksgiving*—I would like simply to underline and emphasize this one phrase. "To thank" means to acknowledge the great things God has already done for us. I believe that we need to begin here if we wish to come to rest in God, in whom alone we find confidence and courage. And I think that it is precisely at this starting point of thankfulness before God that many of us fail. Otherwise, there wouldn't be so much spoiled downheartedness and disquiet among us in this time of testing. I want to implore you with all my heart that instead of wasting so many hours in worry and distress, we ponder anew just how much has been granted to us in our free, strong Switzerland. Indeed, with what greater certainty and confidence we may look forward to the future of our soldiers at the frontier than may all of our neighboring nations.

In particular I implore the many women who are now thinking of their absent husbands and who are unable to dismiss from their mind the question, will he come home again? and to remember for a moment the millions of women whose husbands are now in Alsace, in Belgium, in Poland, in Galicia, on the Danube, or somewhere on the high seas encountering a bloody battle, or those who possibly on this beautiful Sunday morning are right in the thick of battle or have already fallen for their country on foreign soil. This is the most wretched misery. It is also what will certainly take place there in the next few weeks. Step back now from the deep questions in your hearts and think about *this*, for then you will know what you have to be thankful for. Hasn't God indeed dealt mercifully with us up to this point, better than we deserved? Do we not lapse into the sin of ingratitude if we continue to moan and groan about what might also happen to us? And how thankful must we be, if we reflect how unworthy we are to have fared better than millions of others? Are we any better than they? I want to leave the question with you to pursue further. Ask it in the silence. Begin by being thankful to God. Then, by yourselves, you will come to meet God with a deeper trust and obedience. Then you will look steadily to God's mighty and holy rule, awaiting God's power and goodness unfalteringly, without worrying.

And if God should then ordain for us real suffering and misfortune—which God graciously seeks to prevent—then we will be strong and victorious over deprivation and death. *Now*, as we become calm and still in God, we will watch and pray so that we "do not fall away in the time of testing" (cf. Luke 8:13)!

Amen.

August 16, 1914

Sermon at Safenwil

John 15:14–15: You are my friends if you do what I command you. No longer do I call you servants, for the servant does not know what his master is doing; but I have called you friends, for all that I have heard from my Father I have made known to you.

Dear Listeners!

All men and women stand under God's will. All men and women are creatures of the eternal Father and can do nothing other than help to carry out God's holy plans. All men and women are finally able to do nothing other in all they think, say, and do, than to make God's intentions a reality at a given time and place. There is no real resistance to God. No one can actually flee from God's presence. No one can be God's real and final adversary. God cannot be disgraced by humankind. Nothing in the human realm happens without God. When God wills something, it takes place; and when God speaks, "it comes to pass" (cf. Ps. 33:9).

There are two kinds of men and women and, accordingly, two ways of relating to God's will. The first kind of people are involuntary instruments of God. They do not know whom they serve and obey. They are simply used. As in a dream, sighing and sad, or in constant haste and disquiet, or gritting their teeth and furious, they must simply submit and let God's will be accomplished in them and through them, whether they wish it or not.

The second kind of men and women are alert, vibrant, and joyful in God's will. They recognize God's will and delight in doing it. They too must obey, but they would not want it otherwise, for they have found their blessedness in yielding totally to this obedience. Moreover, in the critical time we are now experiencing, these two kinds of people are easy to distinguish. All men and women stand under God's will today as well as always. Of all the memorable, sad paths that we must take, in this ever so, for all time, unforgettable year of 1914, we must all carry out God's intentions and purposes somehow, just as the stars, the wind, and the water for millions of years have followed the course that God established for them. What a comfort, what a joy this fact could be for us amid the darkness and the worry of this day! How joyful and happy we could be in all the disquiet, if we looked steadfastly and with certainty at this one truth: God wills it!

But why is this really no comfort and no joy for so many? Why is there so little of the peace and bliss that could be in us? Because even now, this *one* kind of men and women still submits to God's will involuntarily, just as if they were asleep. They go their own desperate, selfish, crooked way. Through their greed and thirst for power and their mutually blind hatred for one another, they have carried sticks of wood for the ghastly conflagration that has ensued. They have not been courageous [?],[1] serious-minded, and watchful to prevent this catastrophe before it broke out. They have fanned the flames with their passions. And now we see, on the one hand, the ferocious beast in humankind unleashed and, on the other hand, the pale, pathetic fear within the countries, even in our own country. They stand face to face out there at the frontiers of the world empires, full of hateful and revengeful thoughts, or even full of apathy and indifference, desperately fulfilling their duty. And there is so much weakhearted anxiety and agitation, so much foolish and thoughtless opinion within the countries, even in our country; it is "each man for himself, each woman for herself," so much superficial chatter and arguing back and forth.

And yet God also guides all these men and women. God uses their passions, their weaknesses, their petty thoughts for his great purposes, as God uses the lightning and the hail, the toad and the snake, in the great economy of nature. They know nothing of the order of things in which they live and of the purpose that they must also serve. If they knew it, then they would be permitted to play a wholly different role in God's plan. That means, not on the shadow side of evil and human weakness, but on the light side, where one has good intentions and may do good deeds in the service of God. And they would not have to stand there comfortless amid the sad and terrible things that happen around them, and perhaps also to them, but as those who have a hope that "does not disappoint" (cf. Rom. 5:5).

Those are the *others*, the men and women whom God has recognized and come to love, who do not have to obey God without knowing and willing it, in defiance of themselves, but who obey with free, joyful consent. They are the ones who have lifted their eyes and thoughts to God even before the great injustice and misfortune occurred. As long as they could, they hoped and prayed and worked for the victory of the good. They refused to accept the coming calamity to the very end. And where the calamity occurs, it is these persons who now accept and fulfil their duty bravely and gladly, as that obligation is now suddenly thrust upon them under these particular circumstances. If then it now shall so be, these are the ones who now in the field out there with heavy hearts yet with firm, unflinching courage are determined to defend their country with their lives. Or, above all, those at home, who want to help the weak with active love, bandaging wounds, filling a gap that has occurred. Or those who are determined to bear their lot, however dark and heavy, bravely and without complaint. Those are the others in this present time.

Moreover, they must let themselves be led and used implicitly by God in accordance with God's purpose and plan. But they are content with that; they desire nothing else—even in this situation, in this triumph of evil, in the thick of this misfortune that humankind has brought upon itself—but to be of help to God, to make God's intentions their own intentions. Possibly with effective words and deeds, possibly simply with calm minds and prayer, possibly with weapon in hand, possibly with some simple, modest work of peace that is still as necessary now as previously—possibly even through their suffering and dying. But they want to do everything with God and for God. And because this is where they position themselves, they stand even in these dark and incomprehensible works of God still on the light side, where one not only does the good, but where in spite of everything one also feels good, where one can still be happy from one day to the next, though beset by worries and tears. They even know the goal of all human ways, and they know that they are on the way to this goal.

Jesus names the one kind of men and women in this passage *servants*, the other kind *friends*. He describes the *servants* with the words, "*A servant does not know what the master is doing.*" Fortunately for us, there are also male servants and handmaids who are at the same time friends of their master. They are not thought of or mentioned here; but only those who serve solely because they must, or those who serve solely for the sake of a reward, fit this description. Their master's affairs are fundamentally a matter of indifference to them. They live their lives for themselves, have their own particular interests, their hidden, private ways. They do not place themselves inwardly near their master but, rather, distance themselves, if not in a hostile way, yet contrary to the master. Their relationship to the master is no more than an external, accidental necessity.

If they have to obey, contrary to their mind and intent, they do so because they have no choice in the matter; but they are inwardly resentful because they cannot imagine themselves even for a moment in the position of their master by considering the matter from his standpoint. At the next opportunity they will do it their own way. They have no love for the one whom they must obey, and because they have no love, they also have no trust, and because they have no trust, they also cannot understand him; and even if they could understand him, they would not want to do so. Their relationship to the master is formal and superficial, and they are quite distant from him. They must know it and be conscious every day that he is over them, but deep in their hearts they are desperately unhappy about it. Their whole life is a constant friction, a continual dissatisfaction. Their master must suffer knowing it, and they must suffer most of all. There are enough such male servants and handmaids in both the city and in the country.

Hence when it now comes to our relationship with God, we can, if we wish, be God's coerced, sullen, dissatisfied servants. Yet there are servants who at the same time are God's friends. The ancient prophets of Israel liked to describe themselves as servants of God, and in several places in the New Testament Jesus is also called the servant of God. For the moment we will set this aside: we are speaking of those who are in God's servitude only, who are merely God's slaves or debt-slaves. It is their own fault that their situation is so grievous! Basically, they know nothing of the things of God: nothing of truth, justice, and love; nothing of the high aims of life for which we may strive; nothing of the great future and hope that God has in store for the human race. They have a mind and sense of their own; they go their individual way as such servants do whenever they can. They seek their well-being and their ease, what promises them pleasure and tickles their fancy; basically, they love and care only for their own welfare. They know full well that there is a Higher Being whom they must obey. The urging of their hearts and the warning of their consciences draw their attention to the One who has created them and to whom they belong. From childhood on, they hear time and again God's Word spoken to them of what is right and what God demands of them. They note that it is indeed a disgrace that one makes oneself unhappy by heeding the voice of one's lower nature, by pursuing one's selfish interests. They find themselves in situations where they, even if they really so desire, cannot do anything other than fulfill their duty. Sometimes they must be wholly honest; in many cases they must master and control themselves; often they have to be just and moderate; now and then they must even practice a little love and compassion.

But it is only a matter of *must*. They do not actually want to do so. They feel terribly distant and alienated about all these things. Sullen and bitter, they give in to the inevitable. Their only thought while doing so is, "When can I slip away again? When can I be myself again? When can I think, speak, and act just as my own heart desires and pleases, just as a school pupil looks forward during the whole morning to the precious moment when the closing bell rings?" How much of what in human eyes is valued as uprightness and honesty is, at bottom, nothing other than such abject slavery, such a feeling of discontent with God, who they think expects too much from them, so that they also wait for the precious moment when they can again be their own masters!

And now you see that this slavery then becomes apparent in such times as we are now enduring. It indeed shows itself with everyone what that person is and in many it can be seen: he or she is just a slave, a lowly slave of God. Now God expects much, very much from him or her. Their faith, love, and hope are put to a hard and difficult test. Now they should be able to accept blindly what God gives them in the firm confidence that the master knows best and will do the best. Then they would even come through these times safely and happily. But they cannot; basically, they do not have a master. They know the master only formally. They know nothing of the master's thoughts and intentions. Abject men and women, nothing now remains for them except disquiet and distress; now only their wicked and weak instincts remain and dominate them totally. They surrender themselves to their passions, apathy, or anxiety. They follow the compulsion of their selfishness, which was always the strongest impulse in them.

Still, something else moves in them here and there that will not be silenced: trust, kindness, the feeling of obligation, the sense of the divine. But like being swept away by a swelling river, they must drown in their malice or weakness; they will be swept hopelessly over to the other side, to the shadow side, where, to be sure, God rules as well, where one can do nothing against or without God, where everything happens just as God will have it happen, but no more to the salvation but, rather, to the ruin of those who have placed themselves on this shadow side. How much gloom and despair, how many mindless, selfish actions that have occurred in the past weeks, how much mistrust and timidity with regard to the future, have their basis solely in this state of slavery! Whoever is simply a slave of God, whoever wants to remain inwardly distant and separate from God and obeys God only because one must, really cannot act differently. That kind of slave does not know what the master does—especially cannot know it in these times of testing and purgation.

But now there is another kind of person, whom Jesus calls *friend*. How utterly different this word sounds. Oh, if only we could be friends of God! Friends are two persons who feel bound to each other, not out of compulsion but of their own free choice. Friends are two persons who have said to each other by their own free decision, "We desire the same thing, and hence we will stand by each other, we will help each other." If we are someone's friend, then that means that inwardly we will stand close to that person, that we will feel and think with him or her, that we will understand him, that every moment we will be able to put ourselves in her place. The more affectionate and honest a friendship is, the less can anything come between the friends; the more they become, as one says so beautifully, "of one heart and of one soul," the less can there be misunderstanding between them. Where one is completely honest with another, what does one have to hide? Where one does not count personal belongings; things are held in common. No friend credits another friend with evil, because that would be like mistrusting yourself, like harming yourself. Where genuine friendship exists between two persons, it manifests itself externally: one wants only what is beneficial for the other. Perhaps, one has to ask sometimes, "Why are you doing that?" But even if it does not seem completely clear immediately, one still remains calm, because one knows that he or she means well and it will all work out well. The core and essence of all friendship is always love, as the core and essence of slavery is selfishness. Friendship is in every respect the direct opposite of slavery.

And now Jesus says to us that we may be friends, friends of God. Reflect on what that means: persons who have surrendered themselves to God freely, willingly, and lovingly, persons who not only stand under God but want to stand under God, persons who know something wholly different of God than that God is the one above, who demands so much of us and whose hand often rests so heavily upon us. No, God is the one with whom we are of one mind, whose concern is our own deepest concern, who is more important to us than anything else, the one who is also of one mind with us, with whom we are united for refuge and strength!

Think also, if we were the friends of God, how that would play out in normal times and in such extraordinary times as the ones we are now experiencing! A friend of God is one who knows the purpose for which we are created, who does not sigh, "Oh, so much is demanded of us!" but is pleased to ascend so high. A new duty that life often brings unexpectedly does not weigh him or her down; he or she does not think, "O dear God, that too, it's more than I can take!" Rather, he or she thinks, "So that's the way things are! Good, I will give it a good try, and in God's name I will gladly do what I can." The good for him or her is not in the first place something that hovers threateningly somewhere over them every moment, like a menacing cloud raining or hailing new demands upon them, but is an inward motivating force. They must do the good because they are also under a compulsion, as it were, but under an inner compulsion, under their own compulsion. The necessity that they obey is not a distant, alien monster that one would love to escape; it lives in their soul, in their deepest heart. They have positioned themselves; they command and rule themselves. It is their concern, their heart's concern, when they say, "I can do no other, I must—I must follow the truth, I must do what is right, I must practice love."

Such men and women fare well even in the present time. What the time brings to them and will bring is not fate, but something that in any case comes from their Friend, who has their well-being at heart. They cannot protest and complain about it, for they simply have the confidence that it is all part of the order of things and they ask nothing other than, "What is my duty for the next day?" And they become so completely, so certainly, and so wonderfully cared for and blessed as they journey through these times. They are of one mind with the one who leads them according to God's will and protects and shields them anew, so that their feet cannot stumble or slip (cf. Ps. 73:2), come whatever will. They always stand on the side of light, there where the will of God *also* occurs and must occur, as it happens to the bad and weak; but here one says yes joyfully and thankfully to it, while over there one does not really know it, or even rebels against it. And so here is life and peace and blessedness.

Thanks be to God that so much good comes to light in humankind in this dark time. Much undaunted-by-death bravery of men and women, much earnest fulfilment of one's duty, much self-sacrificing love and helpfulness, much heartfelt and God-given prayer have already been stimulated by these horrible events so far. We can count on it, where something good now occurs, where people really prove their worth, where something better than in normal times shines forth from them, that it all has its basis and its cause as a result, perhaps, of such a deeply hidden friendship with God.

Many men and women cannot show themselves like that in normal times; one does not count them among the devout, sees nothing special about them, but in the depth of their hearts there exists that unity with God. They have committed themselves freely and joyfully to God, who is the source of all good; and now in these difficult times they can so place themselves quite certainly and naturally as men and women can who are one with God. They do their duty, they bear their burdens, they do not break down under them, they live by the hope that after the darkness the light has to come. If only we could do likewise!

Yes, now what are we then precisely: slaves or friends? We have now sharply contrasted these two kinds of people in their relationship to God. But it is not actually so simple that one could now, for instance, say about each one of us: that one is a slave, and that one is a friend. Yes, one could not definitely say of any of us: either-or! The same holds true of the millions of people for whom now in these critical weeks and months, so much—to some extent everything—depends on their relationship to God. We are not the one or the other; rather, we have in us a little something of both, of slave and of friend. Or does it not feel like that also for you, that both seem quite familiar?

We yield ourselves to God sometimes very reluctantly and with ulterior motives and then experience all the torment of hell that such behavior inevitably brings. And then again we rejoice in God's will and can gladly accept what God gives us. We have certainly noticed during these weeks how both reign in us: the soul of the slave who cringes in fear before God, and the soul of the friend who loves to praise and glorify God for all that God does for us. But we are not permitted to leave it that way, that is, that we are, side by side and at the same time, both slave and friend. We cannot do it for long. We can only go either forward or backward. Either we sink deeper and deeper into the state of slavery, the false, timid, rebellious relationship to our Father, through which we make ourselves miserable; or we become more and more friends of God, ascending upward to the knowledge of God's will and to the joy thereof, to the conscious, eager obedience of God's commandments in all the situations of life into which God may lead us. What do we want to do now? Do we want to ascend or descend? Do we want to be slaves, and finally and deep down be on the shadow side of life? Or do we want to be friends, children of the light, who cannot do anything other than walk in the light (cf. Eph. 5:9)?

Jesus' saying confronts us with this decisive "either-or": "*But I have called you friends, for all that I have heard from my Father I have made known to you.*" That is the great message that Jesus has delivered to all of us: that we are friends. Jesus shows us God and God's love so clearly in his life and death; he brings God so near to us that we cannot do anything except yield ourselves to God, anything except cross over to God's side out of our own free, joyful resolve. We simply need to listen to Jesus—"Who has seen me, has seen the Father" (see John 14:9)—and must also become the Father's friend. The one who notes this sees that the trembling, agitated, self-seeking state of slavery does not work. "The old has passed away, behold, the new has come" (2 Cor. 5:17).

The predicament of our time compels us all to open our eyes and to realize that we stand before this great "either-or," whether we want to become either real slaves or real friends of God. Grant that it may be given to all of us to hear the saving word of Jesus: "You are friends!" Grant that we may all feel something of the power that goes out from him, a power that makes this promise real, leading us quietly but certainly upward, that truly and really allows us to become what we are meant to be, friends of God, men and women whom nothing in all creation can confuse and frighten anymore!

Amen.

August 23, 1914

Sermon at Safenwil[1]

Revelation 6:4: And out came another horse, fiery red; its rider was permitted to take peace from the earth, so that [people] would slaughter one another, and he was given a great sword.

Matthew 10:28: Do not fear those who kill the body but cannot kill the soul; rather fear him who can destroy both body and soul in hell.[2]

Dear hearers!

    The first of these biblical texts is taken from one of the shocking descriptions of the coming judgment of the world in the Revelation to John. Four grim riders mounted on white, fiery red, black, and yellow horses go out as the first heralds of this judgment (Rev. 6:1–8). They represent plague, war, hunger, and death. Of all of them it is said that power is given to them, given to them by God, to do their unholy work. They may, they must do it. This is how God's judgment begins. From this passage I've selected the words that deal with war: "And out came a horse, fiery red; its rider was permitted to take peace from the earth, so that people would slaughter one another, and he was given a great sword."

    Today let's reflect on the fact that *in this war God's judgment* has come upon us. The war has gone on for three weeks. The initial alarm, as far as I can tell, has given way to a certain calming down among us. We no longer fear the worst immediately. We begin, let's hope, to feel ashamed about a certain selfish folly that has been perpetrated in the past three weeks. We seek with the most reasonableness possible to resign ourselves to the inevitable. We even talk again about things other than the war. Here and there we even hear people laughing and singing again. This change of mood has a good deal of its basis in the fact that we have learned again a little to commit ourselves in heartfelt trust to God. There has been a great deal of praying in these weeks, and God has answered many prayers. It has not been in vain when a troubled soul has called to God from the depths: "Lord, your will be done" (Matt. 6:10). We have become stronger through increased trust and fervent praying. That's the reason we can become calmer again.

Would to God that this were the sole reason for the calming down that has occurred! Then it would always get deeper and stronger. Then we could always look forward more confidently and certainly to all that comes next. But that isn't the only reason. I know it, and you know it as well. We will be completely honest. If it were simply a matter of faith and prayer, we would not now feel so calm and safe. But we have discovered during the course of these weeks that the war is not such a terrible thing as we had originally thought. Admittedly, we've read newspaper accounts of a few bloody battles, but there was nothing in these reports that could deeply upset us anymore than what we heard perhaps earlier of other wars that were distant from us. Above all, we ourselves have yet experienced very little of the war. We live still as in the midst of peace. Our soldiers have gone to the frontier, and money has become a little scarce. That's what affects us. But thank God, we have favorable reports from our loved ones at the frontier, and much seems to indicate that our country will not be directly involved. Moreover, the destitution within our country is not as bad as we had feared. And *for that reason* we are now calmer; therefore we can talk about other things again and can laugh again, not just because of our strong faith! Isn't that true?

My friends! It's not my intention to make you anxious. But I really do want to warn you that we are not now to lull ourselves into a false sense of security by thinking that the danger has passed us by! These thoughts offer us no safe refuge. If we want to reassure ourselves now with them, then the old disquiet will return again, more worrisome than before, should the tide only turn again. Do we not feel that, behind our outward calm, pallid fear lurks: yes, the fear, but what all may still come? We would not be at the risk of such a hidden fear, were our hope set wholly on God. And my friends, the tide could still turn, the momentum could certainly shift. We are not at the end but rather at the very beginning of this period of war. And this time is one of the most serious of all world history. We would certainly act wrongly if we thoughtlessly sleep through it, even if we are not personally affected by it.

What are all the wars we have known, compared with the war that has now blazed up? What are even the Napoleonic campaigns and the Thirty Years' War in Germany, compared with the colossal clash of nations that is now being prepared? We have to go back to the times of the great migration of peoples in order to recall an event of similar significance and extent. Indeed, it has to be a woefully small-minded individual who can be comforted in the midst of it all, saying, that's far away and doesn't concern me! Such a person is one who doesn't experience all this with an alert heart and conscience. In any case, when it comes to this, we ourselves will definitely have to feel these events more than previously.

It doesn't appear as though this war is likely to unwind very quickly; and we do well, at least, to prepare ourselves for a long separation from those who have gone to the frontier. Let's not forget that we are now in the most favorable time of the year. But later on it will be winter, and we will have to realize what it means when the entire life of the economy falters. What sort of Christmas will we experience, how will Easter turn out for us? Until then we can expect that much of the laughter will die down, the laughter of those who instead of placing their confidence in God now reassure themselves that things are not so dangerous for us. I repeat, I do not wish to make you anxious; with you I rejoice over every day we can spend in safety and peace, but I dread a certain carelessness that now after the initial shock would seek to seize a place among us. This carelessness is a folly and sacrilege. I wish that we would look these dangerous facts in the face. I wish we would all understand the signs of the times. This is a unique time of God, a time of judgment without equal. And for that very reason, it is also a wholly special time of grace. Blessed are those who now have ears to hear.

The war, as a bitter, unavoidable necessity, has drawn closer, descending upon us like that unstoppable rider in the Revelation to John: "He was permitted to take peace from the earth that men might slaughter one another." To this day, it is something wholly *inconceivable*, how within a few short weeks the whole of Europe, and even the entire world, has taken on a different countenance. Broken off, all of a sudden, are all the millions of links of feverish, busy commerce that run back and forth among the nations. Cut off are the thousand different sources of prosperity and wealth. Suppressed are all the scientific, artistic, and religious interests that affected distant people and bound them together. Brought to an end, once and for all, are all the false or genuine, polite and friendly encounters, all the human relationships between nation and nation. Icy silence or accusations and defamations have taken their place. Stockpiled with weapons, resolutely determined all of a sudden, each nation withdraws into itself and has no longer any interest other than this: Will we be quick, efficient, well-equipped, and numerous enough to overpower the enemy out there, with whom we are no longer bound together except by mutual hatred? Everything else is forgotten except the claim, we have to defend ourselves! We want to, we must, and we will win.

And now mutual destruction is about to commence. What occurred up to now were only insignificant preliminary skirmishes. Yet they were already able to give us an indication of what is now about to come. Never before have death and destruction been pursued so methodically, so technically, and in so precise and businesslike a way as today. Immense intellectual activity is put into the preparation and performance of powerful armies, which are now in the field of battle with all their resources. In all probability, death will be the harvest of European humanity as never before. Millions will mourn their loved ones and will be in deep distress. What about the things that will be destroyed, the means of livelihood and works of art, what Europe will forfeit economically through American competition, which now all of a sudden and for a long time can develop freely at our expense? And how much can the European nations lose with regard to power and respect in the eyes of other nations in Africa and, above all, in Asia, with all the uncivilized and half-civilized peoples, who have long waited to free themselves from a hated Europe? All this can scarcely be predicted.

And then there is above all the terrible spiritual and moral decline that such a war involves for all participants. It means an awakening of nationalistic passions, the fanatical barbaric consciousness—we are German! we are French!—settling like a wretched fog over the great truth that all humankind are brothers and sisters. It means the supremacy of brutal, impersonal, material power over all other forces in human life; it means these unleashed impulses to hate, kill, and destroy. What kind of a godless catastrophe is it that has descended upon us! Perhaps you still remember how scarcely two months ago, we spoke here about our national Swiss Exhibition[3] and about the great gifts and powers God has entrusted to us. The text on that occasion was from Psalm 8, where it says of human beings, "You have made them a little lower than God, and crowned them with glory and honor" (Ps. 8:6 NRSV)! For us, what have things come to now? Where now is the glory of humanity about which at that time we could gratefully rejoice? Now we can do nothing but hear in silent reverence how God all of a sudden speaks quite differently with us, showing us a wholly different picture of humanity than that which we admired at that time.

I tell you this world catastrophe has come over us like an inexorable *necessity*. All the forces that one would have expected to maintain peace proved to be powerless. They could not prevent Europe from falling to pieces. Mammon, international capital, was unable to do it. Many had expected that in our time business interests in all countries were so strong that they would not let this happen. What a bitter disappointment that money did not make people close friends. It will probably turn out to be the opposite, that the exaggerated business and money interests, by which the nations have let themselves be guided, have marched them into this murderous war. In one respect it is indeed already certain: all the thousands of French soldiers who now must die, die not for their country but for the forty billion francs that the French banks have invested in Russia.

However, the Social Democrats have also been unable to prevent the war. I have been asked once or twice during these weeks by such persons who do not think too much of this political movement, whether the Socialists were not sufficiently strong to resist the war. I had to answer no, they still are not sufficiently strong, and here everyone may ask oneself why they were not strong enough. The will and purpose of millions of the working classes was indeed there, but the authority wasn't there. It wouldn't have been of any use, even if they had opposed it. In the long run they could do nothing else than march under the flags of their respective nations and wage war against one another like everyone else, and now for some time they can only blush when they speak of the brotherhood and sisterhood of all humanity. There is also a serious warning for us: Why did we not let the forces of peace become stronger in tranquil times? Do we not now share the guilt in this time of distress that we failed to do so? However, there is also this admonition: "Put not your trust in princes" (Ps. 146:3), whatever they may be called.

As well, Christianity, at least the Christian churches, have failed vis-à-vis the war that has come about. What has become of the power of the gospel? Why did it not become alive in thousands, so that these atrocities would have been prevented? How is it then that now two thousand years after Christ, these so-called Christian nations, which should be the light of the world (see Matt. 5:14), stand over against one another with the single thought: to do harm, to destroy if possible, with all one's might? I have in mind, among these Christian nations, a nation with so many deeply serious thinkers as the Germans and a nation so puritanical and zealously missionary as the English. Even in the last week of his life, Pope Pius X, who just died, issued an encyclical containing a universal prayer for peace.[4] It was like the voice of a child in the storm, so helpless and ineffective, and yet I'm sorry to say the only luminous point; here at least was a voice that was not the voice of a combatant, that pointed to something higher from a position *above* the fray.[5] This voice is now also silent, and it also wouldn't have made any difference. And what about the other Christians? The German, the French, the Russian, the English . . . ?

Thank God that he sees what is hidden; for what comes to the surface isn't soul-stirring. What do they all now pray for? They pray for the victory of *their* nation, their armaments, each for its own! What would happen if God were just as all these Christians think of him? What would Jesus say, if he now returned and found his disciples offering these peculiar war prayers? See, all human nature has collapsed so deplorably before the rider on the fiery red horse, to whom the sword and power have been given to take away peace from the earth, so that people would slaughter one another. What has befallen humanity is simply stronger than we are, stronger than the best in us. So, let no one boast (1 Cor. 3:21), as Paul would now say, for there is no one who does good, no, not even one (see Rom. 3:10). We Swiss aren't really any different. If we were in the position of our neighbors, we wouldn't be different and wouldn't think differently. Human beings are now all of a sudden in the situation that they can no longer accuse the other. The point is that God can now again speak to us, so that we have to listen to him.

The war is *God's judgment* upon us. Every misfortune is such a judgment. But the greater the misfortune, the more terrible is the judgment that God exercises. And precisely the incomprehensible and inevitable character of the present-day events portends that a greater day of judgment has just begun. Judgment! That means that God wants to tell us now once again that we are in the wrong, that he is not pleased with us. God speaks to us, interrupting in an unprecedented way our usual being and doing, by placing in our midst a fact so hard and inexorable that we must pay attention to it and fall silent before God. We Europeans were of the opinion that we were on the right road. We took it for granted that we were the highest echelon and choicest flower of humanity. We were so keen to increase our wealth and well-being. We had devised such a clever system of achieving success in the world, vastly superior to our grandparents. We were so enchanted with our acquired knowledge. We found so many means and ways to spend our earned income usefully and pleasantly. We did not hesitate to look down our noses on the brutish, uncivilized inhabitants of other continents; we could even look down on our own ancestors. We felt so secure. We were firmly persuaded that we were on the right road.

Now suddenly God comes and says to us sharply and sternly, "No! You are not on the right road!" Consequently, God sends us the inexorable rider on the red horse, who with his great sword takes peace from the earth. In sending us the war, God is saying "No!" to us. God, and not some predetermined power, sends it to us. The war is no surprise, even though it broke out so suddenly and unexpectedly like a phantom. Suddenly it was there in the midst of our unsuspecting world. It came as the inevitable consequence of what we've been and what we've done. It's suddenly there on our path, which we thought to be so right. We should have known it earlier; now we have to reap what we have sown.

This is always so with God's judgments. They do not come as miracles of nature. They come as the natural consequence of our own actions. Suddenly we are faced with the bill. Suddenly we have to realize that we have come to such a pass; here is the misfortune that we've brought on ourselves. So is it also this time. For some time, more perceptive persons have said that if we continue like this, we will bring a catastrophe on ourselves. There's been so much godlessness in our previous doing and being, more than God could continue to tolerate. So much artificiality and sin are hidden in our European culture, even in what one customarily and officially calls Christianity, more than what could survive in the long run.

We have not listened to these voices. There was no time for that. We had to mind our own business and enjoyment. We preferred to listen to those who found everything beautiful and good, to those who went with the flow, who live and let live. God has waited a long time. Now the judgment has come. We ourselves have rushed headlong into judgment. Now the balance sheet is printed out, and it does not read well. Yes, we are more clever and mightier than uncivilized people, more clever than our ancestors; however, our whole culture was no property of our own, and no fraternal and sisterly work but self-seeking. We stood in envy next to one another, all of us greedily working our way up, wickedly piling up tinder for the conflagration between the selfish masses that we call nations, always producing more, always wanting to become stronger—until now finally this explosion of evil had to occur. It cannot have been otherwise in a world in which commercial rivalry is premised on the principle that might is right; a world like that cannot but end up with war, with mutual murder and destruction.

Moreover, if after the war we should again pursue our previous course, then sooner or later still other more shocking events will teach us that we cannot go on like this, that it simply does not work. We now stand there and complain about the evil that has descended upon us, like children who have broken a dish, standing there and looking for excuses. We should not complain; we have created the evil. The arrogance, the selfish and stubborn insistence on our own right and our own power, which were hidden in our boastful, proud culture, have now produced their fruit. Individuals were imbued with it; nations were possessed by it. The peace that we had was no peace; it was a disguised, deceitful, veiled war. It didn't have any staying power.

Warnings were not lacking. But we didn't listen to them. We responded, "There's no danger!" We would even now like to be able to answer, there's no danger—if only we could. Now the hour of honesty has come. Now the long-hidden, existing war has suddenly moved into the daylight. Now one is openly the enemy of the other. Now our culture, our human nature, has received this staggering, perhaps irreparable blow. It didn't come from outside but from inside. This is how God punishes us, my friends. God sends no bolts of lightning from heaven but leaves us simply doing our own thing, until one day we go so far that we punish ourselves through our own action.

What should we do now in this hour of judgment? We might cry with all our heart, "Lord, have mercy on us!" Yes, that we must do, that we would do, that is the only thing we can do. Nothing helps now but that we understand:

it had to come to this through our own fault. That we reverently confess: God has spoken and has once again shown us the fruits of our doings, that God alone is the mighty one. That we bow unconditionally and uncomplainingly, bow under God's verdict and God's mighty hand, which now punishes us. That we implore one thing of God: "Lord, do not forsake us!"

Our second text, a word of Jesus, should show us the kind of attitude with which we must now call upon God in this hour of judgment. "Do not fear those who kill the body but cannot kill the soul," he says to us. "Fear much more those who can destroy body and soul in hell." There is a way to tremble before the judgment of God that doesn't pay off, that leads us only deeper into judgment, into destruction. As long as we look only at what concerns us as individuals outwardly and possibly produces suffering in such extraordinary times, then we have missed the main issue. As long as we allow ourselves to be moved and excited only by that, then we are still blind to the signs of the time. That's not the judgment of God, that men and women now perish; cities and villages are destroyed; financial loss, hunger, and distress threaten. That's only the external. Whoever knows only that, whoever is afraid only of that, is blind. The judgment is what God says to us with all these external signs: "Your ways are not my ways, and your thoughts are not my thoughts" (see Isa. 55:8). Misery and death, all the horrors of war, the destruction of our whole European culture, the yellow and black peril, and what just may be the consequences of our contemporary events—these cannot reach to the very soul of humankind, they leave its soul untouched, they can be overcome in faith, love, and hope.

But it would be terrible if God were to say to us with all this: I am separating from you, I no longer want to know you, I don't have any further need of you. That would be horrible, if God were to destroy us now, we who have so stubbornly gone our own evil ways, destroy us, body and soul in hell. If we now had to hear his "No!" that not only halts us on our way but also finally condemns us to a lost, spiritually wretched life. That, my friends, is what we should fear in the hour of judgment. The immensely great danger among us is that we simply do the other. I think once more about this certain carelessness that now seems to be present among us. In the beginning we occupied ourselves much too eagerly and excitedly with those external dangers that kill the body, as Jesus says. We chose at that time to be comforted out of God's Word that we don't have to fear those dangers, because the soul cannot be killed, since God's love for us remains certain as long as we depend on him. And we want to stay with that. The external danger has temporarily receded to some extent, and now apparently many think that there is now nothing more to fear.

But I must now remind you of something else: "Fear the one who can destroy the body and soul in hell!" Yes, fear the living God, who now says to us, as God presides over this world catastrophe, that God is not pleased with us and God will certainly not be mocked (see Gal. 6:7). It would be terrible if we would now ignore God and through our own guilt separate ourselves from God and God's love. God will not soon come so near to us again as he does now with this generous call to mend our ways and to change our mind. Oh, if we will just once stop this seesaw game of thoughtless and baseless anxiety and worry in which we now find ourselves. We cannot get peace this way. We cannot so survive this time. We want to hear God's invitation and to answer him, "Father, I have sinned and I am not worthy to be called your son or daughter (see Luke 15:19), and I would like, I would like so much to become a different person!" A single sigh such as that, out of the depth of a guilt-conscious heart, is worth more than a thousand long prayers full of mundane, external wishes. Oh, that this sigh for God himself would be awakened in us, who can make us blessed or damned! Oh, that now this sigh would be awakened in millions of souls in our country, in all the poor, smitten countries of Europe! Would that fear before God might greatly move all these souls!

Then we would experience in the midst of fear before God, who is the holy and righteous one, who lets us reap what we have sown (see Gal. 6:7), that God is love, that God's present terrible judgment is an act of his grace. Then, but *only* then, we may be completely calm in the certainty that God will not withdraw his hand from us in all these things, because we are *his*.

Amen.

August 30, 1914

Sermon at Safenwil and Kölliken[1]

Isaiah 30:15: In quietness and in trust shall be your strength.

Dear Friends!

This word of quietness and trust once held good for a small nation in the midst of great powers experienced in war. This nation was the kingdom of Judah, which, made up of the city of Jerusalem and a few regions surrounding it, was scarcely larger than a few Swiss cantons. The northern sister kingdom of Israel with its capital city Samaria was already conquered and occupied by the Assyrians, and this rapacious world power now stood almost in front of the gates of the city of David. And in the south, the driving force and power of the ancient African kingdom of Egypt soon began to assert itself. It glanced jealously over at its Assyrian rival, preparing to oppose its claims with all its might and with the weight of an ancient authority and an established state. Caught between these two world powers and their wars and their ever-renewed craving for war, the small nation of Judah was completely dependent on its own power, its shrewdness—and its God! One day the prophet Isaiah spoke this word to them as a word of God in an exceedingly difficult and dangerous world situation: "In quietness and hope shall be your strength."

It is remarkable to see how much similarity exists between the situation of this small kingdom in Palestine back then and the present grave situation in which our beloved Switzerland finds itself, set as it is in the middle of the great war powers of Europe that were power hungry and jealous for many years and have now suddenly entered into open hostility.

Moreover, we must immediately sense the similarity if we think a little more deeply about what God demanded of the nation through the prophets at that time, and what is divinely right and necessary for us, us Swiss people, in the present world situation. If we understand it aright, we may apply without hesitation the message of quietness and hope to ourselves. Probably more than one among us in difficult circumstances has found comfort and courage in this cheerful and clear message. But indeed most rarely has it applied in its original sense so aptly to us and to all that troubles us right now. It will be of help to us now as we give a proper account in this difficult time regarding God's will for our people and our country.

Quietness is the first thing the prophet demanded from the nation and its government in Jerusalem. The "quietness" to which he refers is nothing other than what today, to use a foreign term, we call "neutrality." They should be on guard against taking sides; they should remain neutral, taking the side neither of one nor of the other. They should keep to themselves and watch. This warning was necessary; there was a strong faction that felt that in order to protect itself from Assyria, the nation should throw itself into the arms of Egypt. The government in Jerusalem had great respect for the strong army of the Egyptians, especially for its cavalry and its chariots, and many expected miracles from such an ally. Isaiah was sensible enough not to allow himself to be taken in so easily. "The Egyptians are human and not God!" Isaiah reminded these politicians. "And their horses are flesh, and not spirit. When the LORD stretches out his hand, the helper will stumble, and the one helped will fall, and they will all perish together" (Isa. 31:3 NRSV). You have better things to do, he wanted to say to them, than to get mixed up in this conflict and thereby possibly be destroyed yourselves. You could now be the nation of the living God in the midst of the quarreling world powers. Trust God and serve God in every respect. When you do so, you will have a secure future before you, and then you will fulfill a special calling among the nations. Hence, you will come out of the present difficult situation strong, pure, and great. Quietness is now your noble principle and absolute obligation.

With that we have actually heard quite specifically what our *Swiss neutrality* is and shall be in the current world war. When this war broke out four weeks ago, our executive federal council hastened to make a statement to the warring nations: Switzerland remains neutral; she maintains friendly relations with both sides and hence will choose no party. In order to secure our independent and carefully considered position, our armies were sent to the borders, and we may be confident that they will fulfil their duty in all circumstances. Yet, with that, my friends, the matter is not settled. Swiss neutrality is by no means only a political and military matter. But behind our highest government authorities, which in this matter are fortunately wiser than the Judean king, and behind our soldiers, a people must stand wholly united and determined to be quiet and not to take sides either for or against, but to wait out the conflict.

And here it is wanting. There may, in fact, be very few among the Swiss people, a few young officers possibly, who wish that we also might still become directly involved in the raging storm. The greater majority is of the opinion that our country and our soldiers should be spared from participating in this war. But it is not enough to have this wish. We should be much clearer than we are in the present moment, that as Swiss we not only have the right but also the obligation to be neutral even inwardly, even in our thoughts and feelings. We commit a great injustice, my friends, and we deprive ourselves of the greatest blessing that we can have in this time, if we do not have the insight that this war going on out there is not our affair, not at all, and if, instead of that, with foolish thoughts and even more foolish chatter we opt for one side or the other. In no respect is it a trivial matter with what kind of thoughts we now read the newspapers, how we respond inwardly to all the reports that come now, and how we speak about it in confidential conversation in the family, on the street, or somewhere else. It is not trivial, because how this war affects us depends a great deal on our present inner attitude.

Our present disposition could have more far-reaching consequences than we can now imagine. Through quietness you will be strong. Much will depend on whether we Swiss become stronger through these unhappy events, and even more when they have ended. Our small nation and country could still have a great mission and future in poor war-torn Europe. If we want to be strong, we must, however, be quiet, honest; and deep down we must be "cool in the depth of the heart,"[2] watching the conflict and desiring victory for neither side. God will see to it that matters will develop in ways that heal.[3] *Why* all this? The present war is largely a *racial* conflict. The ancient antagonism between the German and the French way has broken out openly once more. These nations now believe that their natural differences and jealousies can still be resolved only through slaughter and destruction. And on the other side, in eastern Europe, German civilization is opposed to Slavic civilization. This racial hatred and racial conflict, my friends, do not concern us. We may not, we cannot, and we will not take this or that side, even in our thoughts and wishes. We too are German, from Alemannic stock, and in this respect naturally stand closest to our German neighbors among all the warring sides. But what are we to make of German pride and hatred directed against the French, against the Russians? We have no reason in the least to share this frame of mind. Are not the Waadtlanders, the Genevans, the Ticinos, our Swiss brothers and sisters? And yet they are French, Italian, foreign people, if you will. But we Swiss do not recognize that there has to be hatred and war between foreign nationalities.

We have put together three "foreign" nationalities and said to one another that we want to be a united nation of brothers and sisters.[4] Our unity must now stand the test, not only inwardly but also in our judgment of foreign nations. We Swiss do not understand and do not want to understand why German and French now have to destroy one another. We can have only one thought, whether we are German-Swiss or French-Swiss, namely, that this racial war is not necessary but is an abomination. Calvin and Rousseau were French. I have in mind the noble Russian count and novelist Leo Tolstoy. I think of the men whom Germany has given us—Goethe, Schiller, Kant, and so many others—and all that humanity owes to them. There is no serious reason for the nations that have produced such men to hate or fight one another. Anyhow, so long as we are German Swiss, we have no reason to let ourselves be biased against the nation of Calvin, against the nation of Tolstoy. We are here to unite not in hate but in love.[5] It is the high privilege of Swiss freedom and independence that we see and recognize the goodness and nobility of all nations calmly and impartially, that in this time of violent emotion we may now uphold the brotherhood and sisterhood of all peoples. We do not want to forfeit this privilege through the folly of partisanship. The time could come when one is glad of such a nonaligned, truly international nation as we may be through God's grace.

And on the other hand, the present war is a *power struggle*. For a decade now, this struggle regarding who has or should have first place in Europe or on the world stage has been in its preparatory phase. The war between England and Germany, for example, has no other background than this question of power. Economic reasons play a role. Each nation wants the largest and most splendid "place in the sun"[6] (as they express it) for its world trade. But individual and national ambitions also play a prominent role. France cannot forget how things were in the time of Louis XIV and the period after Napoleon. For almost a century England has played the role of a single world power on all continents, and now in the last few decades Germany has produced similar slogans: "Germany, foremost in the world!" "The world will be saved by the German spirit!"[7] "We Germans are afraid of no one except God!"[8] One nation after another, including Japan, says the same thing.

No nation has much reason to blame the other. They have competed with each other, using grand pronouncements and threatening armaments. Now the hidden power struggle has come out into the open. We Swiss can only say again that this power struggle is not our affair. We have no reason at all to take the side of one or of the other. We simply do not believe that one nation must be the first and the strongest at the expense of all the rest. We do not believe and do not want to believe that the well-being of nations is served in this way by prompting them to say time and again that the other nations out there are your enemies!

There are enough places in the sun for all to be able to enjoy, if once and for all everyone would put an end to their self-seeking and arrogance, if everyone would feel and behave as brothers and sisters instead of as economic rivals and opponents. We can only see this whole power struggle as a terrible insanity, and hence we simply cannot wish that one or the other side should be victorious; for if now one of the two sides should win, the self-seeking and arrogance that cause all the havoc will not be broken but will be strengthened all the more. There would be haughtiness on the winner's side and a sulking thirst for revenge on the side of the loser, as was the case in the period after 1870.[9] And sooner or later, new wars, new havoc and suffering, will come. Whether the Germans or their opponents come out victorious, we have nothing to expect from this power struggle.

Hence, we cannot take sides, even in our thoughts and wishes; we can only stand back and watch with heartfelt sympathy for all the innocent victims, and attempt on our part, so far as it is possible, to convince our neighbors that this power struggle is sheer madness and a sin through which humankind is brought to ruin. Again it is by God's grace that we Swiss are now so able to stand aside and not get dragged into this blind, mad activity of ambition and jealousy. We indeed do not wish to trifle with the grace of God. Nevertheless, if we are quiet, we will become strong, individually and as a nation, to help others. Our interest and strength are not staked on this or that option, but through everything right to the heart of our belief in the unity of humanity. "Blessed are the peacemakers, for they shall inherit the earth" (*sic*; see Matt. 5:9, 5).

Most especially, we should not and do not want to let ourselves be confused because of the many prayers and much talk of God that are heard far and wide. Many items of such news are now coming, particularly from Germany. There we read again and again: "We are certainly right; in our innocence we have been attacked; God himself must definitely be on our side and indeed has acknowledged our worthy cause and so acts to prove it. God has already helped us to win many battles!" Thus speaks the German kaiser.[10] This is what is openly spoken from most German pulpits, and thus speak discerning Christians. A huge wave of religious enthusiasm is moving through Germany. In a reputable journal we read that Germany has again rediscovered its God. And hence the Germans pursue their war "with God, for king and fatherland," as it is inscribed on their soldiers' helmets.[11] And now we hear this and we think that these Germans must surely be a pious people, and instinctively we cannot help thinking that God is certainly with them!

You believe me, I hope, when I say that I have nothing against the Germans but indeed respect them highly. I received so much intellectually from the Germans during my student years[12] that I can remember them only with the deepest gratitude and esteem for this splendid and highly gifted nation. I have dear friends there who even now are in armed combat, whose feelings I fully understand and whose fate is close to my heart. But I urge you not to let yourselves be taken in by this talk of Germany's innocence and justice in this war and its idea that God must and will help the Germans, however fine and confident that may sound. The very same thing is also said by the other nations. They also all want to be right and innocent, and they also all ask God to support their armies. Not only the unleashed war mania all around us, but also the particular religious frenzy to which the nations are succumbing at this time, can be a stern admonition to us to remain quiet, not to be infected by this excitement and to wait that God may let his justice roll down, a justice that is wholly different from human justice, a justice that humankind has often enough trampled underfoot.

And let us not forget that God shows himself as a master very different perhaps from the one who is prayed to on both sides. It seems to me that one of the most distressing things to see in this difficult time is how one nation now accuses with the ring of the holiest conviction the other nation of all possible wrongdoing, while each nation still has so much to mop up at its own door. And equally distressing is how God's name is now bandied around and drawn into the sinful, impassioned activity of humankind, as if God were one of the old warrior gods to whom our heathen ancestors appealed.

It is simply out of the question that God "helps" the Germans or the French or the English. God does not even "help" us Swiss. God helps justice and love. God helps the kingdom of heaven, and that exists across all national boundaries. "God is Spirit, and those who worship him must worship him in spirit and in truth" (John 4:24). The foolish mixing of patriotism, war enthusiasm, and Christian faith could one day lead to the bitterest disappointment. "He who sits in the heavens laughs; the Lord has them in derision" (Ps. 2:4). We will not join in drinking this intoxicating potion. We want to look steadfastly and unwaveringly here to God, who loves everyone equally, who is above all the nations, from whom all have similarly departed, and from whose glory they have fallen short (see Rom. 3:23)—the God who in like manner wants to draw all people to himself and gather them under the rule of his good and holy will.

Blessed are we once more, that we may now be quiet, quiet before God, that we stand aside from the dangerous delirium into which millions are now plunged, that we may see God as God is in his full majesty. It is by God's grace, and not because we deserve it, that we may do this. On our own, we could not handle carefully enough the precious treasure of this position of independence, this incorruptible decision that God has made possible for us. Again, on our own, we cannot tell ourselves clearly enough what kind of great responsibility rests upon us, because we are so privileged. Great tasks await us. What great pains we must take to preserve this freedom and neutrality—a gift given to us by God—in the deepest and innermost sense! We must remain quiet in this clamor-filled, turbulent time, in order to be strong in the coming days!

"Cool within our hearts," watching as bystanders, is how I expressed it. For no nation do we desire victory or defeat. They are all dear and precious to us. We hate no one and should hate no one. We hate only the war and the selfishness and pride that have ignited it. But with passionate, burning hearts we should put ourselves, and want to put ourselves, on God's side. With our innermost thoughts and desires, with our prayers and thoughts and wishes, we should walk, and want to walk, on God's side, on the side of truth and justice and freedom.

Here is the second thing that Isaiah certainly demanded of the people in Jerusalem: *hope!* Isaiah was no narrow-minded nationalist who warned his fellow citizens simply out of small-minded shrewdness: Stay out of the games of the world powers. There's nothing in this for you. In fact you could come to grief! His warning had a more profound basis. You are the people of the living God, he wanted to say to them, the nation to which it is given to hold fast, instead of getting mixed up in the world's turmoil. You are the people to which it is given to submit to and to follow the one who will become one day the master over all the turmoil of the world. You may be the vessel in which in a rough, stormy time, justice and love remain stored for a better future.

Keep yourselves worthy of this high responsibility! Do not cast aside this holy vocation! If you remain faithful, you now already have this future. Through hope you will be strong. In majestic words, Isaiah, a prophet of God's grace, has spoken of this better future. In that day there will be a highway from Egypt to Assyria—from one of the now-hostile nations to the other. The Assyrians will come into Egypt and the Egyptians into Assyria, and the Egyptians along with the Assyrians will serve God. In that day, Israel will be the third party with the Egyptians and Assyrians, a blessing in the midst of the earth. Then the Lord of hosts will bless them and say, "Blessed be Egypt my people, and Assyria the work of my hands, and Israel my heritage" (Isa. 19:23–25)!

How strong could this nation have been, my friends, if it had done what the prophet in the name of the living God had demanded of it; if it had hoped and looked forward to that day when the conflicts and the rivalries were ended, when the Egyptians and Assyrians and Israelites will all serve God in genuine righteousness and holiness; if it had told itself with all gravity that only one thing can now be valid in the midst of the misery and worry of the time: we must equip ourselves and prepare for this glorious end that God will bring about after all the suffering; we must be the holy guardians of this holy faith, for ourselves and for the others, so that it can develop very soon into its full reality for the blessing of the whole world.

Here, my friends, we also have the mission of our *Swiss people* in this time of iron and of blood. Oh, we should not be indifferent in the face of the events that are now going on around us. Neutrality does not mean indifference. And what is also to be avoided is the deplorable, cunning business sharpness that perhaps now could suggest, keep yourselves nicely aside, it doesn't pay to take part, and afterward when the others have bled to death, you will make all the more profit. Shame, shame on you! If that is Swiss neutrality, then indeed I would envy the Germans and the French, who plunge themselves in blind passion into the present destructive war, but do so for a great idea. We want to be neutral, not out of fear and not out of bourgeois shrewdness, but because we know and hold dearly and passionately to a still greater ideal, a still higher good, than what the nations out there call "the fatherland."

We believe in another world rather than in this present evil one. We believe that humankind, in spite of different origins and competing interests, will live on the earth as brothers and sisters, as one united people, as we Swiss want to and now already can live as brothers and sisters in our small land. We believe that righteousness and peace are possible in the world, that war and bloodshed will one day lie behind us as a bad dream, that one day the self-love and the conceit in men and women will be subdued and rooted out. We believe that Germans, French, and Russians will one day find themselves as those who belong together, that a highway will go from one to the other, as Isaiah prophesied concerning the nations of the ancient world, that instead of fighting for their country, all will one day work together for the fraternity, sisterhood, and unity of humankind. We also believe that God will lead the world through all the horrors of the present time to these goals.

It all really had to come to this. Human guilt had so accumulated that it had to come to this terrible catastrophe. But in the divine order, redemption comes after the guilt and after the punishment. Even if it is in the midst of many tears and wrongs, this war must be a stage in the coming peace of the nations and the still higher peace of God for which all hearts long. Whether the war will be this stage now depends on us, particularly on us Swiss, who are now comparatively so calm and undisturbed by personal misfortunes and national passions that we may devote ourselves to this hope. Where living hope exists, there also God's kingdom and lordship have always drawn closer. I repeat, we shoulder a great responsibility because we are now so privileged. One day we will have to give an account of this: What have you done with your privilege? Were you right-living people of hope, people of the future, as you could be in this grave time, or did you go through it thoughtlessly, in a superficial state of mind, blathering away? Did you remain the light of the world, the salt of the earth (see Matt. 5:13ff.), or did you become inward-looking, as this world is?

What will we give as an answer? O my friends, if we are true Christians, only then will we be able to give a satisfactory answer, only then will we be strong, only then will we be reckoned as real Swiss, who have understood the neutrality of their beloved country. Only a Christian can be truly quiet and hopeful. The one who has come to know life through Jesus has what is more precious than anything that conceit and selfishness promise us. Whoever has experienced the living God through Jesus—the God who stands above all German, French, and Swiss national and war gods—lets himself or herself be filled by Jesus with the confidence that the kingdom of God is coming and that even all the injustice and evil of the world must finally serve its coming. Are we true Swiss?

We would now ask, are we true Christians? Is it not marvelous that our nation is now specifically called, in virtue of its neutrality, to preach the gospel—yes, truly to preach the gospel to this disquieted, torn humanity!? But it does not suffice that our soldiers are guarding the border. This neutrality, this being quiet and hopeful, through which we are strong and through which the weak will be made strong, must become our innermost possession; it must possess us in flesh and blood when once the day for it has come. The spirit of Jesus, from which alone the real Swiss spirit can now spring, must now become alive in us. And now each one of us seeks how it is to be found. Let us seize it humbly and joyfully in our hearts, which know so little of love and joy. Let us ask God for it every day anew. Then we are strong. Then we will have a great future before us. For so does the Lord prosper the upright (see Prov. 2:7).

Amen.

September 6, 1914

Sermon at Safenwil

Psalm 102:26–28: Of old you laid the foundation of the earth, and the heavens are the work of your hands. They will perish, but you endure; they will all wear out like a garment. You change them like raiment, and they pass away; but you are the same, and your years have no end.

My Friends,

This past week no day went by in which we did not read about *victories* and *defeats*. This powerful push of the German armies has proceeded on both the western and eastern fronts, one blow after another. How this progressed had in itself something uncanny about it. What a mass of human intelligence, ingenuity, organization, and discipline, how much earnestness and energy, how much endurance and self-sacrifice were required in order to achieve this! We had the feeling, it is all that; but also that everything is calculated and prepared in advance, and now apparently everything is working out to the last detail. The efficiency of the German military, of both its officers and soldiers, has possibly proven greater than anyone anticipated, although everyone expected it to be considerable. Like a monstrous machine they have set themselves in motion, along with all their sophisticated equipment on sea and land, and the terrible work of destruction that they have to attend to has already made a good start. Woe to those who come under the wheels of this machine! Uncanny, I say, and yet against our will it compels admiration.

And now at this very hour in all churches in Germany praise and thanksgiving resound to God, who has so obviously helped the Germans, as well as prayer for even further victories over their foes. The German nation had told itself from the outset: we will win or perish. Accordingly it had summoned all its strength, and now, on these glorious battlefields, on the stormed or heavily shelled fortresses, it can already see its advancing troops marching directly toward the French capital. And now this awareness: Those are our people! They are our own! It's working! We will become the master of Europe! This rejoicing is only all too understandable. If it happened to us, we would also feel the same way. In that moment, we would also probably be aware of nothing greater than this proud self-confidence! What about those on the other side who suffered defeat? What did they lack? Was it leadership? Was it organization? Was it the necessary esprit de corps? This will all first show itself much later.

In any event, the contest is not yet lost. They are fiercely preparing themselves for a new offensive. But is there not already something desperate in this fierceness? They encourage themselves with great exhortation to endure, but one still senses that they have become somewhat subdued. They had not thought that things would begin like this. There are probably now countless persons in these nations who, if they are permitted, already say publicly, "This disastrous war! If only we had avoided it! Nothing good can come from it." And now also the godly in these nations pray fervently in the face of the disaster that threatens to engulf them, "My God, my God, why have you forsaken me?" (Ps. 22:2). We also understand them. If, like them, we belonged to the losing side, we would now also be subdued, we would now also implore God in our need.

But we must go deeper. In this regard, what can we now really say about all of this, we who now stand neither on the one side or the other? What are we now to say about these initial victories and defeats, and then later, when the war is over, and one emerges from the dreadful struggle as the victor and the other as the vanquished? Do we want to act like young rascals who at a match cheerfully and gladly latch on to this or that side? Then we would have nothing else to do each day but to be pleased or annoyed and distressed with those whom we have favored. I still recall how once in school we all passionately took a side in a war and greatly entertained ourselves by doing so. But that is what young rascals do: "When I was a child, I spoke like a child, I reasoned like a child; when I became a man, I gave up childish ways" (1 Cor. 13:11).

There should not be anyone among us adults and Christian Swiss who takes sides in such a childish manner. I repeat what I said last Sunday: it is our task unfailingly to remain neutral in this conflict, down to our deepest thoughts. It is none of our business. It is not up to us to decide which side is more just or unjust. We can only hate and judge the war itself and all that has triggered it, but not the warring nations. With respect to these victories and defeats, we have something better to do than to rejoice with the one or weep with the other. This settles nothing. One can politicize about this endlessly in the pub or elsewhere, but it has no worthwhile value; it also does not change the events out there. Look, we Swiss are now offered an unparalleled opportunity as we are allowed to watch this terrible course of events so calmly. We may reflect more deeply about God's ways, and through this acquired insight then become inwardly more firmly united with God. For the nations beyond our borders, there is, as it were, understandably nothing other than this question: Who is going to win this war? If we want God to bless us in this critical time, we cannot let ourselves get stuck on this question. We must enquire further—as many of us have already surely done in the stillness—"Yes, and if now one side wins," as we say, if it becomes steadily clearer that the victory is now tilting to one side, what then does this mean? What is its deeper meaning? Is it really the case that now the victor may say, as it is said today, "God has embraced our just cause and has helped us. God is on our side"?

Of course, in the Old Testament, especially in its most ancient passages and also in many Psalms, this is how the matter is undoubtedly viewed: a victory means that God helps a nation, a defeat means that God has withheld help. But is this now true? If we think of the God who has revealed himself in Jesus, the God who in his righteousness prefers no nation before any other, who in his love and holiness definitely does not will that the nations hate, wage war, and vanquish one another, is this true? Can one really approach this God and pray, "Lord God, we thank you that we have conquered Belgium and are vanquishing the French and the British and have taken 70,000 Russian prisoners,[1] and we beseech you also to give us the means to soon occupy Paris"? I have in mind a verse in Psalm 136, where it is said of God: "[God] overthrew Pharaoh and his host in the Red Sea, for his steadfast love endures forever; . . . [God] smote great kings . . . and slew famous kings . . . Sihon, king of the Amorites, . . . and Og, king of Bashan, . . . and gave us their land as a heritage" (Ps. 136:15, 17–21). This is powerful, it has impetus, this sounds like the roll of drums and the blast of trumpets summoning the nation to war and victory. Doubtless a nation with such a belief in God will be powerful and brave in attacking its foe.

If the ancient Israelites thought and prayed in this way, then this is not surprising. They did not know any better. But what are we supposed to say to that, if, now in our day in the seemingly most pious way, this war-and-conquering god of the Old Testament—we could even say this ancient storm god, Wotan, of the pagan Germans—is brought forth again and made into the true God by all sides, while all that we could know of God through Jesus Christ is put into the junk room, so to speak, until a later, better time? We do not want to express an opinion and pass judgment, since we would scarcely do any better. This condition is like a sickness that has now befallen all of them, even the best of them. But we cannot and do not want to let ourselves be infected and carried away by it. The idea of God should remain pure for us. And it should be clear and distinct, unclouded by human partisanship and passions. We want to see how God is actually disposed toward such human successes and failures.

Another passage from the Psalms that speaks neither of victory nor defeat, and not of war at all—above all, not of human nature and of its distortion—provides us with the proper guidance: "Of old you laid the foundations of the earth and the heavens are the work of your hands. They will perish, but you endure. They will all wear out like a garment. You change them like raiment, and they pass away; but you are the same, and your years have no end!" You see, here we are told what God is in reality. *God is the creator* of heaven and earth, of everything that exists. It is good for us, especially in this anxious time, to think of the infinite sphere of God's power, of the expanse without limit or end in which we live, of the eternity from which we come and to which we return, and of which our personal life and the life of the whole of humanity is only an infinitesimal, tiny portion.

We speak of a "world war" with regard to present circumstances. We may call it that, yet how truly small our Europe is in relation to the whole earth. There are millions of people who will never know anything of this world war or be affected by it in the least. If we think of all the billions of years since our earth began its course around the sun and in which it and the beings that inhabit it have already experienced so much, what does this world war mean? What does it mean for the universe of the suns and stars of heaven of which our earth is one of the smallest—a universe for which we lack both the numbers and the concepts to describe its vastness?

All of this comes from God, from God who is love, a God who desires to be glorified in all God's creatures. Of these, we human beings in particular carry a spark in our soul that should glow and become a flame, so that we participate in God's eternal being. This God who is holy, who has created men and women for freedom in God and for a life in God's steadfast love and perfection, is a God who mourns when we succumb to the slavery of selfishness. Everything comes from this God, who is a God of justice and order, to whom oppression and conflict are a horror, precisely because in God there is essentially only love and freedom. Everything is from God, heaven and earth, present as well as past and future, all that is greatest and least. How should this war and also these victories and defeats not also be from God, of God's doing and making, as is everything else that has happened, happens, and will happen between the poles of heaven from eternity to eternity! We must proceed from this fact, and we must always return to it: God rules over everything, and nothing is apart from God.

But if a nation on this small planet triumphs over another, should we then really be able to say, "Behold, God has helped it!"—indeed, on the basis of a few agitated and self-serving prayers? Does it have the right to be jubilant and claim, "God is on our side; with God's power we have defeated the enemy, for God's steadfast love endures forever"? Oh, into what a cramped and stuffy room we draw down the great God! It is sheer blasphemy to relate God to our human strivings in this way. Yes indeed, God is Lord over success and failure, and also over this war, and everything that it brings can, in the last analysis, be nothing other than a carrying out of the peaceful purposes that God has for us.

But do we really perceive how it is with everything that God has created, from the greatest to the least? "They pass away but you remain," says the Psalm singer. "They will all wear out like a garment. You change them like raiment, and they pass away." What does this mean? This means that the creation remains forever dependent on the Creator. There are always imperfection, limitation, weakness; and hence there are always alteration, change, and transience. Heaven and earth, sun and stars, do not have an eternal existence. They have their time, their vast time compared with our human time, but they also pass away; they become something other than what they were in the slow process of change as well as in terrible catastrophes. There is nothing that lasts forever, just because there is nothing that is perfect, nothing that is God himself. Only life from God is eternal, life that is active in all things. Only God himself is eternal. If this is true of the universe and of nature, with its enormous vastness of space and time—and contemporary science has shown us how unconditionally this is the case—how much more must it be true of our small human realities, even of this war and the successes of which we now hear so much! "They will pass away, but you remain."

We can and must be clearer with regard to the matter of *war successes* than with regard to anything else. For they bear a human stamp, possibly far more clearly than other great earthly things, and are thereby transitory and provisional. It is not God's purpose to let this or that side win. This is a fact that is also an aspect of God's ways, but God certainly does not stop with this, since it is not the end for God, only one thing; for God has wholly other purposes than the victory or defeat of this or that side. This occurs now, but again afterwards something completely different will certainly happen, and these events that now seem to us so colossal and laden with consequences will be over and done with. God uses them for the time being, as one uses a tool, but then they have no further utility. God's acts continue, and the places where they happen are no longer known (cf. Ps. 103:16).

What then is war? What is a victory? Look at the battlefields of Lothringen, Belgium, East Prussia, and Galicia; then you know. Thousands upon thousands of men have had to slaughter one another. That was only the beginning, and who knows how much longer it will continue this way? Confronted with these things, with the horror that is still to come, and the heartbreak that is experienced now and will continue to come, can we say, indeed this was God's purpose, God willed it, God has helped one side to attack the other—the God who is love, freedom, and justice?

What hand does God have in the greater cunning and ruthlessness, the more numerous battalions, the more powerful cannons of those who have now won? Does God will all that? Does God will that they kill one another in huge numbers? But now someone says: "Yes, the war is horrible, but if it is a matter of a just cause, yes, it is of God. Indeed, God helps those who have a just cause." Yes, this is how human beings seek to excuse themselves. This was how such a man as Luther himself, who was so close to God's heart, could speak in this way. He wrote a specific work on this subject, affirming that Christians may wage war with a clear conscience.[2] A war was nothing other than the action of a hangman, who at the command of the magistrate brings about the death of a scoundrel. But in the case of war the command of the magistrate brings about the death of a whole slew of scoundrels! And the claim is that it was a just cause.

What then do "unjust" and "just" mean here? As far back as we can recall, in every war, self-seeking and pride on both sides have been cited as the causes. If there was a just cause among human beings, if it was true as the nations now say of themselves, "God is with us!" then they would not need to go to war. That is especially clear about the present war. We cannot speak of a just cause on one side or the other. The great powers that now stand opposed to one another in the war have mutually feared and threatened one another for decades with ever more powerful armaments. Who started it? Who feared the most? Who threatened the others most forcibly? Who is finally at fault that the overly full barrel has overflowed? Probably the most resourceful and impartial historian will not be able to decide, not to mention all the entirely prejudiced individuals who now write so favorably about their own nations in the newspapers.

In the end, we will only be able to say that at the conclusion of the nineteenth century and at the beginning of the twentieth century there was among these European nation-states an immense ambition, a jealousy, and a wholly unparalleled arrogance. Thus they all created an atmosphere so tense that they hated one another, armed themselves against one another in a fit of madness, and thereby caused a world war that finally had to erupt. One cannot speak honestly of a just cause on either side, and for that reason it cannot be said that God is now on this side or that side and grants victory to the side with the just cause.

None of this is God's will, neither the selfishness and arrogance in human beings, nor the mutual hatred of the nations, nor their anxieties about one another and their threatening armaments, nor finally that they mutually attack life with both precise and heavy firing power at sea, on land, or in the air. All of these things are completely alien to the innermost being of God. If, nevertheless, they now occur, there is then only one explanation for it: God's innermost being is also completely alien to humankind. In these actions from beginning to end they do not behave with the mind and direction of God, but against God. For this reason they also cannot expect that God will take their side; hence, they cannot plead with God and call upon God's help. God is as distant from them as from their enemies in the wrath with which their actions fill God. But God is also as distant from them in the love that God wants to bestow to draw both sides out of their confusion. And this indeed remains the same in victory or in defeat. They can perhaps win, but they still stand under the heavy wrath of God, which will show them sooner or later that "God is not mocked" (cf. Gal. 6:7). But they could also lose and thereby have the experience that they have drawn nearer to the kingdom of God.

And so it is none of our business to pray, "Lord, give us victory!" Who then is the one to whom we pray for such a victory? And if we are on crooked, godless ways, how can we pray for success? If being far removed from God we have achieved success, how may we thank God? What a deplorable blindness is displayed in these prayers and thanksgivings! We laugh when we hear that street thieves in southern Italy never neglect to offer their prayers and gifts to the Madonna, both before and after their robberies. But then do the Christians of the warring countries around us do anything particularly different with their prayers for victory? Oh, if indeed through this terrible war there would only come an awakening of the spiritless and wretched Christian world, an awakening so that we were constrained to realize that it cannot go on like this! We have now offered prayers and given thanks for victorious battles for the last time! We have drawn God down into our wicked scheme to become master over others, over our brothers and sisters, for the last time! For the last time will we be deluded into thinking that we have to hate and to kill for the sake of justice and by the power of God! All this is too terrible a deception, we cannot do it anymore.

What, then, does it mean to be victorious? To be successful in an evil course of action! And for this reason should we pray for such success, should we be thankful for it, should we, above all, be able to look up above to God with a calm conscience? We cannot do it anymore; it is too blasphemous, too hypocritical, too godless!

And because we still want to look up above to God, we therefore no longer want hatred, intimidation, and war. We want to repent of our wicked ways, we want to become inwardly changed persons, a new people that obeys God's holy will. If only the war would have this outcome, that humanity or at least a greater part of humanity would come nearer to this understanding: God does not want war! Nations cannot pursue war with a clear conscience any longer. They can only make themselves miserable with war. When they resort to war, they can only fall into the most deplorable hypocrisy! And if then only the powerful and universal resolve would awaken within thousands and millions of people: we do not want war any more, we do not want all those things in our hearts any more, the circumstances that make for war. If this realization and this resolve would arise among us through the war, what a blessing this would be for us! Indeed, a blessing!

A little while ago we noted that war, even this war, was not without God. That can strike us as puzzling after what we've just heard: God does not want war. Yet it is certainly no puzzle. God lets us human beings go our way—that is how it is—*our* way. We start with selfishness, we proceed with hatred, and we end up with a bloody, murderous war. Sin is repeatedly multiplied, and suddenly we punish ourselves in the most terrible way. That is what God wills. This is God's order, even though God does not will the war. Instead God wills that we will get sick of our sins because of the war, for the war is nothing other than the consequence of sin. If sin and its consequence increase, then grace increases all the more (cf. Rom. 5:20). When we see clearly what confronts us, we realize that this is what comes from following our own way, that this is how we end up in the most frightful insanity, injustice, and misery. Then God's power can begin to work in us, leading us on the neglected way of truth and peace. So war, even this terrible war, has its place in God's purposeful design of peace for us.

Hence, for us men and women, what matters is that we have a living experience of the wrath and of the unspeakable grace of God, to which the European nations now tread so near. Nothing else will help us. In this time, victory and defeat can again be quickly reversed. For thousands of years the history of humanity has simply been a story of alternating victories and defeats. God has permitted time and again that humanity would go its way and on its way find only misery. Victory and success should no longer be what they want; what do they get out of them? Surely, we should all let God speak to us through the present storm, for which human beings are at fault. This will pass away, but you remain! As long as we keep on praying only for victory and success, God will not hear us, and we will continue to be confronted by new storms through our own fault.

Moreover, we Swiss should not think and pray in this manner. Yes, we want to pray for our beloved country, but not to a god of war and victory, in accordance with the practice of the ancient Jews and the pagans. Nor are we to pray that narrow-minded, selfish prayer: "Spare our house; instead, burn down someone else's!" Yes, and if the situation were to become serious, in no way could we boast about our just cause! Nor could we at all demand without question that the good Lord stand right behind our soldiers and cannons. We also are culpable in our whole being for the present world's situation. Rather, we must pray as Jesus taught us: "Your kingdom come! Your will be done! And forgive us our sins! And deliver us from evil!" (see Matt. 6:10ff.).

Lord, set us free, not from the enemies but from the powers of darkness that are in and around us, from falsehood and arrogance, meanness and thoughtlessness. Lord, let us be victorious, not over foreign nations but over ourselves, over our selfishness. Lord, let us triumph, not in outward success but in letting ourselves be filled and empowered with your love, freedom, and justice. Dear friends, let this be our war prayer, the war prayer of a neutral nation. Oh, how wonderful it will be if we were all to think and to pray from our hearts in this way. Oh, how wonderful it will be if one day the other nations surrounding us, who are now intoxicated with hate and passion, were also to pray again with us this war prayer for God's peace. Will it ever happen? Will we all, we Swiss and the others, have a living experience of the wrath and grace of God? Through the turmoil of this time, will we attend again to the one thing needful (cf. Luke 10: 42), to the one true religion?

May God grant us this. If we *so* pray, God hears us. For then we stand on firm ground. Then our hearts are there where change and transience rule no more, but in their place are stability, security, and steadfastness. What is human is transient. What is divine abides. In this time, what could we wish for that is more precious than that our hearts be strengthened (cf. Heb. 13:9)?

Amen.

September 13, 1914

Sermon at Safenwil[1]

Matthew 8:23–26: And when he got into the boat, his disciples followed him. And behold, there arose a great storm on the sea, so that the boat was being swamped by the waves; but he was asleep. And they went and woke him, saying, "Save, Lord; we are perishing." And he said to them, "Why are you afraid, O men of little faith?" Then he rose and rebuked the winds and the sea; and there was a great calm.

Dear Friends,

We are about to observe the Swiss national Day of Penitence. Our devout ancestors decreed that on this day the entire nation should thankfully, contritely, and prayerfully remember that a higher power rules over Switzerland and that we are God's handiwork. The Day of Penitence has been observed for a good many years without too much seriousness and conviction. We took the old practice for granted. On the third Sunday of September we listened to a sermon about our beloved country, God's providence, and our human folly. We also observed the Lord's Supper. Still, all this was often more outward than inward. We could scarcely say in all seriousness that it was our obligation and necessity. We did not feel that it was altogether fitting that these matters should belong together: God and fatherland, Jesus and our nation, the Gospel and the proper Swiss mentality. Moreover, if we went to church on this day out of a sense of duty or moved by a certain yearning, we still always thought in the recesses of our hearts that one could probably exist without the other.

But this year, for the overwhelming majority of our nation, things will be different. This year, openly or in the stillness, hardly anyone asks, why a Day of Penitence? We understand all this without further explanation, or we have a fairly good idea. We have had continuous repentance for the past six weeks, having to think constantly of everything that this Sunday was supposed to suggest to us: the work of God in the nation's life, the holiness of God's commandments and their validity for both the nation and the individual, the seriousness and severity of the judgments we bring upon ourselves when we fall away from God, and the unshakable fact that even our dear Swiss people and Switzerland can be exalted only through righteousness, while sin must be a reproach to our people (cf. Prov. 14:34). If on the Day of Penitence this year church bells ring out, how should we not sense immediately what this means: a God exists, a holy will lives, although the human reels. The thunder of the guns on our borders have told us the same thing for a long time, much more forcefully and clearly than all the church bells. But just as we do not want to rest content in this deeply critical time with the first superficial thoughts and feelings of excitement, so on the Day of Penitence we also want to penetrate to the heights and depths of what it has to say to us this year. Let us be on our guard against all merely external stirrings of the emotions! Let us be on our guard against all purely empty speech! It is the living, holy, and all-loving God with whom we have to deal. Let us reflect about what we want to seek and also find from God on the Day of Penitence.

A *storm* has descended upon us just as it did upon the little boat carrying Jesus' disciples. It broke out suddenly, howling and blowing on the still water in which the sun was reflected. Only God knows from which bad-weather area it came. All at once it was there; we did not see it coming up. The sky is black, and the land is not visible. The waves come up in unpredictable sequence, blow after blow, every one of them threatening and somehow bringing destruction. And we are en route, right in the middle of it. It is not a dream. It is the bitter truth. Oh, if only we could save ourselves! If only we were on a safe shore! But it is not a matter of choice; the billows do not ask us whether they please us, and there is no way to shore other than through the midst of the surge. What will become of us?

The *war* has descended upon us in a similar way. The nations were startled out of their calm abruptly and unexpectedly. First, we were compelled to notice the signs of approaching, unavoidable disasters. Then came the sudden standstill of all previous life, the shocking interruption of work and pleasure, of cultural activities and sins of peacetime, then the sharp anxiety: What will now happen? What shall we eat, what shall we drink (cf. Matt. 6:25)? And then the departure of all the millions, these enormous movements of men that must result in conflict, and always new conflicts, each always ending with thousands upon thousands of bodies covering the fields. And behind the line of combat, new armies will always be directed forward into battle. And behind the armies, other millions will follow the events occurring ahead of them with an intense focus that excludes every other interest. So now billow after billow surges there.

Who would determine who has unleashed the storm? All accusations against individual persons and nations are puerile prattle before God. Such catastrophes do not come about overnight, and the guilt for them lies deeper than something one could rashly attribute to either side. Of all the millions who have now waged war or who pursue it in their thoughts, who could really say why it is actually being fought? "For the fatherland," they would all answer in every language. But most people do not know what to say, nor can they give a satisfactory reason why the fatherland of one people must fight the fatherland of another. What do the drops of water that are formed into a billow by the wind know? What does the air that under the pressure of the atmosphere becomes a wind and then a storm know? What do the clouds that form lightning and thunder that must condense into rain and hail know? They all have to do what they do. And so now there must be war. We know only that it is here. And that it is awful, terrible.

War was always something terrible. The voice of history tells us of many bloody battlefields, of innumerable ravages. But where war in ancient times was a kind of leisurely activity punctuated from time to time by a massacre, an atrocity, today it has become *one* continuous mass murder. If the uses of war have become more humane, while war itself has only become much more inhumane, because it has become more thorough, what does it mean? Weapons have become more powerful and more precise, and as a consequence pain and suffering on both sides have intensified proportionately. And what especially makes war unbearable these days is the contrast between this thoroughly calculated destruction and killing and the height of civilization that the European nations have attained today, at least outwardly. If brutal savages fall upon one another with spear and stone ax, we are not all that much surprised by it. But what shall we say if we bring to mind the image of our Swiss Exhibition in Bern[2] and almost immediately afterward picture the nightly bloodbaths of Mühlhausen[3] and Löwen?[4] Shall both represent a picture of European humanity? And is it supposed to be true that Europe wants to be both of these things: the flower of spiritual and material progress and a band of robbers who under the delusion of race and power mutually attack and kill one another? Must this awful contradiction not cause one to lose faith in everything that has been believed and accomplished over the centuries?

In this past week I have heard more than one person say that he or she would prefer not to pick up a newspaper anymore; so depressing is the news of which its columns are now so full. And if we, as the ones who still for the time being stand on the periphery, are trembling in our very souls with regard to these events, feeling ourselves transplanted into another world, a world of shock, just think how it must feel above all in the hearts of those who are directly involved in these events or are confronted by them! What is going on now in the minds of all the soldiers who have been torn from the midst of their peaceful employment in order to fight, kill, and destroy? What is now going on in the scenes of suffering on the endless battlefields, in the military hospitals? What an outbreak of fury and meanness! I recall what went on and still goes on in Belgium. The inhabitants took desperately cunning measures of defense against the invaders who attacked their neutral country. Then in turn the Germans took fierce revenge. Who is just, and who is unjust? It is futile to decide on the matter. One can only say that it is shocking that human beings should behave in such a way toward one another, but this is war. How many human lives are now suddenly and randomly destroyed in the prime of their development! What unused powers, unfinished tasks, unatoned guilt, unredeemed consciences lie dormant in all the souls that are now suddenly called to eternity! Nothing remains of their striving toward growth that should find fulfilment in a productive life, perhaps in a better life than it had been at the start. Nothing will become of this. The end is a mass grave in a foreign land. God is gracious, but why are human beings allowed to do this to one another?

We see with deep grief how even educated Christian people on both sides now lose their minds and moral bearings completely by letting themselves be pulled into the maelstrom of war frenzy and appearing to know nothing nobler than the savage slogan: hate, fight, and vanquish. Blame and excuses fly back and forth. Only the honor of one's own nation is praised to the skies, and God is called upon as the supporter of its cause. And hence only rarely do they let anything of the more profound things be heard, things that *all* nations alike lack and that would bring healing alike to all of them. Although bloodless, these are also sacrifices of war.

And we think with particular sympathy of all the wives, children, and parents who have seen their loved ones march out into battle. Alas, if the nations are still poles apart, still so hostile in confronting one another, the picture is now the same everywhere in Germany, France, Austria, and Russia—the picture of those remaining at home, who now have to struggle through such terribly anxious times, grasping at every sign that their loved ones out there before the enemy are alive, and waiting to receive with every mail delivery a report of their death. What an ocean of misery now already exists in all these countries, in the cities and villages, in the mountains and at sea! Should not this alone, this unspeakable suffering of widows and orphans, already make the nations stop in their tracks? Has saying not "dead," but "fallen for king and fatherland," made things any easier? When will human beings wake up and become human beings?

They do not seem to think about it, so it all continues blindly: the killing, the dying, the despair, the need, the hatred, the prematurely broken lives, the insane war frenzy, the blasphemous prayers, and the flood of tears of those who were robbed of their loved ones. It all still continues. Injustice is piled upon injustice, sorrow upon sorrow, and speaking candidly we have to say that all this is only the beginning. How will it continue? What will the end be like? With the enormous forces that are in place and engaged on both sides, is an end really possible? If our thoughts were to stray into the future, they would verge on insanity. We know less than ever what the next day will bring us, and it is in the midst of this storm that has descended upon us that we shall observe the Day of Penitence.

What should we seek from God on this Day of Penitence? The most obvious thing is that, like the disciples in the small boat on the Sea of Galilee, we sigh and cry, "*Lord, help us: we are perishing!*"

In such a time of anxiety and panic, our thoughts instinctively turn to God with the plea, help us! Innumerable persons who otherwise cared little about God, or who in their Sunday best honored God with their lips and a few feeble feelings, but who have not known God in heart and deed, are suddenly again reminded of God. They come defiantly before God with the question, "If you are a God of love, why do you allow all this?" And others in anguish of soul hasten to churches with the plea, "Surely, O God, you will not also permit the most horrible things to come upon us!" Many such thoughts and prayers rise up to heaven on the Day of Penitence. What shall we say about this? All serious, honest Christians have so thought and prayed; so they still think and pray. In such a situation, this cry—"Lord, help us; we are perishing!"—is the first natural impulse of human hearts. All of us—even the more serious and more honest, not just those who only now on this occasion produced their Christianity like an old useful tool in case things should turn out very badly—all of us, in our thoughts and our entire being, were often very far from God. We honored and respected God, but basically we did everything to some extent apart from God without knowing it. We felt so secure. We were so pleased with ourselves and our circumstances.

Now, all of a sudden, we are shaken. Now suddenly we realize how weak and dependent we really are. How vain! How criminal our human nature! We see ourselves now on the edge of an abyss. And now suddenly we call again, "O Lord God, please help!" Just like children, after *we* have slept a long time and were rudely awakened, we think that *we* must wake up the dear *God*, so that God puts everything back into order. It is good that God is greater than we are and that God does not take offense at everything at which he could. Jesus also did not take offense at his disciples when they so anxiously awakened him. God also hears such anxious and muddled prayers, pitiful and self-centered though they often are. Before God, nothing is lost that comes from the human heart helplessly seeking the way to God. God also hears those who now angrily protest, "Where is God when such things can happen?" That can also be a kind of prayer, even though a rather defiant one. God takes no offense at this either.

And hence also on the Day of Penitence, the cry, "Lord, help us; we are perishing!" may become audible—pitiful here and defiant there. God knows his manifold children and knows well how the cry is meant. This cry may become audible as the *beginning* of true gratitude to God and a proper prayer to God. But, of course, only as a beginning. This cannot be final. We cannot want to stop here, praying to God that God might bring an end to our need and the need of the destitute world, or find fault with the fact that God has not done it a long time ago. If we have nothing but these thoughts, then on the Day of Penitence we must let it be said to us what Jesus said to the disciples on the sea: "*You of little faith, why are you so terrified?*" These thoughts are also a kind of faith on their part at that time and on ours today. But just a little faith, a pagan faith, a faith that is not worthy of a Christian. It has no stability and no depth. It has no seriousness, and it provides no hope and power. We can see this in ourselves.

Many people came to church on that first Sunday in August—which certainly all of us will remember—in order to pray, "Lord, help us!" In the week before that, the same people went trembling to the savings bank and dashing to the specialty shops in order to care for the precious "I," although they knew how injurious these actions were for the whole community. Are that prayer and this selfish action compatible? This was the "little faith," the faith that is not serious. And how would such people react who know nothing else than to moan to God, "Lord, help us!" or to accuse God that for such a long time God has allowed it to happen? How would they react if a really serious ordeal should befall them? We are by no means certain that it will not happen. Oh, how powerless then would they be standing alone, those who knew only how to moan and protest, powerless with their "little faith."

And what will these same people do, once the danger and the disaster have passed, so that one quietly breathes a sigh of relief and is able to think seriously about matters other than the war? Oh, I see and hear it already, and I am often really worried about this time of calm after the storm, when they then again will continue as they did, secure, content, and smug, considering everything and doing everything just as they did previously. A small faith, a fearful faith that bears no fruit, dares to emerge only a very little from the morass, and once calm has returned after excessive misfortune, immediately jumps back again to where it came from. Oh, if only it were a few of us or none from among us who would deserve this reproach: "O you of little faith, why are you so afraid?" You who have earned it! If we would all just realize on this Day of

Penitence that my faith is too small, it is not sufficient. I need more faith and a better faith. With this meager faith I will not get through time and eternity. We may begin with it. We may pray this prayer, "Lord help us!" as a first step to God, as it were, whom we had forgotten and who has roused us in such a frightful way through the thunder of artillery, the sighs of thousands of dead, the tears of the desolate, and all the million forms of injustice and misfortune that have now broken out. But we can't stop there. At all costs we must go further and higher. If we stop at this point, then we have not yet found God, we have not yet found what we need.

Further? Where? Now what then should Jesus' disciples have done, instead of just so excitedly lamenting and wailing? They should have remembered that Jesus was with them. Whoever believes does not fear. Whoever is certain of God has a firm defense against all misfortune and danger. Such a person knows God, who is Lord over everything that happens, and knows most clearly what to expect from this Lord. Such a person knows God as the one who is holy and righteous, as the one who is wisdom and love, and knows that this God must and will become master over all things. Why then be afraid of the wind and waves? There are much better things to do. Such a person can have only one goal: to remain wholly certain of this God, and indeed not to lose sight of God. As long as we know God, as long as we can say to God from the bottom of our hearts, "My Father," all is well; the worst misfortune and the greatest danger simply have no power over us. Of course, we see these dangers, we see them with clear eyes but, so to speak, from the standpoint of God—there below, deep down, wind and waves on the Sea of Galilee. What do they signify before God?

If it is God's will, how little is needed to bring calm. And certainly it is God's will. It is quite impossible that in the middle of his ministry Jesus would have been drowned in the Sea of Galilee, and the same applies to his followers. This cannot be the end. It implies instead, persevere! Row and wait on God. But no wailing and no complaining. This is how Jesus would have wanted his friends to behave. If they had thought of him, this is how they should have acted. And in order to show them how they should have acted, he did something that amazed them: *he stood up and commanded the wind and the sea, and it was completely still.* For us, this is astonishing. It was also astonishing for the disciples. For Jesus it was self-evident, natural. Jesus was completely one with God's will. In the deepest, truest sense, he called God his Father. He thought about everything, even about the danger and misfortune just as God thinks about them. Therefore, he was able to act against them as God acts. He could be master over them. He was able to master them.

Look, my friends, this is where we have to go *further* than our "little faith" and our moaning, beginning-to-pray attitude—to where Jesus stands, to Jesus himself. That is what we have to seek from God, that we become certain of God and so are able to see God face to face. That is what we need to seek on this solemn Day of Penitence. Then it will be completely natural and self-evident for us that we will not perish in this present storm but head securely through the waves to our appointed goal. O my friends, would that this may happen now, that Jesus would rise up before our eyes and would become eminent in our hearts and lives. Then, from the perspective of God, we could now also look down to see with clarity and confidence a Europe ransacked by war, bathed in blood and tears, with our little Switzerland there in the middle. Then we would know that there is a way through all of this, and this is the way we would take because God goes with us.

All this must happen—yes, it must. And the basis of this "must" lies much deeper than the superficial attitude suggests. The events are much too serious and too important to be the topic of casual political conversation: they have this and that matter, these and those matters, on their conscience. They have their deepest basis in a false attitude to life that the European nations have adopted for the past hundred years. These nations and our nation—every single one of us included—have heard the gospel of Jesus for thousands of years but with only half an ear. They have built churches for Jesus and appointed pastors and established institutions and sent missionaries to the poor heathen, but all of this was mere words and superficial veneer. In reality, they were still poor heathen themselves. The gospel says, "Give everything away in order to hold wholly to God." In response we European people said, "We want the good life." The gospel says, "Love your neighbor as yourself'" (Matt. 22:39). We loved money in place of our neighbor. The gospel says, "Those who will be my followers must deny themselves" (Matt. 16:24). We said that what counts in this world is the gospel of power and unbridled competition. The gospel says, "You are all brothers and sisters." We said, "Everyone is his or her own neighbor." The gospel says, "The kingdom of God is coming; wait for it and prepare yourselves to enter it." We responded by raising world empires, one like the other founded upon cunning and force, on guns and bayonets.

Few objections were raised against this. Those who dared to object were left to be derided as enthusiasts and rebels. The genuine disciples of Jesus seemed like fools and idiots in the eyes of this world, one that was so completely different from what they believed and hoped. Even the pastors, the Christians, the church members knew nothing different. They frequently wanted to hear nothing different, were many times the most anxious, thinking, "Just don't get mixed up in all this." It was quite natural for them that, in spite of all the gospel says, one should do precisely the opposite.

Now this catastrophe has come. Can we be surprised that it had to happen? Is it not foolish now to cry, "Lord, help us; we are perishing!"? Is it still not much more foolish to complain, where is God now in all this, the one God who wills to be love? Yes, God is the God of love, and we are blessed if we at least still remember this! But where do we stand with our faith in this God of love? Where do we continue with the obedience that we owe God? This is the end of *our* ways, the end of things happening out there; the end of our ways, which on winding paths were leading us past and around the gospel. The paganism to which we secretly were clinging while we called ourselves Christians has now broken through to the surface, as formidably as perhaps never before; and it could not burst out except in insanity, murder, and death. What does this tell us? That there is no God? No. Rather, that there lives a God who is holy and righteous, a God who is not mocked (cf. Gal. 6:7). God's wrath is revealed from heaven against all ungodliness and wickedness of those who by their wickedness suppress the truth (Rom. 1:18). All this had to happen.

If we now look out at the world with Jesus, from the standpoint of God, the other thing that we will be able to see is that *it all does not have to remain that way*. It needs to remain so only if we insist on sticking to our own ways. We have come to know its end. It will be different if we desire to become what God wills. What God wills is stated clearly enough for us in the gospel, namely, in the gospel of Jesus, the simply expressed gospel of the New Testament, not in the watered down, warped, and worldly thing that the different churches have made of it. Here, only love for God the Father matters. For this reason there can be no more idolatry of money and power. Here, the only thing that matters is the self-denial that is based on truth, and hence there is no more racial arrogance and no militarism.

The only thing that matters is the mind that with one's brothers and sisters seeks community and cultivates community in all things, thereby signaling the end of all rivalry and conflict between nations. This is what God wills. God has stated it clearly enough. This is God's redeeming Word to needy humanity, revealed two thousand years ago, living among us in Jesus Christ, the holy and righteous one. If we desire what God wills, then there is no longer war. Then there is immediately an end to all that now frightens and terrifies us. This is the major question to us in this time, the vital question, the moral issue: whether we take up a new position in relation to this essential will of God, whether we will say yes to the redeeming Word that God has already offered us for such a long time.

If we do it, then what the disciples experienced with the storm and surge will also be fulfilled in us: *and it was completely still.* Everything that now causes us sorrow and anguish will be restored to order. We do not know when that will occur. It will also depend on us. God waits for us as to whether we finally want to understand God. When we do, then God's gracious purposes will be fulfilled for us.

This then is how we will want to meet God: wanting this meeting to happen, instead of being afraid; wanting to hear what God has to say to us; accepting the gift of God's redeeming message that we have ignored for so long. This should be the meaning of this year's national Day of Penitence, and also of the celebration of the Lord's Supper, for which we are gathered together today and next Sunday. Why do we go to the Lord's Supper? For no other reason than to keep the image of Jesus before our eyes, to let him speak to our hearts. Oh, if only such an encounter with God would really be granted to us! "And Jesus stood up," we read in our story. When he will rise up in our hearts, when he will take a living form in our souls, then the storm will be over. Once again: God is waiting for us.

Amen.

September 20, 1914

Sermon at Safenwil[1]

Mourning, National Day of Penitence

Jeremiah 22:29: O land, land, land, hear the word of the Lord!

Dear Congregation!

Hear the Word of the Lord! O land, O Switzerland, O people of Switzerland! Hear the Word of the Lord! This is the message that is proclaimed to us, that ought now to awaken, grasp, and overpower us. We have come together here to observe the national Day of Penitence, and united with us everywhere are our fellow Swiss nationals from every canton, confession, and party. With thanksgiving we will acknowledge on this day all that we have received from God. With humility we would like to ask ourselves about our faithfulness to God. We will pray in a childlike way to God, remembering to ask God to continue to guide us by God's strong hand.

This time the Day of Penitence, unlike that of other years, is particularly noteworthy. *God himself* has spoken to us. God always speaks to us, but we have difficulty understanding God. God was often so distant and vague to us. And for this reason, for us the national Day of Penitence was also not what it was intended to be. Now this year God has spoken to us so clearly for almost two months that it would be difficult, it seems to me, *not to understand God*. In this short time we have been able to gain more knowledge and experience of God than we did earlier over a period of ten or twenty years.

God himself is delivering the national Day of Penitence sermon to us this year. We would also like to pray with our whole heart, "O land, land, land, *hear* the word of the Lord!" Hear the Word of the Lord that has come so palpably within our reach in the powerful events of this time. With what an awesome *responsibility* we burden ourselves if we do not listen to God now! Hear the Word *of the Lord*—not the word of human beings, not even the word of the pastor. On many national Days of Penitence in previous years, we went to church to listen to the pastor's political views. We agreed with them, or we shook our heads about them. This was always a folly. This year it would be an impiety.

Do not think now of the man in this pulpit in front of you. He is of no importance whatsoever. It has to do with something much greater. I would have preferred to keep silent all these past Sundays as well as today, rather than speaking. If I speak, I do so only in order to serve as a signpost of what is infinitely greater than my opinions and words. Now it is no means a matter of opinions and words. The Word of the Lord to us, to which we must listen, is a chain of facts that we have to perceive and experience. They must rouse us inwardly; we must struggle and wrestle with them; they must master us. They must become the possession of the most profound depths of our soul. High as the snow-capped mountains dwarfing our small hills, they soar above all opinions and words. Hear the Word *of the Lord*, you Swiss people, delve into the depths. Do not remain content with criticizing and politicizing, with superficialities, trivialities, and vanities. Let *eternity* speak to your soul through the events of the time. It will *not* draw near with such fullness of blessing *so soon again* for a long time.

This day invites us *to be thankful*. Is there really a single soul among us who does not know for what it is that we have to thank God anew, today and every day? Indeed, it lies on all our lips: we thank God that to this day God has graciously preserved us from the terrible surge of war that is now moving through the world. We did not deserve this. We are no better than the other nations that are now suffering so unspeakably. We excel many of them not by our virtues but rather by our failings. We also cannot say that it had to develop in this way and that it is self-evident that we continue to be spared. Do I need to remind you of the first days of August and all that we feared at that time?

The fact that our fears have not yet materialized is not our doing. Nor is it the doing of our army, in whose operations and competence we trust so confidently. The guns that reduced the stronghold of Liège to rubble[2] could do the same to our hastily constructed fortification, if it came to that. And compared with the armies of our neighboring countries, which by their achievements compel admiration, we will not boast as if they had been kept far from our borders by the fear of our bayonets. "Not to us, O Lord, not to us, but to your name give glory" (Ps. 115:1)! It all could have happened differently, and it still can. If until now it has not come to pass, then we will thank the Lord of the world and of the nations, who did not will it. While there is now scarcely a small village beyond our border in which the dead are not mourned, we can trust with confident hope in a future meeting with our loved ones who are now at the frontier.

While out there the harvest of the grim reaper of death always grows larger and the tears of the desolate flow more and more, we can become more confident day by day in thinking that the worst has been averted as far as our loved ones are concerned. And whereas outside Switzerland a good many flourishing tracts of land populated by hardworking people are razed to the ground, we on the other hand, after the first frightening blow to our economy is over, can gather in the gifts of the summer and autumn harvests peacefully and no less abundantly than in other years, as well as the profits from industry that will surely begin flowing again. No word of complaint should pass from our lips if we look at the situation of others and what has befallen them. "God has done great things for us" (see Ps. 126:3), without our being able to give the slightest reason why God has now so graciously blessed us in particular.

But we must probe more deeply. It would be ungenerous of us if we did not know any better than to thank God that indeed our neighbor's house has burned down, while ours remained untouched. We should definitely not thank God for this, as that would be completely deplorable, selfish, and small-minded. The other nations that have had so much suffering to bear could indeed in the end certainly despise us and say that we are now passing through a school of harsher discipline, and we are learning something in this school. We are learning seriousness and surrender, sacrifice and brotherly and sisterly love; we are coming to know God in the storm of the disaster that has descended upon us. Will you Swiss also learn a thing or two in this time? Will you learn what suffering and struggle mean, which you do not know and which you only observe comfortably from a distance? What would we answer? Could we really have a good conscience before others when we offer the selfish prayer, "O God, I thank you that our small house is not burned down!"

We have more profound reasons to be thankful than this. It is worse to act unjustly than to suffer unjustly (cf. 1 Cor. 6:7ff. and 1 Pet. 2:19ff.). We thank God above all that God has heard our prayer, "Lead us not into temptation" (Matt. 6:13), and that up to now we have not been put in the position of acting unjustly. It is a great gift of God's grace that until now Swiss guns have not had to be *fired*, that our hands are unbloodied, and that our soldiers have not participated in the huge and terrible breach of brotherly love. Yes, we would certainly love and respect them no less if it were otherwise, but it is still a matter of great importance that up to now we can know that they have not killed! It is quite impossible that there is a blessing either for the individual or the nation in the waging of war, in killing. And somehow it has to be a blessing in the conduct of a nation that has weapons in its possession but does not use them—a blessing that we can now lay hold of. For this we want to thank God because it is a gift.

And still for something else: for this, namely, that we must not let ourselves be inwardly *dragged into* the storm or frenzy in which all these warring nations presently find themselves. What a mass of hatred and contempt now lives in millions of hearts! How many evil words fly back and forth across the borders! What incorrigible self-deceptions regarding one's own innocence and excellence are now indulged in among the masses, and even among the circles of the educated and of Christians! This is a wretched state of affairs, almost as great as that of the soldiers at the front shooting at one another. This also belongs to the ugly breach of human love. And we may keep ourselves free from all of this. We can be sober amid the general drunkenness. We may, for it is, again, a grace and not a merit. Were we Germans or French, we would feel not a hairbreadth less passionately, and like them we would sink into this dark night of barbarity. But we must not do it. We are able to hold on to our moderate, neutral position, acknowledge good where it is found, and name evil as evil, regardless of which side it is on. In the middle of this unspeakable general outbreak of national selfishness, we can also stand aside to love and hold high the unity and solidarity of people and nations. We would be thankful for this, much more than for innocent hands, for this free heart, which we have been able to preserve until now and want to preserve at all costs, and which is not to be protected through foolish partisanship and politicizing. "Do not become slaves of human masters" (1 Cor. 7:23 NRSV).

Furthermore, we still want to be thankful that as Swiss and as Christians in general we may experience such a time of great importance. For indeed it is an important time, and one must state this again and again, in spite of all the devilry that is exposed and in spite of all the distress in which it places us. Above all, it is a time that has once again produced great thoughts. We have often prayed, "Grant us great thoughts in the petty concerns of the day." But this has come unsought and apart from any merit on our part. Think about how much *pettiness* and foolishness we have stirred up just here in our small village, what a wretched web of gossip and hatred we have spun from week to week and year to year. How is it that all at once a whole throng of people have been compelled to be silent, simply because we noticed that their gossip is terribly unimportant, compared to what is now affecting the world? There are still, of course, those incorrigible enough to carry on as before, but many of you do not. In these weeks, almost everyone has been strongly affected by weighty thoughts and questions. We have experienced something of what humanity is and how it is interconnected in joy and suffering, as well as in sin and righteousness. The eternal questions of justice and injustice have become burning ones for us on account of the course of outside events. The question, of what actual value is modern civilization? has arisen anew to confront some people who previously regarded it as self-evident that civilization and education are heaven on earth.

The sight of vast numbers of dead on the battlefields has certainly led not a few persons to reflect carefully once again on the ancient riddles of life, death, and eternity. And in so many, in how many people beyond number, the life-and-death question of God has arisen! Who is God, the one who is behind everything, however God wants to be called? And what are God's ways? This is what millions of souls now ask and inquire. Much thoughtless indifference to God has been transformed into hard reflection, and many superficial opinions and dogmas about God have been quietly corrected in this time. Should we not be thankful to God for this time of greater thoughts that has put an end to so much junk and drivel?

And of course it has not stopped just with great thoughts. Enormous *tasks* engage all of us in this time, both our Swiss nation and also every single individual among us. How much energy and readiness for sacrifice there suddenly must be when it is said that the fatherland is in peril! How much love and loyalty have now suddenly shone forth in many families, in which perhaps for sundry reasons they were long buried! How have a large number of principles of brotherly and sisterly love and solidarity suddenly become necessary and self-evident among the different parties and classes in our nation, which in peacetime we valued, at best, as the rhetoric of the pulpit and the orator! Should we not be thankful to God that God has now once again compelled us to be serious about our Swiss federal oath: we want to be a united nation of brothers![3] And what great tasks must await us in the future!

We do not wish to engage in the art of prophesying. Still, it is definitely certain; we are approaching a time in which it will be necessary more than ever for all of us together to look above to heaven, attempt to understand each other better, and joyfully stand side by side in doing good. There are sufficient signs that indicate that many, perhaps very many, will change. Even the most bristly opponents will have to shake hands, and the selfish will have to perceive that not all things can continue as previously. The most narrow-minded creatures of habit will have to realize to some extent that there are higher life tasks and goals than they had previously perceived. Will we not be thankful to God for this, that God has chosen to let us face a time of greater tasks? "O land, land, land, hear the word of the LORD!" O Swiss nation, ponder profoundly how great God's goodness is to us, how we have ample reason to confess, "The LORD has done marvelous things for us in this critical time, the LORD has done great things for us, for which we are glad" (cf. Ps. 126:3).

Repentance is the other theme to which this day points us. We are accustomed to hear a sermon on repentance on the National Day of Penitence. Indeed, many of those who come to church mainly only on the National Day of Penitence fully expect to be subjected to a solid sermon on repentance, to an exhaustive enumeration and elaboration of our nation's failings and its sins. I would not like to dwell on this theme too long. If I were to begin to sing this familiar tune about extravagance and pleasure, it would be tantamount to carrying water to the Rhine. Every reasonable person agrees that, on account of the mad passion of these aims, in wide circles of the population every notion of economy and moderation has disappeared. Where this must lead many know, who because of their own guilt look into the future with heavy apprehension; I do not need to draw it to their attention. There is also no doubt that here the events will come to *their own conclusion*, and rightly so. In this regard, each man and woman to whom this applies can preach repentance to themselves.

If once again we keep our eyes on the conduct of the majority of us in the first days of the war's hardship, we are led to more serious and weighty considerations. This will now remain as a fact of Swiss history that the River Aare will not wash away, namely, that in these days in which God has allowed a great time of testing and blessing to come upon us, our mobilization for war generally proceeded without fault. Still, at the same time, a quite miserable anxiety and self-seeking convulsion came over the majority of us. Above all, I think of the senseless hoarding of money and foodstuffs in our homes, whereby many people betrayed the fatherland and the general public. This fact is now established, and we may not and do not want to forget it—not even afterward when on our hilltops we can again light bonfires in celebration of peace. Then we will sing:

> Hail to you, Helvetia,
> You still indeed have sons, yes.
> As St. Jacob saw them
> Full of joy for the fight![4]

Hence we want to ponder that indeed our military organization succeeded better than at St. Jacob, but that the majority of fathers and mothers of Swiss households conducted themselves rather differently in the hour of destiny than did the old confederates. We want to and must also reflect on this today. It became apparent on those days of alarm that we are a grasping, selfish people, a people that is accustomed to seize opportunity, but above and beyond this, even more prepared to disregard all other considerations. The last decades have very much strengthened us in this fatal characteristic. We have become a prosperous nation through the flourishing of commerce and industry. We really have no idea of how well off we are. Only rarely do we think of comparing our situation with that of our parents and grandparents. But who among us can seriously claim that this whole development works only for good? There is now among us a kind of spirit that has arisen and become powerful. It is the spirit of "everything has its price"—health, dignity, and character—the spirit that says, each person is his or her own neighbor![5]

This spirit of feverish, ruthless acquisitiveness has returned again in society from top to bottom. But it certainly started at the top with the upper class, and from there it descended to the others. This spirit is not of God. It is not the spirit of truth, righteousness, and peace. Basically, it has not even made us happy. Already, in normal times, our whole condition—seemingly so flourishing—did not fail to have its dark and shadowed sides. I do not want to get into this subject more deeply. This spirit gradually became a curse that lay heavily upon us. Everything that one can otherwise fault in us—our inordinate love of pleasure, our vanity, and oddly enough also our lack of thriftiness and home life—was somehow connected with this. And now, in the first days of the need brought about by war, there is the curse, the basic curse that besets us, that has evidently become obvious once again to all who want to see, so obvious that one could grasp it with one's hands.

And we now immediately go more deeply into what "to repent" means for us. What we suggested here regarding the moral failure of our nation is in the end only the external symptom of an evil that dwells deep within. We do not stand *before God* as we should. This relationship of a nation to God is something that is hidden. It has now suddenly been disclosed, and we must admit to ourselves that it is not as it should be, after we had perhaps long abandoned all sorts of illusions. We had churches and pastors, organs and church bells, and a sermon every Sunday; we had Christian societies, charitable organizations, and foreign missions. But what has all that to do with God and with obedience to God?

God is indeed love. How is it that we can have so easily set aside the consideration of our brothers and sisters? God is indeed order. How, as if we were thieves, can we be so intent on plundering? God is indeed goodness and wisdom. How did it come about that so quickly, so surprisingly quickly, we threw away confidence in God (cf. Heb. 10:35) and could give ourselves up to a childish anxiety and nervousness? Here it has come to light that on that day our relationship to God was all superficiality and veneer. Obedience to God's will was in large part a matter of habit, something shallow, not our inward possession. Hence also, in the hour of testing, it has largely fallen away from us, and here we stand as we really are. In spite of much speaking and singing about Jesus, I believe the gospel and the person of Jesus in particular are still very foreign to us. We have still perceived little of the redeeming power that radiates from this man and his message. Hence, in the decisive moments, as when it is a matter of standing the test as a Christian, we think and act differently than Jesus would in our place.

All things considered, for a long time God has not been sufficiently real, alive, or present in our lives. We do not stand close enough to God. We do not let ourselves be inwardly embraced and filled by God in such a way that in every life situation our understanding would be clear and certain: then we would think, speak, and act, not according to worldly wisdom, but according to the wisdom that comes from God and overcomes the world. If God were to be to us what God wants to be, then we would be quite different people from what the war's misery has brought. We would not be so anxious, not so complaining, not so agitated, not so selfish and thoughtless.

So now it should be clear to us what "to repent" means. Above all, it means immediately to face one's own faults with honesty and humility. And what then? Such faults as ours cannot be laid aside from one day to the next. What can help us face them is simply the *return* to God, who is the source of all good, and who above all grants the power not only to perceive the good but also to do it. In a shocking way, present events demonstrate how true this is. We have heard it said on so many national Days of Repentance, without perhaps rightly believing it, that sin is a reproach to a people (Prov. 14:34). God cannot be mocked. What we sow, we must also reap (Gal. 6:7). If the European nations had stood before God differently, if they had taken Jesus' gospel seriously, then this insane war would not have occurred; it would have been nipped in the bud. Now judgment has overtaken us. It has not yet hit us Swiss with its full force, although we are certainly no better than the other nations. Do we want to wait, thankless and lifeless, until it also befalls us? Do we then not want to hear the call of God, who with such power still invites us to turn to God with our whole heart as long as there is still time, to lay hold of that one thing that alone can ensure our freedom?

"O land, land, land, hear the word of the Lord!" O people of Switzerland, go immediately into the depths and discern how much you still lack of the best and most important thing, and where it is to be found! For once, be serious about what you have already known for a long time! It is a time of repentance. The time of repentance means the time of grace. To repent does not mean to be sullen and depressed. Repentance is a joyful, jubilant apprehension of the greatest thing there is, a childlike, grateful acceptance of the redemption from evil now offered to us. Repentance is in the end nothing other than proper gratitude for God's great goodness to us.

So do we still need to point out in detail what this day, as a national Day of Repentance, has to say to us? In the horror of present events, is it not true that we would want to pray for protection, for God's shield and protection for our dear Switzerland—for God's gracious guidance and preservation in the difficult and confused times that we face? Yes, we also want to pray for these, that these may be the beginning of our prayer today. Hence, in the storm of this time, we ask God to preserve our freedom and independence for the future. We pray to God on behalf of our soldiers that God will watch over them and that they may return to us safe and sound in body and, above all, also in soul. We ask God to spare us too much distress and too heavy a burden of worries during the coming winter! Why should we not pray for this? We know that we find in God, with all our requests, a benevolent Father.

But in this regard, without delay, it must also mean for us that we go more deeply and enter more profoundly into prayer and, in particular, more deeply into what prayer really is: one's inward communion with the one who is the Lord of the world and of our life. I could imagine that earnest Christians could now pray rather differently than as follows: No, Lord our God, let the surge of your judgments simply befall us, so that finally, finally, we hear you and remember who you are and what you demand of us! Just let our Swiss freedom now come into great danger, so that we perceive it is not a possession to be taken for granted, but a gift of your goodness, which we must carefully protect and of which we must prove ourselves worthy again and again. If it is necessary, let the time of distress be extended and become more burdensome than before, so that we cannot breathe freely again so soon and fall back into the same old rut. We would not like, and we could not wish, that you speak less plainly and sternly with us than with the other nations. We do not have the right so to pray, since we should not and do not want to prescribe how God will deal with us, either in good times or in bad.

But this is certain: when this day enjoins us, Pray, free Swiss citizen, pray! Then our life shall be something deeper and better than petitioning and begging that God might spare us while all others must suffer. It is rather for this reason, above all, that we will pray for all others that the gratitude we owe to God and the repentance to which God invites us may be true and genuine, that there again may be a return to a full union of our soul and the soul of our nation with the holy and righteous God. We will want to say to God: Lord, what our Switzerland needs now is that you are in covenant with us, not as a God of battle but as the God who inspires all rulers and citizens with great thoughts, who unites the parties, classes, and confessions not in a foolish and thoughtless tolerance of each other, but in a common love, in a common zeal for what is good and needful, and as the God who establishes and preserves justice and righteousness and smashes and destroys all that is petty and selfish.

Lord our God, we pray not for victory, not for power and wealth, but that we might be a nation in which also the weak and the poor find their rights undiminished and can enjoy their existence. Deliver us from all disorder and despotism, rescue us from the pride of the great and the rich and from the thoughtlessness of the lowly and the poor. Let your good spirit of seriousness and strength break forth among us. Show us ever anew and always more clearly what we have in the shining image of our Lord Jesus, through whom you speak to us. Open our ears and our hearts, enter into us, make us truly your children, and fill us with your glory!

This is how we want to pray. To pray really means to seek God thankfully when we look at God, and humbly when we look at ourselves. Oh, if only now everywhere we prayed like this, if only God's community in Switzerland would seek to pray to God like this, what a blessing would then proceed from this national Day of Repentance, from this wonderful time of repentance! "O land, land, land, hear the word of the Lord!" O people of Switzerland, take note and consider how you now have to pray in your church, in the privacy of your room, in the solitude of nature: "God, you great and living one, I want to be yours; and then do with me what you will!"

Dear friends, God gives us everything we need—not just for today, but for the grave times we face, for our whole life: the right gratitude, the right repentance, even the right prayer to God. It has to be all *God's doing* if it is to be good. God *wills* to give this to us. The Holy Supper again speaks clearly and tangibly to us: "I want to give you the greatest thing you need." And God knows the way to each one of us. "Behold, I stand at the door and knock" (Rev. 3:20). Do you hear God? Will you open the door? "O land, land, land, hear the word of the Lord!"

Amen.

October 11, 1914

Sermon at Safenwil

Mark 10:17–23[1]

Dear Friends!

It surely must have been a marvelous moment in the life of this man when the question welled up in his soul, "What must I do to inherit eternal life?" What may have been going on in his mind earlier? Probably for years he had no idea at all that one could ask this question. He had other questions: "How shall I gain wealth and honor? How can I make my life comfortable? How can I arrange it so that others fear me and must do my bidding?" He had wondered about eternal life at one time or another, but never for long, and then he briskly brushed it aside and thought of something else. Perhaps he was also so sure of inheriting eternal life that he never thought to question it at all. He seemed to be one of those godly persons who makes every effort to live a life pleasing to God and therefore could confidently think that, as far as eternal life was concerned, everything was in good order. Suddenly that changed. His good life of peace and security was shattered. Misgivings arose when earlier he had never entertained them for a moment, and doubts arose where beforehand everything was certain. A secure person had changed into a questioning one. It's wonderful when that happens to someone.

I believe something similar has occurred in our time to countless persons. They also had not troubled themselves greatly about eternal life. They had other concerns. They had their great and small worries and joys. They loved and hated. They lived and let live. Eternal life was distant, something airy, nebulous, uncertain. And even though they were uncertain, they still conducted themselves as if they were certain. They thought there was no hurry. They relied on the church, on the gathered community, which they attended.

They relied on their Christianity that surely had to guarantee eternal life, and they heard quite gladly at appropriate times the mention of it. Or they trusted in the education and culture that human beings have achieved in our day. And so they went their way as confident people, untroubled by any concerns about eternal life.

And now all of a sudden this world war came. And something happened to them, something like what happened to that rich man. They were shaken out of their peace and quiet, eternal life became important to them, and the question crept up on them: "How do things stand with me?" They noted that they had no cause to be so certain. I know there are many now who are already finished with the world war. The French did not come, which was a real blessing, like a due reward; what more is needed? They scarcely think any more about what is going on beyond the border. We are not speaking now about them. They are not to be envied. But since this war has occurred in the world, there are others in whom something has begun to work and develop. Ever since this event of great magnitude began, many things have become less significant to them, as if their old way of being has suffered a shock. They feel as though the ground under them is shaking. They perceive that the sort of life that was so dear to them is a fragile, frail, fleeting thing. They perceive that, if left unimpeded, the devil and hell that are hidden in human nature may take their own course. They perceive that the little measure of Christianity and culture we have is only a thin veneer over our beings, on which we cannot rely.

All of a sudden they have lost the confidence they possessed earlier. The world has taken on a different appearance. Mists that we took to be sky have dispersed. The idols we worshiped are deposed. The questions "Where do we come from?" and "Where are we going?" have suddenly become living and burning ones for us. We ask, Is this all there is? Is this what life now is, this human life that is displayed before our eyes more frightfully from week to week: the hunger for power of the Russians, the self-righteousness of the Germans, the revenge-seeking of the French, the cold commercial spirit of the English, and the brutish cruelty of the Belgians . . . and the petty meanness of us Swiss. Is this all there is? Is this life? Is this what people are? Is this what we are?

We pose the question and know the answer well enough: "No, that *isn't* all there is. There is something else. There must be something else, something that is completely opposite to what we now see. Something that is not war and not racial hatred, not mass murder, not senseless destruction." But it is also not the narrow, limited, loveless, and fundamentally unhappy existence that we contentedly lived during peacetime. The war has after all revealed only what we really are. It tells us more clearly than any sermon: it is *not* this; your human nature is *not* this. This is *not* the true life; you yourselves see how it degenerates into madness and horror. There is something different, and it is the complete opposite of your whole being. There is eternal life, life free of hate and suffering and death, life in happiness and truth and love, life in God.

And now the yearning, the longing for this other life, is awakened in many people. They are wrenched out of the tranquility into which they earlier settled themselves. In spite of the fact that they are devout and educated, they are no longer of the opinion that they already possess it. They no longer want to content themselves with the scant comfort of a dull, superficial Christianity. They see themselves as utterly famished and miserable. They would like to begin afresh with the ABCs in the great school of God. And now their souls search and fumble to and fro: What shall I do that I may inherit eternal life? What shall I do in order to lay hold of and possess what is greater and stronger than all of the suffering and injustice of the world, the firm ground when every other place becomes doubtful and uncertain, the place we call home in the foreign country of this world, the light in the impenetrable darkness of such events?

We do not know what it was that led this man to Jesus with this question, or what made him fall on his knees before Jesus. In any case, it must have been a powerful experience. His former nature became humble, completely humble. He became uncertain in the depth of his soul; that innermost, most hidden part in him pressed toward the light, sought, inquired, yearned for the new order, for a better world, for a different life. Such a powerful experience may now also be ours. How can those be helped who do not seriously desire to be helped? It is incumbent upon us that in these months we experience something of the miraculous—which our superficial nature spoils for us and our illusory Christianity makes repulsive to us—so that the question overpowers us and takes hold of us like an armed man: "What shall I do that I may inherit eternal life?"

But it is not achieved by awakening, questioning, and seeking. Where do we search for the eternal life that we lack? The man knelt down there before Jesus and said to him, "Good master, you must tell me: how am I to do this?" It can indeed surprise us that this was not the right approach. Many readers of the Bible have already taken offense that Jesus answered, "Why do you call me good? No one is good but God alone. You know the commandments: Do not commit adultery. Do not steal. Do not kill, and so on." Why does Jesus speak this way? We think of the well-known saying of Peter, "Lord, to whom shall we go? You have the words of eternal life" (John 6:68). And now Jesus actually refuses to give him such a word but instead reminds him of the well-known Ten Commandments. We think of Jesus' saying to Philip, "Whoever has seen me, has seen the Father" (John 14:9 NRSV). And now Jesus does not want to have the simple, little word "good" applied to himself: "No one is good but God alone." Why did he decline the appellation? Oh, we have to understand it correctly. It is not a matter of taking offense; on the contrary, here we get to know the greatness of Jesus from a perspective that perhaps is still quite new to us.

With one voice the prophets and the philosophers, of course, would have answered differently, had they been in his place. They would have been pleased about the trust that the man showed them and then possibly would have given him a small bit of good advice: you have to believe this and do that. This was also what the man expected. He had expected to find a new religion with Jesus. If only the longing in his soul would be stilled, he was willing to believe new doctrines from God, to accept new duties for himself. He was prepared for all human possibilities. How easily Jesus could then have pacified him. Jesus refused to do this. This man had no need whatever to "do" this or that. Oh, how well it would have suited him if he could "do" something, in order to calm himself! But this is not how he would have found eternal life. After a time the dissatisfaction and uncertainty would have returned to him. For everything that we human beings can "do" is necessarily insufficient, since human vanity and pettiness also always play a role. The best that we "do" has always a negative side. We are not able to find eternal life therein, because if we are honest enough to observe it, one abyss after another opens up at our feet, and we must constantly admit that what we do is patchy and botched work. It is so with our best thoughts, our most noble deeds.

Jesus wanted to spare the man this disappointment. This is why he declined to give him good advice. Hence he also did not want to be called "good master." There was something not right, something insincere in the way the young man called Jesus "good master," however serious he seemed to be, and however sincere he seemed in asking for his help. Jesus should save him from having to ask and to seek for eternal life. He should be a good master to him and somehow pacify him in his misgivings and doubts. The confidence he showed Jesus was fundamentally an evasion before something much greater that he anticipated and before which he was afraid. And hence Jesus also rejected this feeling of confidence. He did not want this man to honor him personally, and meanwhile to leave aside the most important thing. Yes, Jesus was a good teacher, the best who ever lived; but whoever wants to call him such must let himself or herself be directed to God by him. This is precisely the incomparable goodness of Jesus, namely, that he sought and found goodness in God alone. Whoever desires something from him must follow him precisely in this respect. Otherwise, all honor that we offer to him is hypocrisy.

If we are seeking to find eternal life, we must think about this refusal. It is something great and wonderful if all at once we become anxious and perceive that our human nature lacks something, that we need something different. But it takes great caution and wisdom now, with all our yearning for something better, to avoid getting bogged down once again in something human that can finally satisfy us just as little as that from which we would like to escape. We ought not to grasp for some answer too quickly and think, that's it now, there I have it now, I have gained eternal life! Jesus must say to all the many individuals who in their anguish of soul have been touched in this time of need, "It's *not* that, however well-intended it may be."

Have you not observed how, after the initial shock of the war, it was immediately said by all sides that we must do something: collect for the Red Cross, knit socks for the soldiers, organize aid committees for the needy? In fact, our Aargau church council has addressed a letter to all its pastors to this effect. This is all definitely well and good, and of course I have nothing to say against this. I might only point to the great danger we run if we think that the main thing in our present situation is that we should do this or that. The danger lies in the fact that then, with the best will in the world, we get bogged down in the very place from which we want to be delivered. So we then remain the same people we were earlier, except that now we strive to do some of those things that were set before us as good and necessary: we save a little more, we take part in this or that good cause, we go to church somewhat more often!

However, what happens when one day we perceive that in spite of all this activity we are still the same individuals, and that our human nature, of which we were so sick, is not the least unsettled or changed through it all? What a terrible disappointment that is! We want to guard against this danger. The longing for eternal life is now awakened in many persons. It is wholly right that we do all that is our duty and even more, but this matter does not depend on our doing all sorts of things. Moreover, it could happen to us that through all our good intentions and undertakings, the decisive moment in which God speaks with us clearly passes by without our having heard God.

I would also like to point out emphatically that it is not accomplished by resolving to pray more, read the Bible more, go to church or the assembly more often. Indeed, that is all fine and good and not to be despised, but *this* also is not what is now needed. Moreover, these belong after all to the things that one can "do." And what we do always remains something human, and one day we discover that it is human and imperfect, and the same dissatisfied longing appears again. All this inhibits us from inheriting eternal life. We need to think about the man who came to Jesus himself and thought he could "do" something, even by calling him "good master." With all our good intentions and ideas that may now move us, we definitely need to ponder whether, like the young ruler, we do not evade the one thing needful from among the things that should now actually happen.

What answer does Jesus give that man? He tells him, "You know the commandments!" He then reminds him of what he long knew, of what is quite obvious to him. Imagine his astonishment! He thought of discovering a new religion with Jesus, a new faith and a new code of ethics—perhaps in the same way Muhammad brought the Arabs a new religion, or as it happens when a new community of believers appears in a district and now people come and make an effort to understand the new faith that is being taught, how it is practiced, and what is demanded of them. There is nothing like this with Jesus. The way to eternal life is nothing new. "You know the commandments!"—the simple Ten Commandments that every child knows. And out of the Ten Commandments, Jesus mentions precisely the most obvious of all of them: "You shall not commit adultery, not kill, not steal, not bear false witness, and you shall honor your father and mother"—as if to say to him, "I really mean just the simplest, just those commandments that you think you have known inside out since childhood."

Do you think there is one of you who perhaps as a result of the war has now come some little way to an awakening, to other thoughts, to a hunger and thirst for eternal life that stands above this futile and pitiful human life? Perhaps also in another way, it does not depend on this. It is a matter of asking, seeking, and feeling one's way: Where do I find support and strength and light for my life? And now comes the answer: Be honest in the responsibility entrusted to you! Have esteem for your neighbor's life and soul! Take particular care to tell the truth! And show gratitude and respect to those to whom you owe gratitude and respect. These are matters that are clear, advice that one would give to children in Sunday school. Hence this will be the response to the question, what shall I do that I may inherit eternal life? Is it not true that there is something in us that rebels? We almost become angry. What, should it now depend on this? But you do not need to tell me this! I know this too well! Why does it upset us so much when our attention is drawn to the simplest things as the way to life?

The young ruler here also began to lose his temper. He did not want to be told that the Ten Commandments had anything to say to him! He thought he did not need to come to Jesus to be told this. "Master, I have kept them all from my youth!" he said. Naturally, yes, indeed he was from a good family; of course, he was recognized and honored by the people; to be sure, he was the kind of person whom one could not reproach in any way. Even more so, he could bring into the calculation so much additional good work that is not stated in those laws. The Ten Commandments: not stealing, committing adultery, or killing—he could still set them aside as having nothing really to do with him. Yes indeed, but why? Is it really only with the right of injured pride, when he, and when we along with him, politely disregard these simplest commandments of God: yes, yes, to be sure, one must keep this, I also keep this, but surely the way to life must be different than that?

Is it really only on account of justifiable pride if we long for a more refined way to life? Or is it not a hidden fear that takes hold of us when these simple words ring out: truth, purity, love, the neighbor's goods, life, and honor—the fear that something lurks there with which we are not yet finished, not finished with by a long shot, and by which we do not want to be bound. Woe, if the lion awakens, this lion that lurks in the Ten Commandments, and for a long time seemed to have nothing more to do with us, until all of a sudden we notice: here there is indeed a lack, and as long as there is no change in this regard, all the paths I pursue to eternal life are simply detours and byways.

Yet to allow it to be otherwise is incredibly difficult. How much easier it is to "do" something! How much easier it is, for example, in our present situation to lay five francs or even more on the table for the Red Cross than once and for all to make sure that there is harmony in the home! How much easier it is to go to church every Sunday than to change one's tone of voice with one's spouse or one's children! How much easier it is to knit many, many pairs of socks for the soldiers than to remember to be no longer so close-fisted! How much easier it is to read a gruesome book about the approaching end of the world than to stop the evil backbiting chatter that causes so much mischief! We know full well that God always demands exactly the latter things of us, always exactly what we have known for ages and what for this reason we are so unwilling to do. We know all too well that there is no other way to eternal life than by again taking these simple things seriously. God's will, indeed God himself, is found in these simple things.

If the European people had been obedient in these simple matters in the Ten Commandments, we would not have a war now. Obedience to the Ten Commandments would be deliverance from all evil. We are fully aware of this, but what is demanded of us here seems so overwhelming that we prefer the easier way, choosing to do something rather than obey, just as children often do. And so, with an authoritative look on our face, we then say, "I have other things to do, and I would like something different, a different way of salvation"—always something other than what God wills! What shall we say about this? Is our foolishness greater than our hypocrisy? Look, this is why Jesus refused that man. He saw clearly that he had awakened from the sleep of indifference and security. But he also noticed that the man was not completely serious about eternal life, that he was secretly afraid of what now had to happen within him. Jesus reveals this fear to him—not in order to torment him but to help him. Jesus holds up the Ten Commandments before the man because he knows there is something lacking in him! And the rich man asks only, "What shall I do?" because he does not want to know what fundamentally he knows all too well.

But the man did not understand Jesus, or, rather, he didn't want to understand him. He did not want to see the clear, straight path that Jesus opened up to him. He answered, "I've kept them all from my youth!" Therefore, he meant, of course, you have to tell me something better, something higher. Just as we also do. What should Jesus say now? He could perhaps have asked him: "Really? Is that so? Did you keep every one? Are you serious about the majestic will of God that is behind each of these short commandments?" Jesus did not ask him these questions. A great back-and-forth conversation would perhaps have taken place in which the man would have tried to absolve himself, to prove that in everything and in all respects he kept the Ten Commandments. And through it all he would have forgotten that he had come to ask about eternal life. We should note this: we are never further removed from God's kingdom than when we make excuses and pardon ourselves, no matter whether we are right or not.

Jesus did not want to give him any opportunity to argue. He did not want to let him go. The passage says, "He looked upon him and loved him." He looked at him, seeing that he cared to attain something better, even if he still was not completely sincere. He looked at him and saw that, strictly speaking, he was not a bad person. And for this reason he wanted to bring him further. And this is why he now spoke these remarkable words: "You lack one thing; go, sell what you have, and give to the poor, and you will have treasure in heaven; and come, follow me, and take the cross on yourself!"

Well, what is this, this outrageous demand that turned his world upside down? As we said earlier, unlike other founders of religions or leaders of sects, Jesus brought no new thing. What was new about him was precisely what he said: that which is long established must carry weight—that which is long known, plain, and self-evident, the simple, divine commandments of love and justice. But it must really be ruthlessly and unconditionally valid. There should be no doubt whatsoever about taking God's will seriously. Is this not indeed something new that he brings here: "Sell what you have, and give it to the poor; follow me and take up the cross?"

Does this also belong to the simple things that we know of ourselves, and concerning which the only question is whether we are also serious about it? Yes, that is really Jesus' meaning. He did not want to add an eleventh commandment to the familiar ten. He simply wanted to say to him, "See, if you will really keep the Ten Commandments, this is what it will involve." Then this is what it means, yes, what it means: to give up everything for God's sake, all the visible possessions to which your heart is attached; to make yourself completely free; to put all you have in the service of your brother and sister; to go with me in the way of poverty and of love and take the cross upon yourself, which means being ready to suffer. Whoever does this, whoever gives up all one has, has eternal life; whoever does not do this, whoever cannot give up everything, does not have eternal life.

But now the man became puzzled. Now he perceived what previously he had not noticed or had not wanted to admit to himself, namely, that the Ten Commandments caused him anxiety, that he was too far away from them to have really fulfilled them from his youth. Will he gain mastery over himself? Will he extricate himself from his anxiety about the will of God, to arrive at a happy resolution? He could not bring himself to do so. He was not yet ready for this. Sadly, he departed, for he had many possessions. He was still too attached to them. He was still too much at home in the world. He longed for salvation, but he had not the strength to receive it when it was offered to him.

Yes, my friends, what then are the Ten Commandments this man could not fulfill, and before which he stood back, dismayed, when Jesus told him what they should mean for him? The Decalogue, the unadorned will of God, which we all know is nothing but the law that we are to be men and women who serve God and our neighbor. This is what God wants. Whoever obeys this law cannot continue to use the possessive *I* and say that is *my* right, *my* honor, *my* property; he or she cannot continue to say, no matter whether rich or poor: this is *my* money and property. This "*I*" and this "*my*" no longer exist. This "*I*" and this "*my*" cause all the injustice and suffering in the world. Because of the "I" and the "my," human beings torment one another. Because of the "I" and the "my," they wage war against one another. The "I" and the "my" are the emblem of this world, its glory and its unspeakable shame. Whoever longs for salvation, whoever longs for eternal life, has to be able to give up the "I" and the "my." So the Ten Commandments say, "You shall not kill!" means that I shall sacrifice my life for my brother or sister! "You shall not steal!" means that what is mine, shall also be his or hers. "You shall not bear false witness!" means that I shall not think and say and want anything except what is right, what can stand up before God.

Where this law prevails, there is the kingdom of God. In God's kingdom, there are no longer poor and rich. Moreover, this happens without any revolution, because it is impossible in that kingdom for the rich to let the poor be in need; that is, all the injustice on which riches are now based is impossible within it. And hence, there is no longer any strife or war in God's kingdom. This is so, not on account of arbitration tribunals and international treaties, which one again and again tears up when it is expedient, but because in God's kingdom the selfishness and hatred from which wars arise are impossible. Do we indeed doubt that where this law prevails—this law of the Ten

Commandments, where everyone is then a servant of God and of neighbor—there is eternal life? We should certainly try to apply this law, and we will immediately feel that we are in the very midst of eternal life.

Think what would happen in this moment if the nations would each say not "I" and "my," but God and neighbor—in other words, this great old newness that Jesus has brought us. The guns that are now raised by thousands of brothers on fellow brothers would be lowered. The artillery that is now permitted to spit out murder and destruction would be drawn back and dismantled. The actions of men who now attack one another, in the air like vicious vultures and in the trenches underground like malicious moles and ferocious foxes, would stop. All these insane thoughts, speeches, and actions, all this senseless activity to which well over half of humanity devotes itself today, would come to a standstill with one blow and would make room for a universal "No!" to so much blindness. And all of us, who make life often so difficult for ourselves and for others, would once again perceive that life is something simple, something wonderfully beautiful, when we take God seriously, when once the "I" and the "my" are no longer valid. Eternal life would descend upon us even here and now. Life in blessedness. Life in love. Life in God, who is perfect and who wills that we also be perfect (cf. Matt. 5:48).

Why doesn't this happen? Why does eternal life remain so distant from us, so foreign? Why do we have to speak of it almost as of a beautiful but impossible dream? "He went away sorrowful, because he had great possessions." The "I" and the "my" are still too strong. The fear is still too powerful; we could not endure keeping God's commandments. We still think it could not be otherwise. We are still too much at home in this world.

And now we know the way that leads to eternal life: it means becoming freer from that with which the "I" and "my" are connected, whether it is wealth, ambition, sensitivity, or nerves, or something else. So long as you still depend on this, you cannot be saved, "do" what you will. Look, here is God, who alone is good. God wants only the least from you, which is yet so enormously much, which is everything. God wants that you behold God as God is. You know how God is. You know the commandments. Obey them, and you will live!

Amen.

October 18, 1914

Sermon at Safenwil[1]

Romans 8:38–39: I am sure that neither death nor life, nor angels, nor principalities, nor things present, nor things to come, nor powers, nor height, nor depth, nor anything else in all creation, will be able to separate us from the love of God in Christ Jesus our Lord.

Dear Friends!

We have spoken here only sparingly or not at all of the *great and admirable qualities* and abilities that the war has fostered among people. With good reason! There has been quite enough to read in newspaper reports—especially those that come from foreign countries—of patriotism, bravery, and sacrifice shown by the soldiers of the nations engaged in this war. With the best will, and try as I might, I could not bring myself to agree with this and still cannot. As Swiss and as Christians, we have more important things to do than to admire the war fervor and the war feats of contemporary humanity around us, however great and admirable they may be from time to time. It is for us a matter of letting ourselves be permeated still more deeply with the truth that the war and everything connected with it is an unspeakable injustice and a deplorable disaster in every way, now that the wild beast within human beings is unleashed and may bring about the most terrible destruction to the horror and shame of humanity.

If we want to hear what God has to say to us and what God requires of us, this clear knowledge that is enjoined on us through our conscience and through the gospel of Jesus must be the firm ground on which we stand unflinching in this turbulent time. But I believe this discovery, that war is sin and guilt and punishment; and the volition that goes with this discovery concerning the war and everything connected with it, the decision to declare with all one's heart in obedience to the God of peace and love that the war is sinful—this discovery and this volition can only become clearer and stronger once we calmly concede that, yes, the war actually also has its honor; it is in fact not only a night of baseness and suffering. In millions of our fellow human beings we now see noble, pure, and strong character traits—indeed, in a certain sense, also in entire nations—where earlier there was no evidence of these.

The war is a great *magician*. "They were eating and drinking, marrying and giving in marriage" (Matt. 24:38), and now, if we do not want to judge them too narrowly and harshly, all of a sudden they have become persons with positively good characteristics that we must undoubtedly recognize as such. Precious jewels that were long hidden under the dust and dirt of everyday life have suddenly begun to sparkle. People who have gone their way in a dreamy, indifferent, and apathetic mood have awakened, and the best within them has come to light. A heroic age has dawned, a time of great things following long decades of dull pettiness. And hence we also see all the nations, notwithstanding all the shed tears, in a "Sunday best" *mood*. Therefore, no one in Germany, for example, dare say, "This time is a dark age; its events are a judgment of God." No, indeed, they rejoice in these events, they speak of holy experiences, they feel themselves definitely not in discord with but in the perfect harmony with the will of God, and they do not pray "Forgive us our debts" (Matt. 6:12) but say, "The ancient God is still alive!";[2] and they thank God that they are permitted to live at this particular time.

The French, the English, and the Austrians feel the same way. *A feeling of ecstasy* has possessed all these nations. This intoxication of spirit is not a pretense but is something that we must acknowledge as absolutely genuine. External, material, and private interests have largely given way to great thoughts and common ideals, and for me that is the greatest thing about this awakening of the nations. As one man, the whole of France is engaged in the conflict with the holy conviction and intention to complete the great liberation of the French Revolution by overcoming German military superiority, under which Europe has groaned until now. For its part England has the same purpose in mind; humankind ought to become free of fear in face of the German threat. Small nations need protection from the despotism of their larger neighbor. We see Belgians defending with the courage of desperation what still remains of their homeland. It is of Germany that we hear and see most clearly that enthusiasm that depicts this war as a holy cause. "We are defending," they say, "the most sacred possessions and qualities of humanity against the rapacious assault of brutal barbarians. They hate us because they envy us, and they envy us because we are strong. But God wills that we be strong, and for this reason God is on our side."

And Russia? There is no question at all that this great, enigmatic nation is a singular mass of murderers and barbarians. We do not know it well, and so it is exceedingly difficult to understand it, and we should be wary all the more of joining in hateful condemnation without taking other things into account. Russia also has principles. It is convinced of its rightness in this war. It keeps its treaties by protecting the Serbians, just as Germany keeps its treaties through its alliance with Austria. What is more, I could not simply join in the general condemnation of the Serbians, even though they have provided the external causes of the war. There lives in this nation a strong, unified will that we Swiss especially must appreciate. Through difficult struggles, they have become an independent state, and as such they want to stand their ground. The ill-fated murderer, Princip,[3] committed his dastardly deed out of love for his country. We could and should condemn his action, but who will condemn his patriotism? Within the surging sea of nations around us, there is definitely no lack of high and noble sentiments and convictions. Here they are more clearly pronounced, there they are less, but they are present everywhere.

And there is not only enthusiasm, not only exalted thoughts, but also *deeds* at home and on the field of battle, for which we can only truly have the highest admiration. Scarcely a day now goes by without the newspapers bringing us new, stirring ordeals of dauntless and sacrificial deeds of men and women on all the warring sides. What indeed does this huge influx of volunteers tell us, hundreds of thousands who in Germany, in France, in England now voluntarily mobilize themselves under their national flags without being conscripted, even though they have nothing to look forward to except exhaustion, privation, and enormous danger to their lives?

We now experience something similar to what must have occurred during the most troubled times of world history. "The people rise up, the storm breaks out!"[4] Who would have imagined that contemporary humanity, which often seems so senile, so feeble, would still have so much selflessness, fearlessness, and fidelity alive and active within it? Think of what all the millions of women have accomplished at present, and what they are still achieving, by letting their husbands and sons go forth, with the firm resolve not to make their separation and absence from home a burden! Behind every fighting army, is there not a second, invisible army of women and children and of the elderly, of poets and scholars, who by their involvement, their confident spirit, their love, joy, and courage give support to the fighting armies there on the front?! What impetus has this produced in all nations, that everywhere now there is also this second invisible army to assist with the immense work there is to do!

I do not want to speak of what is being done on the battlefields themselves. We simply cannot in any way imagine what a soldier has to do to carry out his duty unhesitatingly, in all circumstances, face to face with the enemy. Millions now unfalteringly *fulfill* this duty to the point of bitter death. What immense energy is deployed here, and what would it have taken to bring this energy to bear on the long, enduring task of producing peace! We should also think of how much love and helpfulness have already been brought to life through this war. Many a closed purse has now suddenly opened, many lazy hands have now suddenly become active for others. People now feel they are obligated to one another. We must "bear one another's burdens" (cf. Gal. 6:2), to the best of our ability; we must act as brothers and sisters toward each other.

And is not this *unity* in the nations and states that has now come about something rather marvelous? Think how Germany itself, how France also, was earlier torn apart by many petty conflicts of parties, classes, and confessions, and what kind of endless and distressing conflict obtained between the diverse groups of people that are united in our neighboring land of Austria! England faced an imminent civil war, with British pitted against British, for in Ireland in a few weeks' time rifles and guns would have gone off. Then the war came. And it came in a remarkable way everywhere, first as a harbinger of peace. Disputes were ended; the German emperor declared, "I know no parties any longer"; and the socialists held out their hand to him in a solemn pledge of loyalty. In France friends of the Roman Catholic Church and freethinkers shook hands: love of country trumped everything else! The people of Ulster (or Northern Ireland)[5] placed their weapons intended for insurrection at the disposal of the British government. Germans, Slavs, and Hungarian Austrians unite with one another at the frontier. Even Russia, the land of the greatest contrasts, contrary to all expectations is united through the war. It is the same spectacle everywhere: "A band of brothers true we swear to be, never to part in danger or in death!"[6]

Is not all this rather *remarkable*? If all these nations find themselves in a "Sunday best" mood, must we not understand this phenomenon, as I said, in the sense that in all seriousness they see the war as a revelation of God, and as a revelation not at all of divine judgment. but of God's goodwill toward humanity? Must we ourselves not admit that the war has surprisingly conjured up many good and even divine things among people? Yes, we certainly acknowledge this, and we are also completely convinced that all the loyalty and love, all the selflessness and fearlessness, all the heroism and the sense of brotherhood and sisterhood that is now shown so luminously far and wide are certainly not in vain. Everything that is good still comes from God; so this whole awakening is also certainly needed for the coming of God's kingdom, even if it is completely different than human beings envision it. Woe to us, if we now stand indifferently aside, selfishly pursuing our own concerns! Oh, we do not want to harden our hearts against the fine new spirit that now pervades all countries and nations. We want to be part of the great awakening that has come over them. We want to "rejoice with those who rejoice" (cf. Rom. 12:15), whenever there is really something to rejoice about.

However! My friends, this must now be quite clear to every one of us—and hopefully it has become perfectly clear to everyone in the long time in which we have been able to reflect on the war—that as Swiss and as Christians we have to place a great "However!" over it all. For the truth is that we must see the events very, very differently than the warring nations. We have to view these good, divine character traits in humanity that are now evident in *all* nations, not just in a single people. If we lift up a current newspaper from Germany, we see there how the good qualities of German soldiers, indeed, the qualities of the German people, are praised to the skies and defended against every reproach; but of the enemies of Germany we read that they are simply "this world with devils filled," of which Luther sang in his hymn "A Mighty Fortress." This is what one of the most erudite men in the whole of Germany, a Marburg professor, actually wrote! (Professor Natorp, article in the *Christliche Welt*, August 1914).[7] This is how they see the other side. There is nothing but treachery, cowardice, and vulgarity everywhere! And this is exactly how in almost the same terms the French often judge the Germans. And so it goes back and forth in the whole warring world. Invectives are hurled.

We cannot go along with that, and we refuse to go along with it. We rejoice in all the great and uplifting things that this war fosters at present, but we must guard immediately against being deceived by what every nation and every party now seems to think: "*We* alone are truly patriotic and enthusiastic about our duty" or "*we* alone can be heroic and loyal." But when it concerns the enemy, everything that is a reason for boasting is dragged through the mud.

Oh, how simple it would be if on the one side we had nothing but heroes of light and truth, and on the other nothing but devils and villains! Then we would know which side to take. But that's just it: we have to see a great deal of good, spirit, and strength on both sides. We have no other option, because we must see both sides, indeed all sides. And that is exactly what our heart apprehends, namely, that we do not see angels pitted against devils, but, instead, admirable, conscientious, highly gifted individuals contending against one another. These are persons who want and do good in many ways, not cooperatively but *against each other*.

This is the dreadful riddle of war that prevents us, that simply restrains us from joining in with enthusiasm and with hate on one side, and that compels us to withhold our admiration for the good and the divine qualities that undoubtedly take human shape today. All the good in human beings is focused today on being against, rather than for one another! It is hatred that has roused them from the sleep of apathy and selfishness! War is the bait that has coaxed out of the nations all the hidden powers and spirits that now shine so brightly! Everywhere these good intentions and deeds in which we would so gladly rejoice must combine to serve nothing except mutual murder, the most awful work of destruction.

What kind of *ghastly, hellish powers* they must be, that were able with one blow to lure out all the forces of good, and with one and the same blow put them in the service of evil! They must be dreadful, monstrous powers, for they have succeeded when in times of peace all good influences, all preaching of the gospel, and all educational endeavors have not succeeded in summoning a comparable life, zeal, and creativity. Yes, they are hellish powers: for they have summoned not blessings but curses. It reminds one of how in the past Balak, the king of the Moabites, availed himself of the services of the prophet Baalam to curse the people of Israel (see Num. 22–24)! So now all that is good, noble, and excellent in people must stand completely in the service of evil. That is simply the ghastly thing about war. All love of one's country that has now gushed forth so immediately and splendidly has its goal and its zenith in this: to do battle with every available means against other people's homelands. All the fervor, loyalty, and sense of duty with which countless individuals are imbued must serve only the purpose of killing other individuals who are motivated by the same feelings, albeit they are expressed in a different language.

Think of the men and women of *scholarship* and of science. They actually belong to all nations and until now were engaged in joint work and research devoted to the good of all humankind. This has ceased. They have placed their scholarship and their literary work, their hearts and their minds, in the service of the conflict, and now mutual accusations and recriminations are hurled back and forth across borders and even across the sea. One no longer recognizes them; their voices so tremble with violent emotion and bias. "How you are fallen O Day Star, son of Dawn!" (Isa. 14:12 NRSV).

There are also the members of *social democracy*. For decades they have spoken against war and for peace among the nations, and they did so with sacred seriousness. Then the war came, and it was stronger than they were, and it swept them up in its current. Perhaps you still recall how it was reported at the outset that one of them, Dr. Liebknecht[8] in Berlin, refused military service, was shot, and became a martyr for his convictions. It soon turned out to be a deception. He and all the others had no intention at all of swimming against the stream. Soon afterwards, Dr. L. Frank,[9] one of their main and best party leaders, was one of the first to die in action. He died not for peace and socialism; he died not for his convictions, but for the war that he had opposed all his life. And thousands of his like-minded supporters have died with him. There are, for the time being, no more socialists in Germany who hate the war, rather, only Germans who hate the French and the Russians. "How you are fallen O Day Star, son of Dawn!" (Isa. 14:12 NRSV).

And then there are the leaders of the Christian *churches*, Catholic and Protestant. They have spoken, Sunday by Sunday, of Jesus, of that man who at the moment when it was the most just thing to do told his disciple, "Put your sword in its sheath!" (John 18:11). These church leaders have spoken of the God who makes the sun shine on the good and the evil and lets the rain fall on the just and the unjust (Matt. 5:45). And they were truly serious about it. And now? Now the Cardinal Archbishop Amette, standing in front of the door of Notre Dame Cathedral in Paris, delivers a fiery address to the nation in which he calls for a war against the Germans and concludes with the words, "Long live God, long live the church, and long live France!"[10] Now thousands of French Catholic priests are going as soldiers and officers to the front, and they surpass all others in their zeal to fight.

Now an outstanding German Christian declares in all seriousness that for the time being, for Germans, the gospel of hate must take precedence over the gospel of love.[11] Now almost every German church periodical is full of war cries and self-assurance. A large gathering of the Friends of the Foreign Mission took place in Berlin and devoted a whole evening to dragging Englishmen before the judgment seat of God.[12] A distinguished French pastor addressed a proposal to Kaiser Wilhelm's court preacher that the two might mutually sign an exhortation for the humane conduct of war and direct it to the warring armies. The court preacher refused to sign, giving as a reason that he did not want to leave the slightest suggestion that German soldiers needed such an exhortation, since from the highest general down to the lowliest private, nothing was to be expected of them except the best behavior imaginable in their conduct of war. Preferably, one should exhort the French, the Belgians, and the Russians to behave properly.[13]

A number of the best-known churchmen of Germany, two of whom were my dearest teachers, have issued an appeal "To Evangelical Christians Abroad."[14] It is full of accusations and excuses on its own behalf. Repentance is mentioned only once in the appeal, when it is said that Germans also need to repent. But then it is immediately suggested that they have already repented, and all guilt is solemnly laid on the enemies' shoulders, on the enemy alone. So even from the ranks of Christians, from the ranks of *earnest and pious* Christians, they have become soldiers. "How you are fallen O Day Star, son of Dawn!" (Isa. 14:12 NRSV).

What sort of powers are these that have managed to pervert the good so completely and are put in the service of evil? As you can see, my friends, these are the "*angels, principalities, and powers*" of which Paul has spoken. On another occasion he called them the "spirits that rule in the air" (see Eph. 2:2). We understand, don't we? There are evil powers in the world between heaven and earth, between God and human beings. They are powers of folly, darkness, and destruction. They exert a powerful influence upon humanity that we experience daily in our hearts and lives. They are permitted to exert this influence because God has given them the freedom to do so. In the difficult struggle against them, God's kingdom will be established. We know nothing about them except that we have to struggle with them and overcome them. For they obstruct the access of men and women to God. They are the enemies of love and truth. They will not the kingdom of God but the kingdom of folly and malice. They sow lies, injustice, and violence. Their great strength is to work under the guise of good. They rarely present themselves as they really are; they are disguised almost always as messengers of God. They whisper in the ear, "People must do evil, so that good will come out of it." They inspire people to do good, and thereby they use them for their evil purposes. And when they triumph over them, they then end up deep in the night of sin and error, deep in a hell that they create for themselves.

Those are the evil powers that are *now at work*. Not only now, but for a long time, indeed always—but now their activity has once again come to light. One of the best sentiments of humanity is its love of home, nation, and homeland, and also of the state, the instrument of order on earth and the greatest achievement of human beings. But the powers have seized both and transformed them into a work of devilry. They have breathed lies into the state, insinuating that it must create space for itself, that it must prevail, and by cunning and force crush so that it can live. This is its right, even its obligation: namely, to expand at the expense of others. And men and women have heeded these powers instead of listening to the unerring voice of conscience and the gospel of God. And now they rule over men and women, over the world. Oh, how these evil powers now laugh and exult over the blood-drenched fields of battle, over the devastated cities and villages, over the countless graves, over the writing desks of scholars where untiring accusations and excuses are composed, and over the churches in which the gospel of hate is preached in "good conscience"!

And they are allowed to triumph, because none of the warring nations recognizes them for what they are. They all "know not what they do" (see Luke 23:34). They are in such captivity that they actually have a good conscience about their actions. They exclaim, "God wills it!" and "God is with us!"; and they are deadly serious about it. They actually perform deeds of the purest spirit of sacrifice, and thereby they rush headlong ever more deeply into the night of a dreadful confusion from which only new sin and new misfortune can continue to arise!

Could we not also become *confused* about this sorry spectacle and begin to doubt God, to doubt all truth and righteousness, to doubt whether love is really the greatest and strongest thing in the world? Are not the evil "angels, principalities, and powers" much, much greater and stronger? Is not all the divine goodness and grace simply a hypocritical pretext that these evil powers employ in order to drive human beings more deeply and more inevitably into discord, death, and hell? Is this not a weapon that the devil presses into their hand, and that even now they use, as they make use of their guns and rifles and their biting words? When we now see *how* strong they are, *so* strong that they are even able, completely and without resistance, to put into their service the divine goodness and grace, is not everything obscured for us, are we not cut off from everything that stands *above* these evil powers?

My friends, now we may and must say with the apostle Paul, "I am convinced that *nothing can separate us* from the love of God in Christ Jesus, our Lord. Nothing, neither angels nor principalities nor powers, neither things present nor things to come, neither height nor depth, nor any other creature." *Jesus* is now for us the sure, shining point of light in the midst of the dark world. In him we trust. To him we look. From him to us flow powers that are stronger than the powers of evil. He too has battled with them. They also presented themselves before him disguised in the dissembling form of truth and righteousness.

He too was in the midst of the deepest night. The "angels, principalities, and powers" had taken captive all those around him, even the best, even his dearest friends. But not Jesus himself. He has not stopped shining. Good Friday is followed by Easter. A worldwide Good Friday has now dawned. But it is not able to kill the spirit of Jesus. He *continues to live* in those who do not let themselves be taken captive by the spirits that rule in the air; he lives in those who recognize falsehood and injustice and do not let themselves be deceived by the most beautiful disguise. They can remain in a living communion with the love of God. They can remain pure in this suffocating air of falsehood and injustice that surrounds us. They know that the laws of God are unconditionally valid and that this God is "not a God of confusion but of peace" (1 Cor. 14:33). But they also know that God's laws permeate and prevail over everything. It will not help the evil one at all that he has roused and used the good for his blasphemous purpose.

We have already recalled that the good, the true good that is now manifested through the war, cannot be lost. This good will one day overcome evil through its own power, through the power of God that is in it. All the loyalty and love, all the great intentions and holy resolves that have come to life through the war, will rebel one day against the shameful chains in which they now still lie. They will make themselves felt again in the Christian churches, among the socialists, among the educated and profound thinkers in all countries, and they will bitterly repent like Peter that they have denied their Lord (see Matt. 26:69–75). The nations' peoples will awaken from the nightmare that they are now experiencing. "Why are we all against one another, rather than for one another?" they will ask themselves. Why are we in the service of the sinister powers of war instead of in the service of God, who is still the Father of all great and good things, and hence in the service of brothers and sisters, of all brothers and sisters?

Oh, this awakening will come one day; we may be completely certain of that. How did it work out at that time with the prophet Baalam, when at the order of a foreign ruler he had to curse Israel? He had to, it is true, but he could not. He finally had to bless and bless repeatedly instead of cursing. May we not take this to be a promise? That one day hence humanity, through the power of God that works in it, will come to the realization that it can by no means submit any longer to the lordship of angels, principalities, and powers, that it can no longer do what until then it repeatedly wanted, that is, to do evil. A constraint is placed, as it were, upon human beings: to bless rather than to curse, to love rather than to hate. This occurs only when we are always close to human beings who want to feel and be conscious of the quiet, deep effect of Jesus, his effect on the heart and conscience. Yes, with men and women who let themselves receive the living hope from God that God will indeed one day be master—yes, the confidence that God *is* already secretly master over the forces of evil, even though our eyes may not be able to detect it.

Do we belong with these men and women? God has made it so easy for us to belong, since God has let us be born as those who belong to a land that until now has not been dragged into the battle of the spirits and powers. The freedom to look above to behold the God of love will not be denied us. But indeed I still do not know whether we actually belong with the men and women who can now affirm, "I am *certain* that nothing can separate us from God!" It is a tremendous thing in such a time as this to be able to say, "I am certain!" We do not want to boast of being something that perhaps we are not. But we will pray to God that we become joyful citizens of God's future world.

Amen.

October 25, 1914

Sermon at Safenwil

Psalm 119:142: Your righteousness is an everlasting righteousness. (NRSV)

Dear Friends!

At the outset of the present war a remarkable statement was made. In an August 4 [1914] session of the *Reichstag*, the German parliament, the chancellor,[1] the kaiser's highest official, told the nation's representatives how matters had developed. He spoke on the subject of Belgium. In order to take the nearest way to the northwestern part of France, the German troops had already entered this neutral kingdom, which was protected by a treaty signed by all the major powers. When he came to speak about it, the German chancellor said, "*Necessity knows no law!* We are now violating international law. Belgium is right to protest this action, but we cannot do otherwise, and we will endeavor to rectify this injustice as soon as the objective we have in mind is achieved."

Necessity knows no law! The slogan had the effect of a fire alarm. It really took this difficult, critical time, this time in which human beings repeatedly reveal themselves for what they really are, to elicit this admission or confession. Countless persons pricked up their ears when this word was uttered. It was a hard, indigestible mouthful. It was like a huge rockslide boulder thrown on a lovely green meadow.

Necessity knows no law! Is it really so? We had to ponder this, and we shouldn't have disposed of it too quickly. Again and again we need to return to it. If we could only give the phrase a presentable countenance! Some have made it easy for themselves: "He's right!" they've said. "It's the end that matters, no matter whether through legitimate or illegitimate means. If it's beneficial, all such considerations are of no concern." But only a very small minority dared to speak like this, only individuals with a completely constricted conscience. The word "injustice" has disquieted many persons. "We have acted unjustly"—they do not want this left dangling. Indeed, this cannot be, this may not be. A renowned teacher [Adolf von Harnack] has distorted things as follows: There are life situations when it's obligatory to do what helps oneself. When he fled from Saul, did not David take the bread of the presence from the table of the Lord and fortify himself with it, contrary to the wording of the law (see 1 Sam. 21:2–7)? In such situations injustice is no longer injustice but justice, and the German chancellor should not have used the odious word "unjust." But that justification does not satisfy everyone.

Understandably, given this justification, we have the feeling of the ground giving way under our feet. What then is justice? What is injustice? Is it really quite acceptable in certain emergencies to act unjustly? Still others take refuge in another point of view and assert, "If *we* had not invaded that peaceful neutral country, others would have done so. We had to act unjustly in order to prevent them from unjust action. and so in fact we acted justly." One can indeed be anxious as to how long one's conscience could rest content with such a situation. I do not address all of these matters to get involved in a dispute. All explanations and arguments that we have heard on this score always say basically one thing: the circumstances were such that we had to disregard the treaty signed by Germany as simply a scrap of paper. In the situation in which we found ourselves, we could not recognize any law, not even our own given word.

Necessity knows no law! However one might understand and excuse it, the German empire has behaved vis-à-vis Belgium in accordance with this rule. The chancellor is an honest, upright man, to whom the highest respect must be accorded, in that he quite openly expressed this rule, and was not especially fearful of the use of the word "unjust." Consequently, he actually expressed nothing at all except the essence and rule of war—yes, not only of war but of human nature, that is, of the unredeemed world. And hence his statement deserves our closer attention.

We have just as little explanation for all the other *events on the outside* that have so upset and shaken us now for three months as for the German incursion into Belgium—and that is that necessity knows no law! This is the great, the sole explanation of everything that happens in war. In their fury over the incursion, the Belgians are seizing every available weapon and conducting a defensive campaign that is degenerating into the most horrible massacre. What else does one expect? Necessity knows no law! The Germans promulgate this rule of war: any person of the country's population caught with a weapon in hand will be shot immediately. Of course, the

Germans must defend themselves against their enraged adversaries. The rule is harsh but necessary; necessity simply knows no law. On the tower of the Rheims Cathedral is an enemy observation post. We are terribly sorry about the magnificent church, but we must shell it. Necessity knows no law. And with the same justification of necessity, like the English, the French summon their black and brown auxiliary troops to Europe—wild, cruel men about whom it can only be said, "Woe, if they are let loose!"[2] Come whatever help there may be, circumstances constrain us not to refuse any help that may be of use to us.

Necessity knows no law. And so on and on, this is the conviction that circulates on all sides. It serves as the final excuse or proof everywhere: we must, we must, we have to be hard-hearted, cruel, ruthless, cunning. With regard to war, the customary concepts of good and evil don't suffice. Here one has to do many things that would not otherwise be within the range of possibility. In war, one asks only what can secure victory and hence who is the more powerful. And of course, the more powerful one is always right.

What shall we actually say to the contrary? I think there is really nothing at all that can be said against it. This is actually so because now, once there is war, in most cases human beings must behave as we see them behaving. On account of this, it is pointless to accuse nations and individuals now being so convulsed in every way with rage against one another. And now especially it is even more pointless perhaps to condemn a nation or a party particularly for its conduct of war. Besides, one can be very passionate in lecturing one or the other side but then fail completely to see what is truly at the heart of the matter. War occurs, and now everyone simply does what has to be done in order to succeed—the one in a somewhat more civilized manner, the other in a somewhat less; the one more roughly, the other more refined. But all are, without exception, under the same constraint to perpetrate injustice; all find themselves without exception in the necessity that knows no law. The chancellor is quite right: when one must defend oneself and when one must win, of what value is a scrap of paper, even when it is the finest treaty with one's signature written on it? And all the others are also right: of what value are all considerations and second thoughts, once war has occurred? Once again, we must be grateful to this man for having so publicly expressed the fact that if the necessity exists, if a nation or an army is in this situation, then injustice simply becomes justice. True justice then has to be postponed to a later time.

And now what is striking is that this rule is certainly valid, not only for princes and statesmen, for nations and armies at war, but for *human life in general.* The German attack on neutral Belgium, the whole ruthless injustice of war after all, is not at all really something new, unique, or special. It is simply a revelation that should open our eyes to the kind of human beings we really are, to the world, to ourselves. We live, of course, under the imperative of decency, duty, conscience—that is, under the commandments of God. We know them. We accept them as a matter of custom. But very clearly, as we know without exception, we keep them only to a certain extent. If circumstances arise and if they create the "necessity," we know them no longer.

Let us consider something quite simple: telling the truth. We know this is right! From childhood we know how to act in this regard. None of us wants to be a liar! But now a situation arises, a wholly special situation, when I really cannot tell the truth. "They don't really need to know what they are now asking me!" "How would they regard me if I told them how it is in reality?" "What would ensue if I now said quite openly and transparently what I know?" Hence, a pretext quickly arises, something small, just a little distorted, something omitted or something added, a yes qualified . . . you've lied! Oh, how loathsome to call it that! I had no alternative; I really had to be somewhat evasive. Yes, it wasn't quite the right thing to do. Anyway, one cannot always be so scrupulous. Necessity knows no law, and I was compelled by necessity. Note this, in just war or even unjust war, in the midst of peace, in the thick of our daily life . . . it happens every day, doesn't it?

Take, for example, this dictate of duty: to be respectful of one another, not to seek one's advantage at another's expense. It's perfectly obvious! Do we not all boast, "I take care of myself and am careful not to harm anyone"? Oh, how nice this would be! But what if necessity now enters the picture? If, for example, the occasion presents itself to make a favorable business deal—and admittedly, another or many others get a bad deal, yet isn't it true that business is business? We cannot, for instance, be so meticulous about it, for where would we be if we wanted to be so precise about the matter? The fact is that there are exceptions, and this *is* an exception that has suddenly intervened. Necessity knows no law!

Take another example, a dictate of justice: pay what you owe! Of course I do that. Who can contest it, who can prove anything different? Really? How then do you stand with regard to the taxes that you owe the state or the local community? Yes, indeed that is something different, isn't it? Here again is also a "necessity." "As a rule, I have enough to pay; the taxes are far too high, and they assessed me unfairly the last time, and there are so many others around who for a long time don't pay nearly half enough and . . . and . . . and . . ." Here we have reason enough, haven't we, to prove that I must make an exception here, definitely in this case; for once, injustice must be justice. How then can one really say that this amounts to deceit, robbery of the public purse? I will not listen to such frightful words. Besides, I am honest and just through and through, but everything has its limits, and necessity knows no law.

My friends, what I have just cited here are undoubtedly clear, plain duties—matters that are self-evident. If we act *in this way* in relation to them, if *in such matters* we are more than ready to replace justice with a right born out of necessity, or a right born out of war when this is definitely injustice, how then will it now fare with the finer spiritual commandments, those mandates declared to us through the gospel that should be dear to us, such as the obligation of faithfulness to our vocation, or the pursuit of peace, or forgiveness, or of being charitable, or of sacrifice and the capacity for self-denial? Do we not all know a whole series of commandments toward which, so to speak, we are always in a situation of necessity, commandments of which we indeed have a distant knowledge, of which we remind ourselves again from time to time and with which perhaps we took little steps toward accomplishing at one time, but which we constantly postpone to another day: right now, this is not for me. At this time they are of no use to me. Love? Peace? Offering myself and sacrificing? Yes, that's fine and good, but right now I *must* do the opposite. Later perhaps, some another time, I would like to be reminded of them again. Now is an emergency. Necessity knows no law! There is certainly no one among us who has not had to confess, "This is the way I have acted many, many times in the past. This is the way I act time and again in the present. I constantly promote 'war right,' 'necessity right,' injustice, instead of justice."

And like our individual lives, all our relationships and states of affairs are totally and forever subject to the rule: necessity knows no law. Is not our common life in the time of peace also a concealed war, laboriously kept within certain limits by means of law and its enforcement by police? Doesn't this also mean that whoever has power and whoever gains it is in the position of being right when it really matters? How is it that so many get the short end of the stick all their lives? How is it that those who count also command in both the state and the local community? How is it that we allow so much public harm in our national life to take its course simply with a feeling of regret and a shrug of the shoulders, but without vigorously doing anything to remove it? Yes, how does this come about? The reason we give is always the same: things cannot be changed; it must be so; we can't do a thing about it! The same reason is always given: circumstances do not permit anything else. For the time being right cannot be right. Necessity knows no law!

What shall we actually say to the contrary? Again I have to answer that we cannot say anything against it, for it is simply the case. This is the way of the world, this is the way of human nature; and it is good that now, as a result of the war, it is even fittingly painted in large letters on the wall that it is so.

Even those with the poorest eyesight have to notice and grasp it. Notice and grasp what? That it cannot really *be* otherwise, that we lie and steal and kill, that we are unfeeling, cruel, cowardly, and faithless, that we *must* act unjustly if necessity simply requires it. It drives us irresistibly to injustice. We cannot help it. We can only let it happen and shrug our shoulders. We feel sorry, but we can't help it! So we *must* speak as the Germans did, when their cannons thundered in front of the Lüttich [Liège] fortress.[3]

We must. Yes, but then what is really the *necessity* that compels us so that we must? The circumstances, we say, the situation, the special case are what require us to do evil against our better judgment and intent. Exactly, these are the conditions once they come into play. But from what do they arise? Do they fall from the sky like a meteorite? Does the necessity that produces the evil come out of the blue, suddenly leaving us powerless to do anything about it? Is it, for example, written in the stars that in the year 1914 Germany would have the whole world as its enemy and would need to dig its way out of its situation, whatever the cost? Is all the other necessity that now daily causes the injustice of war perhaps based on a natural law? Did God ordain that nations should now fear and hate and hence rage against one another? And all the necessity, the necessity that with its unavoidable violence constantly, day in and day out, causes injustice and sin and unhappiness in the mighty and lowly—is this necessity perhaps inevitable? Does distrust need to exist, the distrust with which we face one another and from which the lie follows instantly and unavoidably? Must there be selfishness that dictates to us, "Charity begins at home [literally, "you yourself are your own neighbor"]; look after yourself first, and as far as others are concerned, let them take their chance"? Does the worship of mammon have to exist, and when it entices us, does it compel our consciences to play nasty tricks on another person for the sake of our precious bankbook? Must all of this amount to the sort of things that allow us to disregard the clear mandates of the gospel: Oh, not this! No, I cannot do that now! I may try later? Must our whole life and our life together have to be such a race, such a struggle of all against all, as in fact it now is, and, once it becomes such, inevitably cause wrongs a thousandfold? Yes, where there is necessity, there of course arise injustice and misfortune, and then, in great and in small matters, we must think badly, speak badly, act badly. But I ask, is necessity inevitable?

What then is this necessity that produces injustice? My friends, this necessity is *not something that comes from outside* the person. This necessity does not arise from the external nature of human beings. This necessity does not originate from the fact that we must eat and drink and live, or from the fact that we are imperfect, limited human beings and definitely not angels. This necessity does not have its basis in circumstances, as one expresses it nicely in order to excuse a person (and one certainly does not realize how deeply one humiliates a person with this excuse). It's an excuse that is refuted by our conscience and by Jesus.

Inevitably and insistently our *conscience* tells us that even in the direst predicament, even in the most inconvenient conditions and circumstances, right remains right and wrong remains wrong, and the two cannot be mixed and confused. I would almost like to say that this is something marvelous. I almost want to speak of the divine aspect of the German chancellor's address, namely, that at the very moment when he excused Germany's perpetrated injustice by attributing it to necessity, to the situation in which it found itself, he still had to admit that it *is*, however, an injustice! *Then* the angels in heaven rejoiced! He showed thereby that God is mightier than the devil and holds humanity by the hand, however much humanity opposes God! And this voice of conscience by which God holds us fast speaks in all of us. We may advance a thousand reasons and excuses; we may say continually, "I must; this and that external circumstances compel me to act unjustly." Conscience simply does not give us the right. It tells us, in spite of ourselves, time after time: you must not do it; the external circumstances could not compel you, if you did not want to yield; the necessity that compels you is different, and you know very well which is right!

Still more powerfully than our conscience, *Jesus* contradicts us. Jesus shows us that our conscience does not delude us with a beautiful but impossible dream. Jesus was a man of flesh and bone as we are. He also had to eat and drink and live as we do. He lived in the midst of circumstances, in the conditions of this imperfect, limited world. He also knew what the difficulties and obstacles of life are. Indeed, he knew even more about these than do all of us. But for him the necessity did not exist, the necessity that does not care to know any law, the necessity that produces injustice and misfortune, the necessity that compels us to be wicked. If we focus on him, what our conscience already tells us will be confirmed in the most powerful way: this necessity is not outside of us; it cannot lie in the circumstances.

The necessity that produces injustice exists within us. It is not in the external but in the spiritual condition of human beings. So it is not an inevitable necessity; rather, the guilt is ours. If we were spiritually different persons, then there would also be no necessity. Then necessity could not produce injustice. Then there would be neither war nor deceit, neither robbery nor cowardice.

The necessity that produces injustice is our righteousness, which is not the righteousness of God or eternal righteousness. Our righteousness is the goodwill in us. It is truly wholly in us. It is in every person. No one actually wills injustice, war, and falsehood. In his or her innermost being every person really wills good, peace, and truth. But this goodwill is not effective. It does not govern us. It ventures forth from time to time to influence us, a little here, a little there; but it does not determine us. It does not determine our personal life, our life together, or consequently the life of nations. Alongside the goodwill in us that would like to be a determining power are other forces in us, that is, within humankind: selfishness, mistrust, mammon, vanity, the lust for power, stupidity, and wickedness. And now the goodwill in us says to these: you really should not exist; I should really defeat you, but you are too strong for me, and anyway you also have a right to exist. So peace be with you; I want to let you have a place alongside me.

Hence, both are in us: a little goodwill and much, much of the powers of evil. And so it happens that time and again, without letup, indeed with regret and groaning, we commit injustice upon injustice and speak falsehood, we take advantage of one another, we hate one another and must wage war against one another. The goodwill in us has told the bad will, you also have your assured right to exist, and on that account, at certain countless points, evil then has free rein in our lives. In this regard it is not that we have the feeling of being bad. Rather, we console ourselves that there is definitely still much good in us and that this good will be done. But at the same time we do not notice how against our will, and yet with our will, we always produce new injustice, new distress. This is our righteousness. Such a will is good, but it is one that does not act seriously. This righteousness of ours, which has the appearance of righteousness, is our necessity.

God's righteousness is *an eternal righteousness*. Moreover, in God is goodwill. But solely goodwill. God's goodwill rules and determines; alongside it, nothing else may prevail. The powers of evil are not too mighty for God. God gives them no right; God overcomes them. Where God is, evil cannot break loose. God is light, and in God is no darkness at all (1 John 1:5). God does not know necessity, God knows nothing of indecisiveness, inactivity, half measures, and hence God's commandments hold good. God wills and God can, because God wills seriously.

My friends, our necessity is *not inevitable*. It must not be so that over and over again injustice and suffering proceed from the false state of our inner being. It does not have to be so that our world is a world of lies and of wars. Our uncertain, hypocritical, and hence ineffective righteousness stands over against the righteousness of God, the eternal righteousness. Our conscience and Jesus not only rebuke us or reveal our condition to us; they also point us in the direction beyond these to the righteousness of God. "Happy are they who hunger and thirst after this righteousness" (see Matt. 5:6)! Happy are they who are awakened, who are dissatisfied with the half-righteousness of humans and the righteousness of the world. Happy are they who may have caught a glimpse of what they can do beyond these in God's world! Something of this world of God, something of God's righteousness, now lives in them. They see beyond the necessity under which we all suffer. They know that the compulsion to evil is not unbreakable. Day by day they become freer from it. They believe that there is complete freedom for us and for our poor world. Freedom will be here when the goodwill in us will become serious, as serious as it is in God. In God and through God our freedom and our true righteousness will be established,

Amen.

November 1, 1914 (Reformation Sunday)

Sermon at Safenwil[1]

John 17:20–21: I pray . . . that they may all be one; even as you, Father, are in me, and I in you, that they also may be in us, so that the world may believe that you have sent me.

Dear Friends!

On this Reformation Sunday, following established practice, we reflect about what the Reformation of almost four hundred years ago brought us. But our thoughts on this occasion cannot proceed along the same lines as in other times.

Now our thoughts will not at all take the old familiar paths, either today or some other time, either here in church or in our everyday lives. Hence, do I particularly still need to remind you that God has new things now to say to us—that is, ancient, eternal truths in a wholly new way—and that we also must prepare ourselves inwardly to be obedient to God? Yes, dear friends, I need to remind you. At the present time, it seems that many of us are already sick and tired of thinking about the war. You now would like to hear again something different in the sermon. You believe that "the honorable pastor should now get back again to the Bible."[2]

I feel sorry for those who can think and speak like this. Such thoughts are a sign of great superficiality—one could even add, of great stubbornness. What in the world shall God do with us? In truth, God has let us experience this great, strange time. It's a vintage time, a time of judgment, but also a time of grace, as perhaps has never yet occurred. The former world in which we lived has been shaken to its very foundations. Again, people have gone to the very limit of their nature and recognize with horror where they have arrived. We are all urgently questioned, "Where do our souls have their true dwelling place, here in this world or in God's world?" God has graciously placed a wide-open Bible before us. Moses and the prophets begin to speak again, as if they were in our very midst. The bright image of Jesus Christ shines in the dark world, as we have never yet seen it shine, and his apostles witness and point us to him: "In no other is there salvation" (Acts 4:12)! But after a brief time of excitement and attention, apparently we've already had enough; now we would again like to hear something other than "about the war"; we long "to get back again to the Bible."

What does that mean? I believe that we harbor a fear of the real Bible, of God's book, that is, of the Bible as the living Word of God, a revelation of God's judgment and grace. We have a fear of the Bible, which is "a sword dividing our thoughts" (see Heb. 4:12), "a hammer which breaks the rock in pieces" (Jer. 23:29), and "a spring flowing with the water of life for those who truly thirst" (see Rev. 22:17). Or possibly, do we notice nothing of how God drives us to the real Bible through the events of this time? Do you seriously think we are speaking here of the war just for amusement's sake, in order to "gain attention," as you say? Hence, are all the terrible and fearful things that we experience something so superficial, so indifferent, that we want to turn the page as quickly as a child does with a picture book?

Do we actually believe that the Word of God is a sort of good old devotional self-help book and that we assemble here for a pious pastime? I cannot hope to dissuade anyone who in spite of everything now still thinks and feels like this. I can only say once more: I feel sorry for those who could think and feel like this, who even now are incapable of seeing beyond the narrow hedge of their previous accustomed way of thinking. One of these days we should pluck up enough courage to see and to hear God as God actually is and speaks, and not as we would like to see and hear God. One of these days, we should venture to go in a new direction with our thoughts, a direction God himself now shows, even though we are still accustomed to the old path. What shall God do with us then, if now we willfully and indolently give up and do not want to be awakened?

The events of our time also constrain us to think of the *Reformation* in a different way now than we did in former years. The Reformation was a war of opposing spirits, and it resulted in a deep division of the Christian world. And when we were pleased to be an evangelical people, heirs of the Reformation, we could not help thinking, above all, of this conflict, of this divorce; thinking of the struggle for free access to the pure gospel, certain comfort for the troubled conscience, and a clear and unadorned religion. Like booty from a successful battle, these Reformation-achieved goods became ours.

Yet there is the divorce, and we must think about it, the division between Catholic and Protestant Christianity and being. As best we can, we have to guard against reviving something of the old fierce enmity that once existed between this and the other side. We searched for our Protestant distinctives, rejoicing gratefully in them, without attacking the other side. And yet this was not possible except by feeling ourselves in this day to be opposed to Catholic Christians. We had to emphasize the distinctives of our faith and, along with that, what separates us from them. We had to, if not erect walls, at least to draw boundary lines. What was essential and distinctive for us on Reformation Sunday was nevertheless always the recognition and confession: we stand here, and they stand over there!

It seems to me our thoughts today must proceed in a different direction. We also think today with heartfelt gratitude for all the things we have been given through the Reformation, and we would not like to give up one iota of that legacy. We are also thoroughly familiar today with the boundaries that divide us from Catholics. But we know something quite different today, something that is greater and more important to us than these dividing lines. We hear the voice of Jesus, the voice of him who sees his followers in the midst of a world full of sin and guilt, a world so dark and so hostile, where they are so weak and helpless, and who now prays for them: "I pray *that they may all be one; even as you, Father, are in me, and I in you, that they also may be in us, that the world may believe that you have sent me.*" If we want to think of Catholics and our relation to them, then we must think today of this prayer of Jesus.

At present, we live in a world that does not believe that Christ is sent by God. Yes, it seems to believe in Jesus. It builds churches in his name. It reveres his cross. It calls itself by his name. But in deed and in truth, it has rejected the prince of peace. It considers it a matter of foolishness that there could be a truly inclusive community of love, of love of all people; instead, it preaches hate and so inflames the passions of one nation against the other. It does not want to be great in spirit and greatest in service but great in the might that is based on power, and it prides itself that it is so dispassionate and free of fanaticism. It does not see that "righteousness exalts a people and a nation" (see Prov. 14:34) but boasts instead in its financial wealth, the number of its soldiers, and the size of its cannons. It supposes that the saber rather than the cross has the last word and proclaims, over against Jesus: "Those who want to follow me must assert themselves and defend themselves as best they can" (see Matt. 16:24). So the world has rejected Christ. And as a consequence the world is now at war.

And now we hear *Jesus' prayer*: "I pray, that they may all be one!" Jesus summons those who *believe in him*, that is, all those who have accepted with utmost seriousness his gospel of peace and righteousness, those who have taken to heart his call to the kingdom of God. Everything that is true, lovely, and just in individuals must now come to the surface. Where there is something of his spirit in humanity, it must now awaken. A decision is now essential. On the one side is humanity with its war; with its selfishness, which has given rise to the war; with its worldly being, which is selfish through and through. This is the humanity that makes itself so unhappy, that must suffer so terribly as a consequence of its unbelief, as a consequence of its falling away from the truth.

And on the other side is the gospel, God's power of truth, which entered the world in Christ. In it is victory over the world. In it is the redemption of the world. The world must learn to believe that Christ is sent by God; it must realize that the real life is the life of Jesus, not wealth or power. And the world will believe the gospel; it will realize and recognize, it will overcome and become redeemed. That is the mission that Jesus shared with and committed to his disciples. But if this is to happen, then his disciples, who have confessed him and who are dearly devoted to him, need to let their light shine (see Matt. 5:16). Then everything that comes from him will become active.

There is so much life from God hidden in human beings that has not yet been realized. There is so much Christian spirit there, which their foe or their work try to trace in totally wrong areas. There are so many Christians who are still waiting for the right motive and the task that corresponds to the deepest longing of their soul. In this grave time, Jesus summons all these latent powers. He shows them the enemy. He shows them the task. The world is full of foolishness, passion, and power. It has to be won for the God of love.

But for this to happen, the forces of good, that is, the divine forces, need above all to be *gathered*. "I pray that they may all be one." As Christ was one with God—that is, as in his human nature Christ was united with the eternal God and God was united with him—so men and women who have discerned the truth have to be one. To be one does not mean to be the same, but it means to understand, to appreciate each other, to feel, to think, and to work together with one another. One can be very different and still be one with the other. Furthermore, you know when we are one in God, God is the greatest friend of diversity, because God is a rich and not a stinting God. Evidently God wanted Christians to be divided into two great communities, the Catholic and the Protestant, to serve him and to discern the truth in distinctive ways. Yet God is a God of unity and always remains a God of unity. While God really wants his own to be separate communities, at the same time God does not want them to be cut off from each other. The one "who scattered Israel will gather him" (Jer. 31:10).

Today is a time in which God in a strongly audible voice calls to be gathered together all those who are serious about doing God's will, all to whom Jesus is dear. There is a time for everything; there was a time when it was necessary to say to the Catholics, "We are here; you are there." Perhaps such a time will come again, but that is not for us to know. Today is no such time. Today we face the blatant contrast: war or peace? selfishness or love? the world or God? And beside these, all smaller distinctions and contradictions, important as they might be otherwise, must take second place. Today we must conduct ourselves in accordance with our Master's saying: "Whoever is not against us, is for us" (Mark 9:40 NRSV). Today, Reformation Day, therefore, should remind us not about what separates us from Catholics but about what unites us with them.

We have many important things *in common* with Catholics, not only with individual well-meaning people among them, but indeed, thank God, with the pope in Rome. Above all, we share a common *guilt*. And that unites us in the strongest way with them at this time. For common guilt means common redemption. The two churches, Catholic as well as Protestant, have incurred great guilt in that they were not energetic enough in standing up for the truth, so that now in spite of them this misfortune has occurred. The present war, before all else, is a defeat of Christianity, and no confessional community can point the finger of blame at the other. Both confessions have been lacking in appropriate gravity vis-à-vis the spirit of the age. They have been content with the contradiction that the cross is set up in thousands of churches and yet is denied everywhere. They have blessed the secular order with pious words and practices, instead of raising a protest against it, as God's prophets have done. All too often Protestants and Catholics have reversed black into white and called evil good. Time and time again, they have become too much like the world. How priests and pastors have interpreted the Christian message, how they have made Christianity an easy matter for the bigwigs in the world, as they have made it an easy matter so many times for themselves! Think of how far they have distanced themselves from the clear confession of their Master: "My kingship is not of this world" (John 18:36)! "Blessed are the pure in heart, for they shall see God" (Matt. 5:8)! This is the common guilt of the Christian churches that we want to accept today and along with Catholics confess, "Father, we have sinned against heaven and before you; we are not worthy, we are all not worthy to be called your children" (cf. Luke 15:21)! Oh, if only in this critical time we Christians would all become one in this confession! Just think what sort of power must soon emanate from us into the needy world!

The second common thing that unites us with Catholics, and particularly at this time must unite us, is the power of *prayer*. On both sides we find ourselves in the same state of depression. Our Christianity has become too weak. The world has triumphed over us. But on both sides, we also know from where our help comes (cf. Ps. 121:1f.). "Out of the depths I cry to you,

O Lord" (Ps. 130:1)! If Christianity has become weak and hence has lost the battle against the powers of selfishness and arrogance, then it must now become strong again; and it will become strong through no other means than that on both sides we go into the depth and into the stillness, that we learn to pray in the way God wants his people to pray, God having now shown us how helpless we are without God.

What is now needed are men and women who know what it means to walk before God, submitting to God's will and letting God's light shine through them. From such men and women there proceeds unfailingly an impact on their surroundings. As soon as there are more such men and women, then there will arise, as it were, a fresh breeze, a breath of air in which toxic fumes could not arise, fumes from which hate and war spring. Thankfully there are already such men and women on both sides. They are the true harbingers and firstlings of a better future. On our side, our only worry is that the flock on their side is always greater! By the way, is it not noteworthy that the great saints of the Catholic Church, to whom today, All Saints' Day, is dedicated, and our Protestant reformers, in spite of all the differences, have this in common: they were all great people of prayer? There was something in the soul of the saints and of the reformers that made them one in God's eyes: namely, the pure flame of God's love of which their prayers were full. If we Christians on both sides would be one in this pure flame, then the world would soon take on a different appearance.

The third common thing between us and Catholics is the goal of our hope, the *kingdom of God*. We all believe that the proud spirit of the world will not have the last word. We see the folly and malevolence of human nature, but we are not content that it must be so; we await a fulfilment. And we are one in the expectation that God's kingdom of peace and righteousness does not come through natural progress or along the way of selfishness that human beings have walked up to now in sophisticated ways. Rather, it comes through the miracle of God, because of a new way of thinking created in human beings, in that they give honor to God through brotherly and sisterly love. This hope lives on both sides, even though the form is still so different. The only thing lacking is that previously on both sides we hoped far too weakly.

Do we not want to rejoice and strengthen ourselves by the fact that we all anticipate this same goal? Could we Protestants think of a more serious motto than that of the late pope: "All things gathered up in Christ"?[3] Could the most zealous Catholic set himself or herself a more profound, a more comprehensive task than that which Calvin set himself, namely, to build the city of God here on earth? If we follow our best leaders on both sides in hope and effective responsibility for the coming kingdom of peace and righteousness, then the victory over the world and its redemption will be within our reach.

The different forms of religion on either side are not the obstacle. Rather, the real obstacle is that we have still not acted with sufficient seriousness on both sides.

My friends, if today, in this critical time of opposition between God and the world, we obey the call of Jesus that we all be one, then in so doing, we will not be unfaithful to the spirit of our reformers. If they were in our position today, they would not act differently, just as the best people of the Catholic Church today would not push our hand away from theirs. If on this Reformation Sunday, we reflect seriously regarding what it means to be a Christian in heartfelt communion with all who would like to be Christians,[4] if we strive for the unity of believers, through which they will become strong for their great battle and conflict in the dark world—then we demonstrate true fidelity to our reformers. For they did not live and labor for their own glory but for the glory of the one whom the world now rejects, yet who holds the scepter firmly in his hand and will finally rule from eternity to eternity. Always becoming inwardly more obedient to God, as they did, this is how we want to attest our gratitude to God for the things God has done for us in them.

Amen.

Notes

Preface

1. The First World War was frequently associated with biblical end times. Philip Jenkins edited a collection entitled *Remembering Armageddon: Religion and the First World War* (Indianapolis: Cardinal Publishers Group, 2015). The same author's introduction to *The Great and Holy War: How World War I Changed Religion Forever* (Oxford: Lion Books, 2014) is titled "From Angels to Armageddon"; in particular, Edmund Allenby's 1918 military campaign in Megiddo, the setting of Revelation's armageddon and the origin of the English term, was frequently referred to as "Armageddon" (ibid., 177–78).
2. See David Stevenson, *Cataclysm: The First World War as Political Tragedy* (New York: Basic Books, 2004).
3. See David Fromkin, *Europe's Last Summer: Who Started the Great War in 1914?* (New York: Vintage Books, 2005).
4. See George F. Kennan, *The Decline of Bismarck's European Order: Franco-Russian Relations 1875–1890* (Princeton: Princeton University Press, 1981), 3.
5. See Karl Barth, *Predigten 1914* (Zurich: Theologischer Verlag, 1974), 433: "Est ist eine Gotteszeit, wie nur je eine." The text is from his August 23, 1914, sermon to his congregation in Safenwil. See also my translation of the sermon in this volume.
6. See page 93 here of Barth's August 23 sermon.
7. See page 125 here of Barth's September 20 sermon.
8. William Faulkner, *Requiem for a Nun* (New York: Vintage International, 2011), 73.
9. Barth reports on this remark in his November 1, 1914, sermon. In his monograph, Jochen Fähler, one of the editors of *Predigten 1914*, attributes this complaint to the woman referred to in Barth's *Homiletics*, p. 118, who begged him to speak about something other than the war. While this is possible, it is not likely, since the former request was more specific: "Get back to the Bible." It is highly probable that Barth's concentration on the war elicited more than a single complaint from the Safenwil churchgoers. Moreover, the sympathies of this German-speaking part of Switzerland would be overwhelmingly on

Germany's side. Barth's strong critique of German war policy and German war theology would be irritating to some of his parishioners.
10. Karl Barth, *Homiletics*, trans. Geoffrey W. Bromiley and Donald E. Daniels (Louisville, KY: Westminster/John Knox Press, 1991), 118–19.
11. Eduard Thurneysen, ed., *Karl Barth-Eduard Thurneysen Briefwechsel*, vol. 1 (Zurich: Theologischer Verlag, 1973), Dec. 1, 1918, letter, 305: "Nun ist der Teufel sichtlich zu ihnen übergegangen."
12. From the title of Hannah Arendt's *Eichmann in Jerusalem: A Report on the Banality of Evil* (first published 1963).
13. One of Romain Rolland's major pacifist works is *Au-dessus de la mêlée* (1915), in English *Above the Battle*, trans. C. K. Ogden (Chicago: Open Court Publishing Co., 1916), available online through the Gutenberg Project at http://www.gutenberg.org/ebooks/32779.
14. See Stefan Zweig, *The World of Yesterday*, trans. Anthea Bell (Lincoln: University of Nebraska Press, 2013).
15. See Bertrand Russell, *Justice in War-Time* (London: National Labour Press, 1915), rev. ed. (Chicago: Open Court, 1916).
16. See F. W. Marquardt's review "Karl Barths Safenwiler Predigten, Jahrgang 1914," *Evangelischen Theologie* 37 (1977): 377–96.

Introduction

1. Margaret MacMillan's detailed description of the Paris Exposition in 1900 can be found in *The War That Ended Peace: The Road to 1914* (Toronto: Penguin Canada, 2013), 3–9.
2. See A. J. P. Taylor, *The First World War: An Illustrated History* (New York: Berkley Publishing Group, 1972), i.
3. Agnes von Zahn-Harnack, *Adolf von Harnack* (Berlin: Hans Bott Verlag, 1936), 443–44.
4. Adolf von Harnack, ed. Kurt Nowak, *Adolf von Harnack als Zeitgenosse*, vol. 2 (Berlin: Walter de Gruyter, 1996), 1441: "Als David in höchster Not die Schaubrote vom Tischedes Herrn nahm, war er ganz und gar im Rechte; denn der Buchstabe des Gesetzes existierte in diesem Moment nicht mehr."
5. Jonathan Brant, *Paul Tillich and the Possibility of Revelation through Film* (New York: Oxford University Press, 2012), quoted in Philip Jenkins, *The Great and Holy War* (Oxford: Lion Books, 2014), 226.
6. Karl Adam, cited by J. McConnachie, *The Significance of Karl Barth* (London: Hodder and Stoughton, 1931), 43.
7. Letter to A. Graf, March 18, 1955, quoted in Eberhard Busch, *Karl Barth: His Life from Letters and Autobiographical Texts*, trans. John Bowden (Philadelphia: Fortress Press, 1976), 44.
8. Karl Barth, *Selbstdarstellung* (Self-portrait), 1964, quoted in Busch, *Karl Barth*, 44.
9. Busch, *Karl Barth*, 39.
10. Busch, *Karl Barth*, 43.
11. Karl Barth, Fakultätsalbum der evangelische-theologischen Fakultät Münster, 1927, quoted by Busch, *Karl Barth*, 44.
12. Hendrikus Berkhof, *Two Hundred Years of Theology* (Grand Rapids: Eerdmans, 1989), 201.
13. Karl Barth, "Moderne Theologies und Reichgottesarbeit" [Modern Theology and Work for the Kingdom of God], *Zeitschrift für Theologie und Kirche* 19 (1909): 317–21.

14. Busch, *Karl Barth*, 53–54, 57.
15. Busch, *Karl Barth*, 61.
16. Karl Barth, "The Word of God and the Task of the Ministry," in *The Word of God and the Word of Man* (London: Hodder & Stoughton, 1935), 186.
17. Ibid., 199.
18. Eduard Thurneysen, "Die Anfänge: Karl Barths Theologie der Frühzeit," in *Antwort* (Zollikon-Zurich: Evangelischer Verlag Ag., 1956), 831; Barth and Thurneysen, *Revolutionary Theology in the Making*, trans. James D. Smart (Richmond: John Knox Press, 1964), 12.
19. In a television interview on the occasion of Karl Barth's eightieth birthday, a Safenwil parishioner recalled: "I had the impression that at that time his sermons were much too profound and many people really did not understand them. But nevertheless the situation in the community, especially with the working classes, was very good one, because at that time already he was a union organizing socialist. He belonged to the socialist party of Safenwil" ("German-Swiss Television Interview," in Karl Barth, *Gespräche: 1964–1968*, ed. Eberhard Busch [Zurich: Theologischer Verlag, 1997], 224).
20. See Münster Faculty Album, in *Karl Barth-Rudolf Bultmann, Letters 1922–1966*, trans. G. W. Bromiley (Grand Rapids: Eerdmans, 1981), 154.
21. See Gary Dorrien, *The Barthian Revolt in Modern Theology* (Louisville, KY: Westminster John Knox Press, 2000), 32. The course that Barth followed in making this transformation could not have made much sense to the Safenwilers at the time, for it began with his conversion to Religious Socialism. Bruce McCormack, on whom Dorrien seems to depend here, speaks of "Barth's conversion in Safenwil to the socialist cause under the influence of Sombart" (*Karl Barth's Critically Realistic Dialectical Theology: Its Genesis and Development 1909–1936* [Oxford: Clarendon Press, 1995], 83), but he is more careful by referring to Barth's earlier socialist sympathies. At the same time, McCormack is inclined to minimize Barth's earlier socialist leanings. Ian R. Boyd has misread McCormack when he accuses him of holding that Barth had little knowledge of socialism prior to arriving in Safenwil. See Ian R. Boyd, *Dogmatics among the Ruins* (Oxford: Peter Lang, 2004), 57.
22. Busch, *Karl Barth*, 31.
23. Fritz Barth, *Christus unsere Hoffnung*, 19f., quoted by Busch, *Karl Barth*, 69.
24. Karl Barth, *Vorträge und kleinere Arbeiten, 1905–1909*, ed. H. Drewes and H. Stoevesandt (Zurich: Theologischer Verlag, 1992), 74
25. Ibid., 75–76.
26. Ibid., 98–99.
27. Ibid., 75.
28. See E. Buess and M. Mattmüller, *Prophetischer Sozialismus: Blumhardt–Ragaz–Barth* (Freiburg: Exodus, 1986). I am indebted to Timothy Gorringe for reference to the monograph: see *Karl Barth against Hegemony* (Oxford: Oxford University Press, 1999), 28.
29. Karl Barth, "Rückblick," quoted by Bruce McCormack, *Karl Barth's Theology*, 85.
30. Hermann Kutter, *Sie Müssen! Ein offenes Wort an die christliche Gesellschaft* (Berlin: Hermann Walther, 1904).
31. See *A Ragaz Reader: Signs of the Kingdom*, ed. and trans. Paul Bock (Grand Rapids: Eerdmans, 1984), 3–15.
32. See Barth, *Action in Waiting for the Kingdom of God*, trans. and ed. Society of Brothers (Rifton, NY: Plough Publishing House, 1969), originally published as "Auf das Reich Gottes warten," *Der freie schweizer Arbeiter* 49 (1916).

33. See George Hunsinger, ed., *Karl Barth and Radical Politics* (Philadelphia: Westminster Press, 1976), 19.
34. Karl Barth, "Jesus Christ and the Movement for Social Justice," trans. George Hunsinger, in *Karl Barth and Radical Politics*, 20.
35. Ibid., 36.
36. Barth, *Final Testimonies*, ed. E. Busch and trans. G. W. Bromiley (Grand Rapids: Eerdmans, 1977), 39.
37. Stephen Evans, "Berlin 1914: A City of Ambition and Self-Doubt," January 8, 2014, *BBC News Magazine*, http://www.bbc.com/news/magazine-25635311.
38. Quoted in the postscript to "Jesus Christ and the Movement for Social Justice," in *Karl Barth and Radical Politics* (Philadelphia: Westminster Press, 1976), 37–38.
39. Ibid., 39.
40. Ibid., 40.
41. Ibid., 43.
42. Ibid., 45.
43. Karl Barth's letter of September 9, 1917, in *Karl Barth-Eduard Thurneysen Briefwechsel*, vol. 1, *1913–1921*, (Zurich: Theologischer Verlag, 1973), 229; (English translation, *Revolutionary Theology in the Making*, trans. James D. Smart [Richmond: John Knox Press, 1964]).
44. See James D. Smart, "Eduard Thurneysen: Pastor-Theologian," in *Theology Today* 16, no. 1 (1959): 74–89.
45. See John Donne, "Meditation 17," *Devotions upon Emergent Occasions* (New York: Random House, 1999), 103.
46. *Karl Barth-Eduard Thurneysen Briefwechsel*, trans. James D. Smart (Richmond: John Knox Press, 1964).
47. Eduard Thurneysen, quoted in Smart, "Eduard Thurneysen: Pastor-Theologian," 77.
48. Karl Barth, quoted in Smart, "Eduard Thurneysen Pastor-Theologian," 75.
49. Karl Barth, "Concluding Unscientific Postscript," 264.
50. See Karl Barth, "Modern Theology and Work for the Kingdom of God."
51. For the German numbers, see Margaret MacMillan, *The War That Ended Peace*, 294 (book cited in preface), and for the French, 296–97.
52. Karl Barth, "The Word of God and the Task of the Ministry," in *The Word of God and the Word of Man*, 196.
53. Colin Gunton, *The Barth Lectures*, transcribed and ed. P. H. Brazier (London: T. & T. Clark, 2007), 20.
54. See Karl Barth, "Past and Future: Friedrich Naumann and Christoph Blumhardt," in *The Beginnings of Dialectical Theology*, vol. 7, ed. James M. Robinson, trans. Keith R. Crim (Richmond: John Knox Press, 1968).
55. McCormack, *Karl Barth's Theology*, 109.
56. The latter was a weekly newspaper devoted to religion, politics, and art, edited by Friedrich Naumann (1860–1919), Rade's brother-in-law, and subtitled "Help for God, help for one's brother [and sister], help for state, help for oneself."
57. Barth, "Past and Future," 37.
58. McCormack, *Karl Barth's Theology*, 109.
59. Ibid.
60. George Hunsinger, "Toward a Radical Barth," in *Karl Barth and Radical Politics*, 199.

61. Friedrich Naumann, *Central Europe*, trans. Christabel M. Meredith (London: P. S. King & Son, 1916).
62. "Germans Can't See Why War Continues," *New York Times*, August 24, 1916.
63. Barth, *Action in Waiting*, 24.
64. Barth, "Past and Future," 37.
65. Ibid.
66. Barth, *Church Dogmatics*, IV/3, *The Doctrine of Reconciliation*, trans. G. W. Bromiley (Edinburgh: T. & T. Clark, 1961), 169–70.
67. Barth, "Past and Future," 43.
68. Ibid.
69. Ibid., 44.
70. Aug. 23 sermon; see, e.g., p. 8: "The peace that we had was no peace; it was a disguised, deceitful, veiled war. It didn't have any staying power.... We stood in envy next to one another, all of us greedily working our way up, wickedly piling up tinder for the conflagration between the selfish masses that we call nations, always producing more, always wanting to become stronger, until now finally this explosion of evil had to occur."
71. Stefan Zweig, *The World of Yesterday* (Lincoln: University of Nebraska Press, 1964), ix.
72. Romain Rolland, *Jean-Christophe*, vol. x (1912), trans. Gilbert Cannan; vol. iv, 504, quoted on the frontispiece of Romain Rolland, *Above the Battle*, trans. C. K. Ogden (Chicago: Open Court Publishing Co., 1916).
73. Barth, *The Humanity of God*, trans. Thomas Weiser (Atlanta: John Knox Press, 1978), 14.
74. William Shakespeare, *Hamlet*, Act I, Scene 2, l. 135–37.
75. Barth, *Predigten 1914* (Zurich: Theologischer Verlag Zürich, 1974), 521.
76. See Adam Hochschild, *To End All Wars* (Boston: Houghton Mifflin Harcourt, 2011), 93–94 and Zweig, *The World of Yesterday*.
77. And punished painfully it was. Austria-Hungary, Germany, and Bulgaria attacked Serbia in October 1914. This small country suffered the highest death toll of all combatants: almost one in five of its military and civilian population; see Hochschild, *To End All Wars*, 194.
78. Barth, *Predigten 1914*, 389.
79. Ibid.
80. For the first time, on the manuscript of his Aug. 2, 1914, sermon, and then thereafter, Barth noted the hymns he had chosen. The two other hymns for August 2 were "Praise and Honor the Highest Good" by J. J. Schütz and "Oh That Still Soon Your Fire Were Burning" by G. F. Fickert.
81. See sermon of Aug. 2, 1914, note 4.
82. See Roger Chickering, *Imperial Germany and the Great War, 1914–1918* (2nd ed.; Cambridge: Cambridge University Press, 2004), 14, 125.
83. Barth, *Predigten 1914*, 402.
84. Barth, *Predigten 1914*, 403.
85. Ibid.
86. Barth's letter to Eduard Thurneysen, September 4, 1914, in *Revolutionary Theology in the Making*, 27.
87. John Keegan, *The First World War* (New York: Alfred A. Knopf, 1999), 12.
88. Henry M. Pachter, *Modern Germany: A Social, Cultural, and Political History* (Boulder, CO: Westview Press, 1978), 67.
89. See Barth's letter of May 25, 1915, in reply to Eduard Thurneysen's negative remarks about Italy's entry into the war on the side of France, Russia, and

Britain. Barth admitted that Italy was acting villainously. Yet that shouldn't cause any more grief than Germany's violation of Belgium's neutrality and the sinking of the *Lusitania*. Politics is politics, Thurneysen conceded. Barth regarded Thurneysen's reason for preferring a German victory—namely, Germany's high values—somewhat disturbing and bizarre (*Karl Barth-Eduard Thurneysen Briefwechsel*, 48). While he was careful not to be partisan, Barth seems here to favor the defeat of the Central Powers.

90. See Christoph Schwöbel, "Theology," in *The Cambridge Companion to Karl Barth*, ed. John Webster (Cambridge: Cambridge University Press, 2000), 20.
91. Sermon of Aug. 9, 1914.
92. McCormack, *Karl Barth's Theology*, 111.
93. Ibid.
94. Karl Barth to Martin Rade, Aug. 31, 1914, quoted in McCormack, *Karl Barth's Theology*, 111.
95. Barth's Sept. 4, 1914, letter to Thurneysen, in *Revolutionary Theology in the Making*, 26,
96. Karl Barth, *Karl Barth–Martin Rade: Ein Briefwechsel*, ed. Christoph Schwöbel. (Gütersloh: Gütersloher Verlagshaus Gerd Mohn, 1981). The letter to Herrmann is recorded on pp. 113–16.
97. Agnes von Zahn-Harnack, *Adolf von Harnack* (Berlin: Hans Bott Verlag, 1936), 460ff.
98. Barth, *Revolutionary Theology in the Making*, 27, Sept. 4, 1914, letter to Eduard Thurneysen.
99. McCormack, *Karl Barth's Theology*, 92–104 and 112–17.
100. Barth, *Kirchliche Dogmatik* I/1 (Munich: Chr. Kaiser Verlag, 1932), 292ff. and 295; English translation *Church Dogmatics* I/1, trans. G. T. Thomson (Edinburgh: T. & T. Clark, 1934), 316ff. and 319.
101. Though he largely ceased to preach about the war, he continued to agonize over the war. His biographer, Eberhard Busch, claims that "the outbreak of [the war] . . . shook him and disturbed him to the depths of his being." See Busch, *Karl Barth*, 81.
102. McCormack, *Karl Barth's Theology*, 92ff.
103. Barth, *The Word of God and the Word of Man*, trans. Douglas Horton (Cleveland: Pilgrim Press, 1928).
104. For an able discussion of Luther's views of God's "strange" and "proper" work, see Benjamin Drewery's chapter on Martin Luther in Hubert Cunliffe Jones, *History of Christian Doctrine*, esp. p. 335.
105. Barth was a student at the University of Bern and a member of Zofingia at the time; in 1906 he became president of the group (Busch, *Karl Barth*, 37).
106. *Barth-Thurneysen Briefwechsel*, 474.
107. For this prediction, see Jenkins, *The Great and Holy War*, 317.
108. A. Shadwell, "German War Sermons," *Hibbert Journal* 14 (1915–1916): 691–704.
109. Cf. Peter C. Matheson, "Scottish War Sermons 1914–1919," in *Records of the Scottish Church History Society* 17 (Edinburgh: Scottish Church History Society, 1972), 203–13: "The term 'war sermon' itself is understood in the more limited sense of sermons making direct or indirect reference to the war" (204).
110. Barth, sermon of Aug. 2, 1914, p. 7.
111. Frank J. Gordon, "Liberal German Churchmen and the First World War," *German Studies Review* (1981), 39–63, quote from 40.
112. Quoted in Wolfgang Tilgner, "Volk, Nation und Vaterland im protestantischen Denken zwischen Kaiserreich und Nationalsozialismus," in *Volk-*

Nation-Vaterland: Der Deutsche Protestantismus und der Nationalismus, ed. Horst Zillessen (Gütersloh: Gütersloher Verlagshaus Gerd Mohn, 1970), 155.
113. Arthur F. Winnington-Ingram, *Guardian*, June 10, 1915, quoted in Stuart Mews, "Spiritual Mobilization in the First World War," *Theology* 74 (1971), 258–64, quote from 260. A slightly later part of this letter is quoted in Jenkins, *The Great and Holy War*, 71.
114. Quoted in Jenkins, *The Great and Holy War*, 95; Lyman Abbott, *The Twentieth-Century Crusade* (New York: Macmillan, 1918), epigraph.
115. Barth, *Homiletics* (Louisville, KY: Westminster/John Knox Press, 1991), 118.
116. Ibid.
117. Ibid., 118–19.
118. Dietrich Bonhoeffer's judgment was that Niebuhr's work was thin, both biblically and theologically. See, for example, Eric Metaxas's biography *Bonhoeffer: Pastor, Martyr, Prophet, Spy*. Metaxas relates that during Bonhoeffer's trip to New York in 1939 the theologian was disappointed in Niebuhr and Union Seminary for including little of the Bible's "light" in their teaching.
119. For a short discussion of Barth's views of the *analogia entis*, see Busch, *Karl Barth*, 215–16.
120. Ibid., 118.
121. David G. Buttrick writes in the foreword to Barth's *Homiletics* that Barth "condemns the whole idea of a 'Conclusion' to sermons, fearing that an ending will either be a 'work' or a weakening of the message of grace through trite summation or minor-key application" (Foreword, from *Homiletics*, 7–10, quote from 8–9).
122. Barth, *Homiletics*, 117: "Especially unhelpful is the method of seasoning a sermon with all kinds of illustrations."
123. Karl Barth, "Die Neuortierung der Prot. Theol. in den letzten dreissig Jahren," in *Kirchenblatt für die ref. Schweiz* 7 (1940): 100.
124. See Barth, *The Word of God and the Word of Man*, 33.
125. See Karl Barth, *Das Wort Gottes und die Theologie* (Munich: Chr. Kaiser Verlag, 1929). Douglas Horton translated the title, *The Word of God and the Word of Man*.
126. Karl Barth, *Church Dogmatics* I/1, 136ff.
127. Hugh Strachan, *The Outbreak of the First World War* (Oxford: Oxford University Press, 2004), viii.
128. While it is generally acknowledged that Barth was the theologian par excellence of the twentieth century, his important role as a social and political thinker is not always sufficiently emphasized. Frank Jehle, however, has devoted an all too brief yet valuable study of Barth's political and moral thought. He states that Barth "was at the same time one of the most significant political and moral philosophers of the twentieth century." See Frank Jehle, *Ever against the Stream: The Politics of Karl Barth, 1906-1968*, trans. Richard and Martha Burnett (Grand Rapids: Eerdmans, 2002), 6. See also Will Herberg, who speaks of Barth as "one of the most influential social thinkers of our time" (Introduction, Karl Barth, *Community, State, and Church: Three Essays* [New York: Anchor Books, Doubleday, 1960], 13).

Sermon: July 26, 1914

1. A village close to Safenwil. Barth filled in for its pastor, Paul Schild.
2. After Archduke Ferdinand, successor to the Austrian throne, and his wife, Sophie, were assassinated and died on June 28, 1914 (see Sermon of Oct. 18,

1914, note 3), Austria-Hungary's forty-eight-hour limited ultimatum to Serbia caused the First World War.
3. Cf. Fr. von Schiller, *Wilhelm Tell* IV, 3 (verse 2683f.):

> The most godly cannot live peaceably
> When the wicked neighbor is not friendly.

Sermon: August 2, 1914

1. The hymns that were sung in the service are noted on the manuscript: no. 266 (*EKG*, 294), verses 1–3: "Commit Your Way" by P. Gerhardt (1607–76); no. 257, verses 1–3: "I Abide with You!" by A. Morath (1805–84); no. 9 (*EKG*, 233), verses 1, 5, 6; "Praise and Honor the Highest Good" by J. J. Schütz (1640–90); no. 168 (*EKG*, 219), verses 1, 6, 7, 8: "Oh that still soon your fire were burning" by G. F. Fickert (1758–1815).
2. Swiss National Celebration Day.
3. These first three sentences replaced the original sentence that Barth struck out: "In the past week we heard a good deal about war and rumors of war and still it is indeed, not out of the question that we could still get to hear and see something rather different."
4. In 1798 the old Swiss confederation was transformed by force into the Helvetic Republic, dependent on France, following the invasion by French troops led by Generals Brune and Schauenburg.
5. The allusion is to the conclusion of the patriotic song "To My Native Land" by Gottfried Keller (1819–90), in *Great German Poems of the Romantic Era: A Dual-Language Book*, ed. and trans. Stanley Appelbaum (Mineola, NY: Dover Publications, 1995), 165:

> When some day I fling away this garment of dust,
> I will then pray to the Lord God:
> "Let your loveliest star shine
> Down on my native land on Earth!"

Sermon: August 9, 1914

1. Verse 3 (*EKG* 232) "Should I not sing to my God . . ." by Paul Gerhardt (1607–76).
2. The origin cannot be determined.

Sermon: August 16, 1914

1. Question mark in original (*Predigten 1914*, p. 420)

Sermon: August 23, 1914

1. For this and the following sermon, see *Barth-Thurneysen Briefwechsel*, 10.
2. Barth's choice of text was suggested by Martin Rade's meditation "God's Will in the War," in *Die Christliche Welt* 28 (1914): 769ff. (no. 33, Aug. 15, 1914).
3. See sermon of June 7, 1914, *Predigten 1914*, 287ff.
4. Pius X, "Exhortation to All Catholics on the Outbreak of the Great War," August 2, 1914, in *Acta Apostolicae Sedis* v. 6, no. 11 (1914): 373.
5. This phrase is similar to the title of Romain Rolland's 1915 pacifist manifesto, *Au-dessus de la mêlée*.

Sermon: August 30, 1914

1. A neighboring village of Safenwil. Barth substituted there for Pastor Traugott Haller.

2. From the beginning of J. W. von Goethe's ballad *The Fisherman*:

   The water rushed, the water swelled
   A fisherman sat thereby,
   Looking calmly at the line held,
   Cool in the depth of his heart.

3. Beginning of verse 1 of Hymn 271 by J. D. Herrnschmidt (1675–1723).
4. Fr. von Schiller, *William Tell* II, 2 (verse 1448): "We want to be a united nation of brothers."
5. Sophocles, *Antigone*, verse 523.
6. The phrase "a place in the sun" got its specific German nationalistic meaning as a result of a Dec. 6, 1897, speech in the German parliament by Count Bernhard (later Prince) von Bülow, foreign secretary (later chancellor), on the occasion of the occupation of Kiaochow by Germany: "None of us wants to be put in the shade, but we also demand our place in the sun."
7. The common inexact citation from the poem "Germany's Calling" (1861), by E. Geibel (1815–1884). Original:

   And it may by German spirit
   Once again the world renew.

8. "We Germans fear God, but nothing else in the world," as O. von Bismarck stated in a speech in parliament on Feb. 6, 1888.
9. The German-Franco war of 1870–1871 led to the downfall of the French empire and to the establishment of the German Reich (Versailles, Jan. 18, 1871). The annexation of Alsace-Lorraine placed a heavy strain on German-French relations.
10. See the promulgation by Kaiser Wilhelm II on the National Day of Repentance, Aug. 5, 1914, the text of this appeal to the public of Aug. 2, 1914, in *Allgemeines Kirchenblatt für das evangelische Deutschland* 63 (1914): 386.
11. "Every militia soldier is marked as such by a white metal cross with the inscription 'With God for King and Fatherland,' which is fastened on the front of the cap" (from King Friedrich Wilhelm III of Prussia's ordinance, March 17, 1813, concerning the organization of the militia, Supplement III, abs. 5, p. 38).
12. Barth's studies in Germany: winter semester 1906/7, Berlin; winter semester 1907/8, Tübingen; summer semester 1908, Marburg. From autumn 1908 to autumn 1909, Barth was assistant editor of *Christliche Welt* (Christian world), again in Marburg.

Sermon: September 6, 1914

1. In the battle at Tannenberg (Aug. 26–30, 1914), 93,000 Russians were taken as German prisoners of war.
2. Martin Luther, *Whether Soldiers Can Be Saved* (1526), WA 19, 623–62. In August and September 1914, Martin Rade published extracts from this treatise in installments in the *Christliche Welt* 34–38. Cf. Barth's critical statement regarding this in his letter of Aug. 29, 1914, to E. Thurneysen, in *Barth-Thurneysen Briefwechsel*, 7.

Sermon: September 13, 1914

1. Barth added in pencil "Kölliken, Sept. 16."
2. Cf. Sermon of June 7, 1914, in *Predigten 1914*.

3. Battle at Mühlhausen/Alsace on Aug. 19, 1914. First, the French, with the approval of the inhabitants, succeeded in the capture of the city by a surprise attack. With the winning back of the city, the Germans took severe revenge.
4. Löwen was falsely accused of participation in the French surprise attack, was bombarded and partially incinerated (Aug. 14, 1914). Cf. P. Natorp, *Löwen, Letter to a Dutch Theologian*, in *Christliche Welt* 28 (1914), 861f., and Barth's critical statement about Natorp's position in Sermon of Oct. 18, 1914, note 7.

Sermon: September 20, 1914

1. The hymns that were sung in the service of worship are noted on the manuscript: No. 8: "We vow today anew . . ." by A. E. Fröhlich (1796–1865), verses, 1, 2, 4; No. 25: "Great God, we praise you . . ." by I. Franz (1719–90), based on the early church Te Deum, verses 1, 7, 9.
2. Aug. 4–16, 1914, under the command of General von Emmich.
3. Beginning of "Oath on the Rütli," Fr. von Schiller, *Wilhelm Tell* II, 2 (verse 1448).
4. From the first verse of (at that time) the Swiss national anthem "You call, my country" (1811), by J. Rud. Wyss (1782–1830):

   You call, my country,
   Behold us with heart and hand
   All to you devoted,
   Hail to you, Helvetia,
   You still indeed have sons, yes.
   As St. Jacob saw them
   Full of joy for the fight.

   In the battle at St. Jacob on the Birs (Aug. 25, 1444), about 1500 Swiss confederates completely wore down the superior strength of Burgundy and French forces. That was henceforth for Swiss consciousness something like a battle of Thermopylae.
5. This slogan goes back to Terence (195[?]–159 BCE), *Andria* IV, 1: *Proximus sum egomet mihi*.

Sermon: October 11, 1914

1. The passage is not written on the manuscript, as Barth typically did with his shorter texts, but the NRSV text reads:

   As he was setting out on a journey, a man ran up and knelt before him, and asked him, "Good Teacher, what must I do to inherit eternal life?" Jesus said to him, "Why do you call me good? No one is good but God alone. You know the commandments: 'You shall not murder; you shall not commit adultery; you shall not steal; you shall not bear false witness; you shall not defraud; honor your father and mother.'" He said to him, "Teacher, I have kept all these since my youth." Jesus, looking at him, loved him and said, "You lack one thing; go, sell what you own, and give the money to the poor, and you will have treasure in heaven; then come, follow me." When he heard this, he was shocked and went away grieving, for he had many possessions.

   Then Jesus looked around and said to his disciples, "How hard it will be for those who have wealth to enter the kingdom of God!" (Mark 10:17–23).

Sermon: October 18, 1914

1. The hymns, which were sung in the service of divine worship, are noted on the manuscript: No. 225: "If God is for me, so step . . ." by P. Gerhardt (1607–76),

verses 1, 8, 9 (*EKG* 250, verses 1, 12, 13); No. 31 (*EKG* 209): "Oh stay with your grace . . ." by J. Stegmann (1588–1632), verses 1, 2, 3, 6.
2. Cf. E. M. Arndt (1769–1860), *Hymn of Trust* (1813), which reads:

> The ancient God is still alive!
> Will you, my heart, despair?

3. On June 28, 1914, in Sarajevo, the fanatical Serbian nationalist Gavrilo Princip murdered the Habsburg successor to the throne, Archduke Franz Ferdinand, and his wife. This assassination was the cause of the First World War.
4. From the poem "Men and Knaves," by Th. Körner (1791–1813).
5. From 1912 to 1914, three times in a row the British Parliament adopted the bill of home rule in Ireland, against the extraordinary efforts of Protestant Ulster. [This editorial footnote by Barth is misleading. Home-rule bills were introduced by Gladstone's government in 1886 and 1893. A third home-rule bill was passed in 1914, but it never came into effect because of World War I.]
6. Beginning of "Rütli Oath," Fr. von Schiller, *Wilhelm Tell* II, 2 (lines 1448f.). I have followed Sir Theodore Martin's translation.
7. Paul Natorp (1854–1924); see note 4 to sermon of Sept. 13, 1914. A similar use of the same Luther citation is made by Martin Rade, "Concerning a Just Self-Consciousness," in *Christliche Welt* 28 (1914), 887.
8. Dr. Karl Liebknecht (1871–1919), since 1912 member of the Reichstag for the SPD, voted in December 1914 and August 1915 against the war credits; he left the party in 1916 in protest against the war-friendly attitude of the SPD. Together with Rosa Luxemburg, he was murdered in 1919 in the course of the social unrest created by their political Spartacus movement.
9. Dr. Ludwig Frank (1874–1914), killed in action at Lunéville, was a leading SPD member in the Reichstag since 1907. Obituary by Martin Rade in *Christliche Welt* 28 (1914): 862ff. and by Theodor Heuss in *Die Hilfe*, weekly journal for politics, literature, and art, ed. Fr. Naumann, No. 38, Sep. 17, 1914, 618ff.
10. Address of Cardinal Amette (1850–1920) during a "Day of Prayer for France and its Armies" on Sept. 13, 1914.
11. The identity is unknown. An American Congregational minister, Lyman Abbott, expressed near-identical sentiments against Germany in his 1918 article "To Love Is to Hate" (Jenkins, *The Great and Holy War*, 10).
12. Rally of the German-Evangelical Mission Circle, on Sept. 21, 1914, in Berlin; see *Short Notices*, in *Christliche Welt* 28 (1914): 902.
13. The principal court preacher was Ernst von Dryander (1843–1922); his correspondent was French Protestant pastor Charles-Édouard Babut (1835–1916) of Nîmes. The response was published in the *Protestantenblatt*, 1914, 895ff. See also E. v. Dryander, *Recollections from My Life* (8th printing; Bielefeld/Leipzig: 1922), 279ff.
14. Published in *Church Yearbook* 42 (1915), 209–13. Barth's two teachers were Adolf von Harnack (1851–1930) in Berlin and Wilhelm Herrmann (1846–1922) in Marburg. See also *Christliche Welt* 28 (1914): 846.

Sermon: October 25, 1914

1. Theobald von Bethmann-Hollweg (1856–1921), German chancellor, 1909–17.
2. From Fr. von Schiller's *Song of the Bell*.
3. See note 2 for sermon of September 20, 1914.

Sermon: November 1, 1914

1. The hymns, which would be sung in the service of worship, are noted on the manuscript: 163 (*EKG* 220): "A flock and a shepherd . . ." by Fr. A. Krummacher (1767–1845), verses 1, 5, 6; 170: "The cause is yours, Lord Jesus Christ . . ." by S. Preiswerk (1799–1871) (v. ½) and F. Zaremba (1794–1874) (v. 3), verses 1–3.
2. Manuscript: There are two large exclamation marks in the margin next to this sentence.
3. "Instaurare omnia in Christo" (Eph. 1:10), the motto under which Pius X had his pontificate.
4. There is an insertion here of three to five words beginning with "gegenüber" ("opposite"), which cannot be deciphered.

Select Bibliography

Primary Works
(church dogmatic major works followed by
other secondary books by Barth)

Kirchliche Dogmatik, 13 vols. Munich: Kaiser, 1932; then Zurich: Evangelischer Verlag, 1938–65.

Karl Barth-Rudolf Bultmann Briefwechsel 1911–1966. Edited by B. Jaspert. Zurich: Theologischer Verlag, 1971.

Karl Barth-Martin Rade, Ein Briefwechsel. Edited by Christoph Schwöbel. Gütersloh: Gütersloher Verlagshaus Mohn, 1981.

Karl Barth Gesamtausgabe, vol. v., *Briefe: Offene Briefe 1909–1935*. Edited by Diether Koch. Zurich: Theologischer Verlag, 2001.

K. Barth-E. Thurneysen Briefwechsel 1913–1921. Edited by E. Thurneysen. Zurich: Theologischer Verlag, 1973.

K. Barth-E. Thurneysen Briefwechsel 1921–1930. Edited by E. Thurneysen. Zurich: Theologischer Verlag, 1974.

Der Römerbrief, 1st ed. Edited by H. Schmidt. Zurich: Theologischer Verlag, 1985.

Unterricht in der christlichen Religion, i: *Prolegomena* (1924). Edited by H. Reiffen. *Unterricht in der christlichen Religion*. Zurich: Theologischer Verlag, 1985.

Unterricht in der christlichen Religion, ii: *Die Lehre von Gott/Die Lehre vom Menschen* (1924/5). Edited by H. Stoevesandt, 1990. Zurich: Theologischer Verlag,

Vortäge und kleinere Arbeiten, 1905–1909. Edited by H. Drewes and H. Stoevesandt. Zurich: Theologischer Verlag, 1992.

Die Theologie Calvins (1922). Edited by A. Reinstädtler and H. Scholl. Zurich: Theologischer Verlag, 1993.

Vorträge und kleinere Arbeiten, 1909–1914. Edited by H. Drewes and H. Stoevesandt. Zurich: Theologischer Verlag, 1993.

Das Wort Gottes und die Theologie. Munich: Kaiser, 1925.

Suchet Gott, so werdet ihr leben. Munich: Kaiser, 1928, with E. Thurneysen.

"'Die Hilfe' 1913, Von einem Religiös-Sozialen." *Die Christliche Welt* 33 (Aug. 15, 1914): 774–78.

Die Theologie und die Kirche. Munich: Kaiser, 1928.

Der Römerbrief, 2nd ed. (1922). Munich: Kaiser, 1929.
Letzte Zeugnisse. Zurich: Evangelischer Verlag, 1969.
How I Changed My Mind. Edinburgh: St. Andrew Press, 1969.
Anfänge der dialektischen Theologie. Edited by J. Moltmann. i, Munich: Kaiser, 1962; ii, Munich: Kaiser, 1963.
Karl Barth-Martin Rade: Ein Briefwechsel. Edited by C. Schwöbel. Gütersloh: Gütersloher Verlagshaus Gerd Mohn, 1981.

English Translations
(in chronological order of publication)

Come Holy Spirit: Sermons by K. Barth and E. Thurneysen. Edinburgh: T. & T. Clark, 1934.
The Word of God and the Word of Man. Translated by D. Horton. London: Hodder & Stoughton, 1935. English translation of *Das Wort Gottes und die Theologie*.
The Theology of John Calvin. Translated by G. W. Bromiley. Grand Rapids: Eerdmans, 1955.
Church Dogmatics. Edited by G. W. Bromiley and T. F. Torrance. Edinburgh: T. & T. Clark, 1956–77.
The Faith of the Church. Translated by G. Vahanian. London: Fontana, 1960.
Dogmatics in Outline. Translated by G. Thomson. London: SCM, 1960.
Deliverance to the Captives. Translated by M. Wieser. London: SCM, 1961.
Karl Barth's Table Talk. Edited by J. Godsey. Edinburgh: Oliver & Boyd, 1963.
Evangelical Theology. Edinburgh: T. & T. Clark, 1963.
Revolutionary Theology in the Making: Barth-Thurneysen Correspondence, 1914–1925. Translated by J. Smart. London: Epworth, 1964.
God Here and Now: Religious Perspectives. Translated by P. van Buren. London: Routledge & Kegan Paul, 1964.
Against the Stream: Shorter Post-War Writings. London: SCM, 1964.
The Humanity of God. Translated by J. Thomas and T. Wieser. London: Collins, 1967.
Call for God: New Sermons from Basle Prison. London: SCM, 1967.
Ad Limina Apostolorum. Translated by K. Crim. Edinburgh: St. Andrew Press, 1968.
"Past and Future: Friedrich Naumann and Christoph Blumhardt." In *The Beginnings of Dialectical Theology*, vol. 7. Edited by James M. Robinson. Translated by Keith R. Crim. Richmond: John Knox Press, 1968.
Fragments Grave and Gay. Translated by E. Mosbacher. London: Fontana, 1971.
Protestant Theology in the Nineteenth Century: Its Background and History. Translated by B. Cozens and J. Bowden. London: SCM, 1972.
Revelation and Theology: An Analysis of the Barth-Harnack Correspondence of 1923. Edited by H. M. Rumscheidt. London: Cambridge University Press, 1972.
Karl Barth-R. Bultmann Letters 1922–1966. Translated by G. W. Bromiley. Grand Rapids: Eerdmans, 1981.
A Late Friendship: The Letters of Karl Barth and Carl Zuckemayer. Translated by G. W. Bromiley. Grand Rapids, Eerdmans, 1982.
The Theology of Schleiermacher. Translated by G. W. Bromiley. Edinburgh: T. & T. Clark, 1982.
Wolfgang Amadeus Mozart. Translated by C. Pott. Grand Rapids: Eerdmans, 1986.
The Göttingen Dogmatics: Instruction in the Christian Religion, vol. 1. Translated by G. W. Bromiley. Grand Rapids: Eerdmans 1991. English translation of *Unterricht in der christlichen Religion*.

Homiletics. Translated by G. W. Bromiley and Donald E. Daniels. Louisville, KY: Westminster/John Knox Press, 1991.

Secondary Works

Balthasar, Hans Urs von. *The Theology of Karl Barth: Exposition and Interpretation*. Translated by E. Oakes. San Francisco: Ignatius, 1992.

Barr, J. *The Semantics of Biblical Language*. Oxford: Oxford University Press, 1961.

———. *Biblical Faith and Natural Theology*. Oxford: Clarendon, 1993.

Berkouwer, G. *The Triumph of Grace in the Theology of Karl Barth*. London: Paternoster, 1956.

Bock, Paul. *Signs of the Kingdom: A Ragaz Reader*. Grand Rapids: Eerdmans, 1984.

Bonhoeffer, D. *Letters and Papers from Prison*, 3rd ed. London: SCM 1967.

Bonjour, E., H. S. Offler, and G. R. Potter. *A Short History of Switzerland*. Oxford: Clarendon Press, 1952.

Bowden, John. *Karl Barth*. London: SCM Press, 1972.

Buess, E., and M. Mattmüller. *Prophetischer Socialismus: Blumhardt-Ragaz-Barth*. Freiburg: Exodus, 1986.

Busch, E. *Karl Barth: His Life from Letters and Autobiographical Texts*. Translated by J. Bowden. London: SCM 1976.

———. *Glaubensheiterkeit*. Neukirchen, 1986. Gottingen: V & R Unipress, 2009.

Casalis, Georges. *Portrait of Karl Barth*. Translated by Robert McAfee Brown. Garden City, NY: Doubleday, 1963.

Chickering, Roger. *Imperial Germany and the Great War, 1914–1918*. 2nd ed. Cambridge: Cambridge University Press, 2004.

Clark, Christopher C. *The Sleepwalkers: How Europe Went to War in 1914*. New York: HarperCollins, 2013.

Clark, Lloyd. *World War 1: An Illustrated History*. Oxford: Helicon Publishing, 2001.

Craig, G. *Germany 1866–1945*. Oxford: Clarendon, 1978.

Diem, H. "Karl Barth as Socialist." In *Karl Barth and Radical Politics*. Edited by G. Hunsinger. Philadelphia: Westminster Press, 1976.

Dorrien, Gary. *The Barthian Revolt in Modern Theology: Theology without Weapons*. Louisville, KY: Westminster John Knox Press, 1999.

Drewery, Benjamin. "Martin Luther." In *A History of Christian Doctrine*. Edited by Hubert Cunliffe-Jones, 311–44. London: T. & T. Clark, 1978.

Dulles, Avery. "Karl Barth: A Catholic Appreciation." *Christian Century*, March 26, 1969, 108–10.

Eberle, M. *World War I and the Weimar Artists*. New Haven, CT: Yale University Press, 1985.

Fähler, Jochen. *Der Ausbruch des 1. Weltkrieges in Karl Barths Predigten 1913–1915*. Bern: Peter Lang, 1979.

Ferguson, Niall. *The Pity of War: Explaining World War I*. New York: Basic Books, 2000.

Fischer, Fritz. *Griff nach der Weltmacht: Die Kriegzielpolitik des kaiserlichen Deutschland 1914–1918*. Düsseldorf: Droste, 1961.

———. *World Power or Decline: The Controversy over Germany's Aims in the First World War*. Translated by Lancelot L. Farrar, Robert Kimber, and Rita Kimber. New York: W. W. Norton & Co., 1974.

Fisher, H. A. L. *A History of Europe*. London: Edward Arnold, 1936.

Fisher, S. *Revelatory Positivism?: Barth's Earliest Theology and the Marburg School*. Oxford: Oxford University Press 1988.

Fromkin, David. *Europe's Last Summer: Who Started the Great War in 1914?* New York: Random House, 2004.
Gay, P. *Weimar Culture: The Outsider as Insider.* Harmondsworth: Penguin, 1974.
"Germans Can't See Why War Continues: Friedrich Naumann, in *Die Hilfe*, Says People Don't Know Now What They Are Fighting For." *New York Times*, Aug. 24, 1916.
Gilliard, Charles. *A History of Switzerland.* London: George Allen & Unwin, 1955.
Gordon, Frank J. "Liberal German Churchmen and the First World War." *German Studies Review* 4.1 (1981): 39–62.
Green, C. *Karl Barth: Theologian of Freedom.* London: Collins 1989.
Gunton, C. *Becoming and Being.* Oxford: Oxford University Press, 1978.
Hall, Douglas John. "Cross and Context: How My Mind Has Changed." *Christian Century* 127, no. 18 (2010): 34–40.
Hamer, J. *Karl Barth.* Translated by D. Maruca. London: Sands, 1962.
Hammer, Karl. *Christen, Krieg und Frieden.* Olten: Walter-Verlag, 1972.
———. *Kriegstheologie 1870–1918.* Munich: Kösel-Verlag, 1971.
Härle, Wilfried. "Der Aufruf der 93 Intellektuellen und Karl Barths Bruch mit der liberalen Theologie." *Zeitschrift für Theologie und Kirche* 72, no. 2 (1975): 207–24.
Harnack, Adolf von. *Adolf von Harnack als Zeitgenosse: Reden und Schriften aus den Jahren des Kaiserreichs und der Weimarer Republik.* Edited by Kurt Novak. Berlin: Walter de Gruyter, 1996.
Hart, Peter. *The Great War: A Combat History of the First World War.* Oxford: Oxford University Press, 2013.
Hochschild, Adam. *To End All Wars: A Story of Loyalty and Rebellion, 1913–1918.* London: Houghton Mifflin Harcourt, 2011.
Hordern, William. "Barth as Political Thinker." *Christian Century*, March 26, 1969, 411–13.
Hunsinger, G. *How to Read Karl Barth.* Oxford: Oxford University Press, 1991.
———, ed. *Karl Barth and Radical Politics.* Philadelphia: Westminster Press, 1976.
Hynes, Samuel. *A War Imagined: The First World War and English Culture.* London: Bodley Head, 1990.
Jehle, Frank. *Ever against the Stream: The Politics of Karl Barth, 1906–1968.* Translated by Richard and Martha Burnett. Grand Rapids: Eerdmans, 2002.
Jenkins, Julian. "A Forgotten Challenge to German Nationalism: The World Alliance for International Friendship through the Churches." *Australian Journal of Politics and History* 37, no. 2 (1991): 286–301.
———. "War Theology, 1914 and Germany's *Sonderweg*: Luther's Heirs and Patriotism." *Journal of Religious History* 15, no. 3 (1989): 292–310.
Jenkins, Philip. *The Great and Holy War: How World War I Changed Religion for Ever.* Oxford: Lion Books, 2014.
Jenson, R. *God after God.* Indianapolis: Bobbs Merrill, 1969.
Jüngel, E. *Karl Barth: A Theological Legacy.* Translated by G. Paul, Philadelphia: Westminster Press, 1986.
Jünger, Ernst. *Storm of Steel.* Translated by Michael Hofmann. New York: Penguin Books, 2003.
Keller, Gottfried. "To My Native Land." In *Great German Poems of the Romantic Era: A Dual-Language Book*, edited and translated by Stanley Appelbaum, 165. Minneola, NY: Dover Publications, 1995.
Kelsey, D. *The Uses of Scripture in Recent Theology.* London: SCM, 1975.

Koch, H. W., ed. *The Origins of the First World War*. New York: Taplinger Publishing Co., 1972.
Kutter, H. *Sie Müssen! Ein offenes Wort an die christliche Gesellschaft*. Berlin: Hermann Walther, 1904.
Lehman, P. "Karl Barth as Theologian of Permanent Revolution." *Union Theological Seminary Review* 28, no. 1 (1972).
Lindt, Andreas. *Leonard Ragaz: Eine Studie zur Geschichte und Theologie des religiösen Sozialismus*. Zollikon: Evangelischer Verlag AG, 1957.
MacMillan, Margaret. *Paris 1919: Six Months That Changed the World*. New York: Random House, 2001.
Marquardt, F. W. *Theologie und Sozialismus: Das Beispiel Karl Barths*. 3rd ed. Munich: Kaiser, 1985.
Marrin, Albert. *The Last Crusade: The Church of England in the First World War*. Durham, NC: Duke University Press, 1974.
Matheson, Peter C. "Scottish War Sermons 1914–1919." *Records of the Scottish Church History Society*, vol. 17, 203–13.
McConnachie, J. *The Significance of Karl Barth*. London: 1931.
McCormack, B. L. *Karl Barth's Critically Realistic Dialectical Theology: Its Genesis and Development 1909–1936*. Oxford: Clarendon, 1995.
McMeekin, Sean. *July 1914: Countdown to War*. New York: Basic Books, 2013.
———. *The War That Ended Peace: The Road to 1914*. Toronto: Penguin Canada, 2013.
Mehl, Roger. "Du Néo-Calvinisme au Barthisme: Quelques remarques sur la théologie d'Auguste Lecerf, de Pierre Maury, et de Jean Bosc." *Études théologiques et religieuses* 52 (1977): 403–15.
Metaxas, Eric. *Bonhoeffer: Pastor, Martyr, Prophet, Spy: A Righteous Gentile vs. the Third Reich*. Nashville: Thomas Nelson, 2010.
Meyer, G. J. *A World Undone: The Story of the Great War*. New York: BantumDell, 2007.
Moltmann, J., ed. *Anfänge der dialektischen Theologie*. Munich, Kaiser, 1977.
Naumann, Friedrich. *Central Europe*. Translated by Christabel M. Meredith. London: P. S. King & Son, 1916.
Niebuhr, Reinhold. "Why Is Barth Silent on Hungary?" *Christian Century*, January 23, 1957, 108–9.
Old, Hughes Oliphant. *The Reading and Preaching of the Scriptures in the Worship of the Christian Church*, vol. 6, *The Modern Age*. Grand Rapids: Eerdmans, 2006.
O'Neill, J. C. "Adolf von Harnack and the Entry of the German State into War, July–August 1914." *Scottish Journal of Theology* 55, no. 1 (2002): 1–18.
Pachter, Henry M. *Modern Germany: A Social, Cultural, and Political History*. Boulder, CO: Westview, 1978.
Palma, R., *Karl Barth's Theology of Culture*, Allison Park, PA: Pickwick, 1983.
Pentz, Wolfhart. "The Meaning of Religion in the Politics of Friedrich Naumann." *Zeitschrift für neuere Theologiegeschichte* 9, no. 1 (2002): 70–97.
Rosenkranz, Gerhard. "Religionswissenchaft und Theologie." *Evangelische Theologie* 24, no. 10 (1964): 512–38.
Rumscheidt, H. M., ed. *Footnotes to a Theology: The Karl Barth Colloquium 1972*. Toronto, Ontario: Corporation for the Publication of Academic Studies in Religion in Canada, 1974.
———, ed. *Karl Barth in Re-View*. Pittsburgh: Pickwick, 1981.
Sansom, Heather R. *Karl Barth's View of War*. Dissertation, McGill University, 1998.
Shadwell, Arthur. "German War Sermons," *Hibbert Journal* 14, no. 2 (1916): 691–704.

Skyes, S., ed. *Karl Barth: Centenary Essays*. Cambridge: Cambridge University Press, 1989.
Smart, James D. *The Divided Mind of Modern Theology: Karl Barth and Rudolf Bultmann 1908–1933*. Philadelphia: Westminster Press, 1967.
———."Eduard Thurneysen: Pastor-Theologian." *Theology Today* 16, no. 1 (1959): 74–89.
Smith, Donald C. *Passive Obedience and Prophetic Protest: Social Criticism in the Scottish Churches 1830–1945*. New York: Peter Lang, 1987.
Sonderegger, K. "On Style in Karl Barth." *Scottish Journal of Theology* 45 (1992).
Stevenson, David. *Cataclysm: The First World War as Political Tragedy*. New York: Basic Books, 2004.
Strachan, Hugh. *The Outbreak of the First World War*. London: Oxford University Press, 2004.
Sykes, S., ed. *Karl Barth: Studies of His Theological Methods*. Oxford: Clarendon, 1979.
Taylor, A. J. P. *The Course of German History: A Survey of the Development of German History since 1815*. University Paperbacks. London: Methuen, 1961.
———. *The First World War: An Illustrated History*. New York: G. P. Putnam, 1970.
Thompson, J. *Christ in Perspective: Christological Perspectives in the Theology of Karl Barth*. Edinburgh: St. Andrew Press, 1978.
Thurneysen, Eduard. *Theologie und Sozialismus in den Briefen seiner Frühzeit*. Zurich: Theologischer Verlag, 1973.
Torrance, T. F. *Karl Barth: An Introduction to His Early Theology*. London: SCM, 1963.
———. *Karl Barth: Biblical and Evangelical Theologian*. Edinburgh: T. & T. Clark, 1990.
Tuchman, Barbara, W. *The Guns of August*. New York: Macmillan, 1962.
———. *The Proud Tower: A Portrait of the World before the War: 1890–1914*. New York: Macmillan, 1964.
Wallace, Stuart. *War and the Image of Germany: British Academics 1914–1918*. Edinburgh: John Donald Publishers, 1988.
Williams, Rowan. "Barth War and the State." In N. Biggar, ed., *Reckoning with Barth*, London and Oxford: Mowbray, 1988.
Zahn-Harnack, Agnes von. *Adolf von Harnack*. Berlin: Hans Bott Verlag, 1936.
Zahrnt, Heinz. *The Question of God*. Translated by R. A. Wilson. London: Collins, 1969.
Zuckmayer, Carl. *Als wär's ein Stück von mir: Horen der Freundschaft*. Frankfurt: S. Fischer Verlag, 1966.

Index of Persons

Abbott, Lyman, 41
Achelis, Ernst Christian, 7
Adam, Karl, 5
Aeschbacher, Robert, 5
Amette, Cardinal Léon-Adolphe, 41, 151, 183n10
Aquinas, Thomas, 31
Arendt, Hannah, xi
Arndt, Ernst Moritz, 183n2 (Oct. 18)
Asquith, Herbert Henry, 27
Athanasius, 31

Babut, Charles-Édouard, 183n13
Bader, Hans, 11
Bainton, Roland, 40
Barth, Anna Sartorius, 5
Barth, Fritz, 5, 8–10
Barth, Helene, 17
Barth, Karl, ix, xv–xvi, xviii–xix, 2, 4–46, 173n5, 179n1, 180n3 (Aug. 2), 180n2 (Aug. 23), 180n1 (Aug. 30), 181n12, 181n2 (Sept. 6), 181n1 (Sept. 13), 182n4 (Sept. 13), 183n5, 183n14
Barth, Nelly. *See* Hoffmann, Nelly
Barth, Peter, xx, 17
Bebel, August, 12–13
Berkhof, Hendrikus, 7
Berkouwer, Gerrit Cornelius, 32
Bethmann-Hollweg, Chancellor Theobald von, xvii, 2, 4, 13, 37, 43, 183n1 (Oct. 25)
Bismarck, Otto von, 20, 181n8
Blumhardt, Christoph, xii, 6, 11, 14, 16–19, 31
Blumhardt, Johann Christoph, 11, 18

Brune, Guillaume, 180n4 (Aug. 2)
Bullinger, Heinrich, 5
Bultmann, Rudolf, 7
Burckhardt, Jacob, 5
Buttrick, David, 42, 179n121

Calvin, John, xvi, 7–8, 12, 19, 31, 44, 46, 98, 170
Castellio, Sebastian, 19
Cohen, Herrmann, 6

Dittus, Gottliebin, 18
Donne, John, 13
Dorrien, Gary, 9, 175n21
Drews, Paul, 7
Dryander, Ernst von, 183n13

Einstein, Albert, 2, 21, 40–41

Falkenhayn, Erich von, xx
Faulkner, William, x
Ferdinand, Franz (Archduke), 20, 22, 179n2, 183n3 (Oct. 18)
Fickert, Georg Friedrich, 177n80, 180n1 (Aug. 2)
Fischer, Fritz, 38–39
Frank, Ludwig, 150, 183n9
Franz, Ignaz, 182n1 (Sept. 20)
Frederick II (the Great), 3
French, John, 2
Friedrich Wilhelm III, 181n11
Fröhlich, Abraham Emanuel, 182n1 (Sept. 20)

Index of Persons

Geibel, Emanuel, 181n7
Gerhardt, Paul, 24, 70, 180n1 (Aug. 2), 180n1 (Aug. 9), 182n1 (Oct. 18)
Goethe, Johann Wolfgang von, 98, 181n2 (Aug. 30)
Gordon, Frank J., 41
Grey, Edward, 15
Gunkel, Hermann, 6
Gunton, Colin, 15

Haig, Douglas, 2
Hall, Douglas John, 8
Haller, Traugott, 181n1 (Aug. 30)
Hardie, Keir, xi, 2
Harnack, Adolf von, xii, 2–4, 6, 10, 15, 21, 31, 45, 156, 174n4, 183n14
Herkner, Heinrich, 10
Herrmann, Wilhelm, 8 xii, xvi, 6–7, 15, 21, 29–31, 45, 178n96, 183n14
Herrnschmidt, Johann Daniel, 181n3
Heuss, Theodor, 183n9
Hillary, Edmund, 39
Hindenburg, Paul von, 18
Hitler, Adolf, 18–19
Hoffmann, Nelly, 7
Holl, Karl, 6
Hooft, Willem Visser 't, 45
Hüssy, Walter, 12–13

Jaurès, Jean, xi, 2
Jenkins, Philip, 4, 38, 173n1, 178n107, 179n13
Joseph, Franz (Emperor), 1
Jünger, Ernst, 36

Kaftan, Franz, 6
Kant, Immanuel, 6, 30, 98
Keller, Gottfried, 180n5 (Aug. 2)
King, Martin Luther, Jr., 40
Kirschbaum, Charlotte von, 14
Kitchener, Herbert, 2
Körner, Theodor, 183n4
Krummacher, Friedrich Adolf, 184n1
Kutter, Hermann, 10–11, 13, 31, 33

Lenin, Vladimir, 12
Liebknecht, Karl, 150, 183n8
Lissauer, Ernst, 21
Louis XIV, 98
Luther, Martin, xix, 12, 30–31, 34–35, 38, 45–46, 110, 149, 178n104, 181n2 (Sept. 6), 183n7
Luxemburg, Rosa, 183n8

Marquardt, Friedrich-Wilhelm, xii, 32
McCormack, Bruce, x, 15–16, 312–32, 175n21
McCrae, John, 40
Michaelis, Georg, 37
Moltke, Helmuth von (The Younger), xx, 2
Moltmann, Jürgen, 36
Mozart, Wolfgang Amadeus, 5
Muhammad, 140

Napoleon Bonaparte, 37, 59, 86, 98
Natorp, Paul, 6, 149, 182n4 (Sept. 13), 183n7
Naumann, Friedrich, xii, xvii, xix, 9–10, 14, 16–18, 39, 176n56, 183n9
Nicholas II, 1
Niebuhr, Reinhold, 8, 42, 179n118

Origen, 31

Pius X (Pope), 39, 44, 89, 180n4 (Aug. 23), 184n3
Preiswerk, Samuel, 184n1
Princip, Gavrilo, 22–23, 183n3 (Oct. 18)

Rade, Helene, 17
Rade, Martin, xviii–xxi, 6–7, 15–17, 29–30, 37, 178nn94, 96; 180n2 (Aug. 23), 181n2 (Sept. 6), 183nn7, 9
Ragaz, Leonhard, xi, xx–xxi, 2, 9, 11, 19
Rendtorff, Franz, 41
Ritschl, Albrecht, 5, 7
Rolland, Romain, xi, xxii, 2, 19–20, 30, 40, 174n13 (preface), 180n5 (Aug. 23)
Rousseau, Jean Jacques, 98
Russell, Bertrand, xi, 2, 40–41

Schauenburg, Balthazar Alexis Henri, 180n4 (Aug. 2)
Schild, Paul, 179n1
Schiller, Friedrich von, 98, 180n3 (July 26), 181n4, 182n3 (Sept. 20), 183n6 (Oct. 18), 183n2 (Oct. 25)
Schlatter, Adolf, 6, 15
Schleiermacher, Friedrich, 5–6, 8, 15, 21, 31–32
Schlieffen, Alfred von, xix, 2, 27
Schütz, Johann Jakob, 177n80, 180n1 (Aug. 2)
Seeberg, Reinhold, 6, 15
Servetus, Michael, 19
Shadwell, Arthur, 40
Shakespeare, William, 22
Smart, James D., 32
Sombart, Werner, 11, 175n21
Sophie, Duchess of Hohenburg, 20, 179n2

Sophocles, 181n5
Stegmann, Joshua, 1883n1 (Oct. 18)
Stephan, Horst, 20

Taylor, A. J. P., 2
Terence, 182n5
Thurneysen, Eduard, xix–xxi, 5, 7–9, 13–14, 17, 27–32, 44–45, 174n11 (preface), 177n89, 180n1 (Aug. 23), 181n2 (Sept. 6)
Tillich, Paul, 2–4, 8
Tolstoy, Leo, 98

von Bülow, Bernhard, 181n6

Weber, Max, 16
Wernle, Paul, xxi
Wever, Margarethe, 4
Wilhelm II (Kaiser), xii, xvii, 1, 3, 10, 15, 18, 20–21, 27, 29–30, 151, 181n10
Winnington-Ingram, Arthur F., 41
Wyss, Johann Rudolf, 182n4 (Sept. 20)

Yeats, William Butler, 15

Zaremba, Felicitas, 184n1
Zuckmayer, Carl, 3
Zweig, Stefan, xi, 2, 19, 22, 40

Index of Places

Aargau, 8, 10, 12, 139. *See also* Safenwil
Africa, 27, 88
   African, 22, 38, 95
Aisne, xx
Alsace, 29, 76, 181n9, 182n3 (Sept. 13)
Asia, 38, 88
   Asian/Asiatic, 21–22, 39
Austria-Hungary, x, xvii–xviii, 1, 20, 22–24, 28, 177n77, 180n2 (July 26)
Austrian, v, xi, xvii, 19, 21, 23, 52, 146, 148, 179n2

Bad Boll, 17–19
Balkan States, 20–24
Baltic States, 18
Barmen, 45
Basel, xv–xvi, 5, 9–10, 19–20, 42
   University of, 5, 42
Belgium, xvii–xix, xxi, 3–4, 17, 21, 27–29, 76, 107, 109, 118, 155–57, 178n89
   Belgian, xvii, xxi, 2, 4, 22, 27, 39, 136, 146, 151, 156
Berlin, xii, 3–4, 6–7, 15, 21, 27, 150–51, 181n12, 183nn12, 14
   Free University of, xii
   University of, 3–4, 15, 32, 46
Bern, 5–6, 22, 117
   Cathedral, 6
   University of, 5–6, 9–10, 32, 178n105
Birs, 182n4 (Sept. 20)
Bonn, University of, 42
Bosnia, 20, 23
   Bosnian, 23

Brandenburg, 4
Breslau, University of, 4
Burgundy, 182n4 (Sept. 20)

Cambridge, University of, xi
Canada, v, 27

England, 6, 20–21, 27–28, 69, 98, 146–48
   English, xiii, xv–xvi, 14, 32, 34, 39, 42, 89, 100, 136, 146, 151, 157, 173n1, 174n13 (preface)
Estonia, 3
Europe, v, ix–x, 2–3, 17, 19–20, 22–27, 34, 37–38, 40, 52, 87–88, 93, 95, 97–98, 106, 108, 117, 122, 146, 157
   European, xii, 1–2, 19–27, 29, 34, 37–38, 52, 65, 88, 90–92, 110, 112, 117, 122, 132, 141

France, xi, xvii–xxii, 1, 3, 6, 16, 20, 24–25, 27–29, 37–38, 41, 59, 69, 71, 98, 118, 146–48, 151, 155, 177n89, 180n4 (Aug. 2), 183n10
   French, xi, xx–xxii, 2, 10, 20, 25, 27, 30, 37, 39, 41, 59, 88–89, 97–98, 100, 102–3, 106–7, 128, 136, 146, 149, 151, 157, 176n51, 180n4 (Aug. 2), 181n9, 182nn3–4 (Sept. 13), 182n4 (Sept. 20), 183n13
Franco-Prussian, 36
German-Franco, 181n9
Russian-Franco, 27
Frankfurt, 16

Index of Places

Geneva, xi, 7–8, 14, 19, 97
  Genevans, 97
Germany, x, xvii–xxii, 1–4, 6, 8, 10, 12, 15, 17, 19–30, 34, 37–39, 59, 69, 71, 86, 98–100, 105, 118, 146–51, 156, 160–61, 174n9 (preface), 177n77, 178n89, 181nn6–7, 181n12, 183n11
  German, xii, xvi–xvii, xix–xxii, 2–6, 12, 16–18, 21–24, 26–28, 30–31, 34, 36–41, 45, 88, 89, 97–103, 105, 107, 118, 128, 136, 146, 148–49, 151, 155–57, 160–61, 173–74n9, 175n19, 176n51, 178n89, 180n5 (Aug. 2), 181nn6–9, 181n1 (Sept. 6), 182n3 (Sept. 13), 183n12, 183n1 (Oct. 25)
Giessen, University of, xvi, 42
Göttingen, 58
Great Britain, xviii, xxii, 1–2, 21, 24, 27, 177–78n89. *See also* England; Scotland
  British, xi, xviii, xxii, 2, 22, 28, 107, 148, 183n5
Greece, 28
  Greek, 3, 28
Greifswald, 7

Halle, University of, 6–7
Heidelberg, University of, 7
Herzegovina, 20
Hungary. *See* Austria-Hungary

India, 22, 27
Israel, x, 1, 80, 95, 101, 150, 154, 168
  Israelite, 101, 107
Italy, 24–25, 27–28, 111, 177–78n89
  Italian, 44, 97

Jerusalem, 95–96, 101, 174n12 (preface)
Japan, xix, 22, 98
Judah (ancient), 95

Kölliken, 95, 181n1 (Sept. 13)

Leipzig, University of, 3, 41
Leutwil, 14
Liège, xviii, 126, 160
London, 41
Löwen, 117, 182n4 (Sept. 13)
Lüttich. *See* Liège
Luxembourg, xviii, 27

Marburg, University of, xvi, 3, 6–7, 10, 14–17, 29–30, 32, 46, 149, 181n12, 183n13

Moabite, 150
Mühlhausen, 117, 182n3 (Sept. 13)
Münster Church (Basle), 9, 20
Münster (city), 42, 174n11, 175n20

Neumünster Church (Zurich), 10
New York City, 8, 17, 28, 179n118
New Zealand, 27

Palestine, 18, 95
Paris, xx, 1, 20, 27, 38, 41, 106–7, 151, 174n1
Poland, 29, 76
Prussia, xviii, 109, 181n11
  Prussian, 3, 36

Rhine, 130
Rome, 169
Russia, x, xvii–xix, xxi–xxii, 1, 3–4, 12, 22, 24–28, 59, 69, 89, 118, 147–48, 177n89
  Russian, xix, 1, 27, 39, 89, 97–98, 102, 107, 136, 151, 181n1 (Sept. 6)

Safenwil, xv, 8–14, 22–25, 29, 44–45, 49, 59, 69, 77, 85, 95, 105, 115, 125, 135, 145, 155, 165, 173nn5, 9; 175nn19, 21; 179n1, 180n1 (Aug. 30)
Scotland, xi, 8
Serbia, x, xviii, 20, 23, 49, 59, 177n77, 180n2 (July 26)
  Serbian, 24, 52, 147, 183n3 (Oct. 18)
South Africa, 27
St. Jacob, 130, 182n4 (Sept. 20)
St. Petersburg, 27
St. Quentin, xix
Switzerland, 2, 6, 10, 17, 24–26, 29, 36–37, 39, 59, 62, 75, 95–96, 115–16, 122, 125–27, 132–34, 173n9
  French-Swiss, 98
  German-Swiss, 3, 12, 26, 98, 175n19
  Swiss, ix, xi, xxi, 3, 5, 7, 9–12, 19, 22–23, 25–26, 29–30, 32–33, 37–39, 41–42, 45, 59, 75, 88, 90, 95–100, 102–3, 106–7, 112–13, 115–17, 125–30, 132–33, 136, 145, 147, 149, 180nn2, 4 (Aug. 2), 182n4 (Sept. 20)

Tartu, University of, 3
Ticino(s), 97
Tübingen, University of, 6, 11, 15, 181n12

Ulster, 148, 183n5
United Kingdom. *See* Great Britain

United States, xii, 22, 27, 37–38
  American, x, xvi, 27–28, 37–38, 41–42, 88, 183n11

Vaud, Canton of
  Waadtlanders, 97
Versailles, 181n9
Vienna, University of, 19

Württemberg, 11, 17, 19

Yugoslavia
  Slavic, 37, 97

Zofingen, 12
Zurich, xi, 5, 7, 10, 12, 19

Index of Subjects

Acts of the Apostles, 6, 166
alienation, 4
American Civil War, 37
Amos (prophet), 28–29, 69
analogia entis, 42, 179n119
angels, 18, 28, 43, 69–70, 145, 149, 151, 153–54, 160–61
"Appeal and Manifesto of the 93 German Intellectuals," xxi, 3–4, 21, 30–31

Barmen, declaration of, 45
Barth's correspondence, xix–xxi, 5, 12–14, 21, 27, 30–32, 36, 174n11 (preface), 174n7, 176n43, 177nn86, 89; 177–78nn86, 89, 95–96, 98; 179n113, 181n2 (Sept. 6), 183n13
Bible. *See* Scripture/Bible

Calvinism, 8
Captain of Köpenick, The (play), 36
Catholicism, 26, 42, 44–45, 148, 151, 166–71, 180n4 (Aug. 23)
Das Wesen des Christentums (by Harnack), 3
Christianity, xix, xxii, 3, 5, 16–18, 21, 31, 35, 38, 40–41, 45–46, 60, 89, 91, 119, 128, 131, 133, 136–37, 145, 149, 151, 166, 168–70
  early, 28, 36, 40, 51, 103
  Hellenization of, 3
  and nationalism, xii–xiii, 2, 17, 22, 26, 30, 41, 52, 60–61, 64, 89, 91, 99–100, 107, 110–12, 118, 120, 122–23, 128, 149, 151, 153–54, 168–70 (*see also* nationalism)
  unity of, xxii, 41–42, 83, 97–99, 102, 123, 128, 148, 166–68, 170–71
Christliche Welt, Die (journal), xviii–xix, 6, 16, 29–39, 38, 149, 180n2 (Aug. 23), 181n12, 181n2 (Sept. 6), 182n4 (Sept. 13), 183nn7, 9, 12, 14
Christian/religious socialism, xi–xii, xxi, 2–3, 9–20, 32–33, 35–36, 44–45, 89, 148, 150, 154, 175nn19, 21
church(es), x, xii, xv, xxi, 2, 5, 7, 9–10, 12–14, 19–20, 23–25, 31, 34, 39, 41, 44–45, 49, 51, 56, 70, 89, 105, 115–16, 119–20, 122–23, 126, 129, 131, 134–35, 139, 141, 148, 151–53, 157, 165, 167, 169–71, 173n9, 182n1 (Sept. 20)
  history of, 3, 5–6, 11, 33, 178n109
  leaders of, 2, 8–9, 12, 39, 151, 170
  World Council of Churches, 45
  See also Catholicism; congregation; Congregationalist; Lutheran Church/pastor; Protestantism; Reformed Church
Church Dogmatics (Barth's multivolume work), xii, 32, 43, 46
Commentary on Romans (by Barth), x, 5
communism, 12–13
congregation, xi, xv, 7, 9, 12, 23, 29, 35, 41, 43–44, 129, 173n5, 183n11. *Also see* church(es)
Congregationalist, 41, 183n11

conscience, 7, 36, 38, 51, 73, 80, 87, 110–12, 118, 122, 127, 145, 152, 154, 156, 158, 160–62, 166
consummation, 64–65
creation, xii, 18, 84, 109, 145
creed (statement of faith), 3, 7

devil, the, xi, 128, 136, 153, 161
  devils, 149, 128, 152
dialectic, x, xii, 8, 15, 31, 34, 175n21
disciples, 41, 44, 66, 89, 115–16, 119–23, 151, 168, 182n1 (Oct. 11)
doctrine, xii, xvi, 7, 30, 42, 138. *See also*, church(es)

ecumenism, 44–46, 165–67
empire, 1, 22, 27–28, 66, 78, 122, 156, 181n9
  imperialism, 22, 50, 39
eschatology, xii, 11, 35–36
eternal life. *See* resurrection/eternal life
evil, xi, 26, 29, 34, 36, 52, 54–57, 63–66, 70, 78–79, 82, 91–92, 102–3, 111, 113, 128, 131–32, 136, 149, 150–54, 157, 160–63, 169, 177n70. *See also* devil, the
exorcism, 18
expansion/Lebensraum, 3, 18, 39
experience of God, ix–xii, xvii–xxii, 3, 8–11, 14–17, 30, 35, 51, 56, 61, 69, 72, 74, 83, 87, 93, 103, 111–13, 123, 125–26, 137, 146, 152. *See also* faith

faith, ix, xviii–xix, xxii, 3, 5, 8, 13, 24, 30–31, 35, 40, 42, 44, 55, 61–62, 65, 81, 86, 92, 100–101, 115, 117, 120–23, 125, 140, 159–60, 167, 171. See also *experience of God*
Final Testimonies (collection of Barth's last essays), 11
forgiveness, 113, 146, 159
Free Aargau (newspaper), 12
friendship, 1, 37, 49–51, 59, 61, 70, 79, 81–84, 87–88, 91, 96, 134–35, 148, 151, 180n3 (July 26), 183n8
  Barth's friendships, xx, 5, 7–8, 13–14, 19, 27, 29–30, 32, 36, 44–45, 57, 61–62, 65–66, 70–72, 75, 86, 91–92, 96–97, 100–103, 105, 121–22, 143, 145, 149, 151, 153, 155, 159–60, 162, 165, 171
  between humans and God/Christ, xviii, 77, 79–84, 95, 121, 168

God, ix–xii, xvii–xxi, 3, 6–19, 21, 23, 25–46, 49–56, 61–67, 69–76, 77–84, 85–93, 95–103, 105–13, 115–24, 125–34, 135–59, 141–46, 148, 151–54, 158, 160–63, 165–71, 176n56, 180n5 (Aug. 2), 181nn8, 11; 182n1 (Oct. 11), 183n2 (Oct. 18)
Christ (Jesus), xi–xii, 3, 11, 15, 18, 34–35, 40–41, 49, 53–55, 61, 73, 89, 107, 123, 145, 153, 166–68, 170, 184n1
  the Father, 3, 35, 41, 50, 64–65, 67, 72–73, 77, 84, 93, 121, 123, 133, 137, 154, 165, 167, 169
  the Spirit, xii, 14, 18, 33, 67, 100, 103, 131, 153
  will of, 26–27, 43–44, 65, 72–74, 77–78, 83–84, 96, 111, 121, 123, 131, 141–43, 146, 168, 170
goodness, xxi, 7, 40, 53, 55–56, 64, 72–74, 76, 78–79, 82–83, 90–91, 98, 100, 102, 106, 108, 119, 122, 127–35, 137–40, 144, 146, 148–54, 157, 159, 161–63, 168–69, 175n19, 182n1 (Oct. 11)
gospel, 3, x, xix, 10, 30, 40, 89, 103, 115, 122–23, 131–32, 145, 150–52, 159–60, 166–68
grace, x, xii, 34, 37, 39, 42, 49, 53, 62, 65, 72–74, 76–77, 80, 87, 93, 98–101, 112–13, 118, 123, 126–28, 132, 153, 165–66, 179n121, 1883n1 (Oct. 18)

hate, 23, 38, 52, 60, 78, 88, 98, 101, 106–7, 110–11, 113, 118, 135, 137, 146–47, 149–52, 154, 160, 162, 167, 170, 183n11
history, ix, xi–xiii, 3, 5–7, 10–11, 14–15, 33, 37, 43, 86, 112, 117, 130, 147
  church history. *See under* church(es)
Homiletics (Barth's book and seminars), xi, 42–43, 173n9, 179nn121–22
hope, ix, xix, 16, 18–19, 24–25, 27, 29–30, 35–36, 40, 44, 50, 53–55, 63–64, 67, 70, 74–75, 78, 80–81, 83, 85–86, 92, 95–96, 99, 101–3, 120, 122, 126, 149, 154, 166, 170

Institutes of the Christian Religion, xvi, 8, 31

"Jesus Christ and the Movement for Social Justice" (Barth's essay), 11, 13, 176n38
Jews/Judaism, 19, 22, 112
Judah, 95
judge/judgment, x, xii, xix, 15, 27, 34, 37–38, 42–43, 85, 87, 90–93, 98, 106–7, 116, 132–33, 146, 148–49, 151, 160, 165–66, 179n118

Index of Subjects

justice and injustice, x, xii, xxi, 4, 11, 13, 33, 37–40, 50, 54, 64, 66, 78, 80, 97, 100–101, 103, 108, 110–13, 119, 121, 128, 133, 137, 142–43, 145, 152–53, 155–62

kingdom of God, ix, xi, 3, 7, 10–12, 14–15, 17, 19, 34–37, 44, 53–54, 64, 67, 75, 95, 100, 102–3, 111, 113, 122, 142–43, 148, 152, 167, 170, 182n1 (Oct. 11)

law, 50, 156, 159
   of God, 50, 52, 140, 143–44, 153, 156, 161
   between nations, xi–xii, 18–20, 24, 26, 39, 52, 60, 66–67, 75, 86–89, 91, 96–98, 100–102, 106–7, 110–13, 116–18, 122–23, 126–28, 132–33, 144–50, 152, 154, 157, 160, 162, 177n70
   of nature, 26, 160
   "Necessity knows no law," xxi, 33, 41, 43, 52, 155–59, 161
letters. *See* Barth's correspondence
liberal theology, xii, 3, 5–7, 11, 14–19, 21, 32, 34, 36, 45–46
literature, ix, xi, 7, 22, 183n9
love, 15, 27, 33–34, 40, 44, 51, 55–56, 61–63, 74, 79–83, 86, 88, 92, 98, 100–103, 118–19, 122, 126–29, 131, 133, 135–37, 141–44, 147–48, 151–54, 159, 167, 169–70
   for country, xix, 22, 30, 67, 80, 95, 102–3, 112, 115, 129, 147–48, 150, 152, 183n11 (*see also* Christianity: and nationalism; nationalism)
   for God, 67, 84, 123
   God's/Christ's, 15, 27, 33–35, 38, 49–51, 53–55, 61, 64–65, 70, 78, 82, 84, 92–93, 100, 107–11, 113, 119, 121, 123, 131, 142, 145–46, 153–54, 168, 170, 182n1 (Oct. 11)
   for the outdoors, 5
   for war, xix, 21
Lutheran Church/pastor, 3, 10, 16, 26, 45

Marxism, 12
mercy, x, 20, 29, 34, 49, 51, 53, 62, 76, 91
militarism, xxii, 2–4, 12, 16, 19, 21, 23, 25, 52, 61, 96, 105, 118, 123, 130, 146, 150, 173n1, 177n77

nationalism, xii, xx–xxi, 3, 16–18, 20, 22, 25, 31, 40, 59, 86–88, 97–98, 100–103, 107, 112–13, 128, 143, 146–47, 151, 155, 180n2 (Aug. 2), 181n6, 182n4 (Sept. 20), 183n3 (Oct. 18)
Neue Wege (journal), xi, xix–xx, 11, 30
neutrality, xvii, xix, xxii, 2, 4, 6, 17, 21, 24–29, 36–37, 39, 71, 96–97, 101–3, 106, 113, 118, 128, 155–57, 178n89
   Belgian, xvii, 2, 4, 17, 21, 28, 118, 155–57, 178n89
   Swiss, 17, 25–26, 29, 36–37, 39, 71, 96–97, 101–3, 106, 113, 128

orthodox theology, x, 4, 6, 24

pacifism, xi, xxii, 19–20, 30, 40–41, 138, 174n13 (preface), 180n5 (Aug. 23)
patriotism, xix, 22, 62, 11, 145, 147, 149, 180n5 (Aug. 2). *See also* Christianity: and nationalism; nationalism
peace, xix, 15–17, 19–23, 25, 27–28, 33, 39–41, 50–51, 53, 55–56, 62, 64, 67, 71, 74, 78–79, 83, 85–91, 93, 99, 102, 109, 112–13, 116, 118, 127, 129–31, 135–36, 146, 148, 150, 153, 156, 158–59, 161–62, 167, 169–70, 177n70, 180n3 (July 26)
penitence33, 115–16, 119–22, 124–26, 129–30. *See also* repentance
Pentecost, x
positive theology, ix, 6–7, 9–12, 15, 18, 34, 146
prayer, 25, 28, 39, 41, 44, 62, 66, 59, 71–72, 75–76, 78–79, 83, 86, 89, 93, 99–101, 105–7, 109, 111–13, 115, 119–21, 125, 127–28, 132–34, 139, 146, 154, 165, 167–70, 180n5 (Aug. 2), 183n10
prejudice. *See* racism/prejudice
Protestantism, ix, 3, 8–9, 26, 29, 42, 44, 46, 151, 166–70, 183nn5, 13
Providence, xii, 31, 115

racism/prejudice, xii, 22, 37–38, 40, 97–98, 110, 117, 123, 136, 160
redemption, ix, 6, 15, 18, 34, 57, 65, 102, 118, 123–24, 131–32, 156, 168–70
Reformed Church, 3, 5, 7–8, 10–11, 14, 20, 23, 45
relevance (in preaching), x–xi, 42
religious experience. *See* experience of God; faith
Religious Socialism. *See* Christian/ religious socialism; socialism
repentance, xx–xxi, 116, 129–30, 132–34, 151, 181n10. *See also* penitence

resurrection/eternal life, 34–35, 49, 55, 109, 135–44, 182n1 (Oct. 11)
revelation, xi–xii, xix, xxi, 14–15, 27, 33, 35, 41, 46, 55–56, 60–61, 73, 75, 85, 87, 92, 107, 109, 123, 136, 141, 145, 148, 155, 158, 162, 165–66, 170, 173n1

salvation, x, xix, 27, 30, 38, 49, 52, 62, 57, 64, 73, 81, 84, 98, 115–16, 138, 141, 143–44, 166, 181n2 (Sept. 6)
science, 22, 105, 108–10, 146, 15
 prescience, 23
 scientific, 6, 21, 87
 scientist(s), 22, 150
 social science, 22
Scripture/Bible, x, xii, 9, 12–15, 29, 32–33, 42, 44–46, 52–53, 56, 69–71, 137, 139, 165–66, 173n9, 179n118
 "New world of the Bible," xii, 15, 33, 45
 themes of, x–xxii, 3, 23, 32–36, 41–43, 129–30
"Simple gospel of Jesus," 3. *See also* gospel
sin, xii, 4, 16, 26–27, 30, 34, 41, 43, 51, 53–56, 63–66, 76, 91, 93, 99–100, 112–13, 116, 128, 130, 132, 145–46, 152, 160, 167, 169
Social Darwinism, 2–3
Social gospel, 3. *See also* gospel
socialism, xii, 9–13, 16–18, 20, 150, 175n21, 179n128. *See also* Christian/religious socialism
social justice. *See* justice and injustice
SPD (Social Democratic Party of Germany), 11, 12, 20, 183nn8–9
Summa Theologiae, 31

theology, ix–xiii, xix, xxi, 2–9, 11, 13–18, 21–34, 36, 42–46, 174n9 (preface), 179nn118, 128
"To Evangelical Christians Abroad," 21, 151
trade unions, 9, 11, 17, 45
transcendence, xx, 26, 33, 35, 42–43, 49–57, 64, 71, 75, 105–13, 129, 162–63, 166
trench warfare, xx, 2, 144

"Unique time of God," ix–x, 13, 34, 37, 87, 157

war, v, ix–xiii, xvii–xxii, 1–5, 9–10, 12–15, 17, 19–46, 52, 54, 59–67, 69–71, 85–92, 95–103, 106–13, 116–20, 123, 126–28, 130–32, 136, 139–41, 143, 145–53, 155–62, 165–70, 173nn1, 9; 173–74n9, 177n70, 177n89, 178nn101, 109; 180n2 (July 26), 180n3 (Aug. 2), 181n9, 181n1 (Sept. 6), 183nn3, 5, 8 (Oct. 18)
 Thirty Years' War, 37, 86
 World War I, ix, xi, xvii–xxii, 1–2, 4, 9, 17, 19, 27–28, 32, 38–39, 41, 45–46, 96, 108, 110, 136, 173n1, 180n2 (July 26), 183nn3, 5 (*see also* war)
 World War II, 1, 19, 39
Weltpolitik, 15, 18
Word of God, xii, 9, 11, 15, 31–33, 43, 45–46, 95, 166. *Also see* Scripture/Bible
Word of God and Theology, The (Barth's 1928 essay collection), xii, 45–46
worry, xviii, 25, 28, 50–51, 59, 62, 66, 69, 71–76, 78, 93, 101, 170

Zofingia (student association), 9–10, 36–37, 178n105

www.ingramcontent.com/pod-product-compliance
Lightning Source LLC
Chambersburg PA
CBHW032034290426
44110CB00012B/804